Neoliberal Reform in Machu Picchu

Neoliberal Reform in Machu Picchu

Protecting a Community, Heritage Site, and Tourism Destination in Peru

Pellegrino A. Luciano

LEXINGTON BOOKS
Lanham • Boulder • New York • London

Published by Lexington Books
An imprint of The Rowman & Littlefield Publishing Group, Inc.
4501 Forbes Boulevard, Suite 200, Lanham, Maryland 20706
www.rowman.com

Unit A, Whitacre Mews, 26-34 Stannary Street, London SE11 4AB, United Kingdom

British Library Cataloguing in Publication Information Available

Library of Congress Cataloging-in-Publication Data Available

ISBN 978-1-4985-4594-5 (cloth)
ISBN 978-1-4985-4595-2 (electronic)
ISBN 978-1-4985-4596-9 (pbk.)

For my beloved wife, Catuska, and dear son, Antonio

Contents

List of Acronyms ix
Acknowledgments xi
Introduction: Living Under the Hen 1

1 Imbricated Spaces: District, Sanctuary, Landscape 17
2 Public Goods, Private Interests, and Stigmatized Identities 39
3 Patchwork: Money, Class, and Patronage 63
4 Knowing What to Do 83
5 Machu Picchu and the Witnessing World 101
6 Protest and Memories of Violence 121
7 Sweet Dreams and Accommodations 137

References 151
Index 161
About the Author 169

List of Acronyms

AATC	Asociación de Agencias de Turismo del Cusco
AGOTUR	Asociación de Guías de Turismo
CONSETTUR	Consorcio de Empresas de Transporte Turistico
COPESCO	Plan Turístico y Cultural de la Comisión Especial
COTUR	Corporación de Turismo del Perú
CTAR	Consejo Transitorio de Administración Regional, Cusco
EGEMSA	Empresa de Generación Eléctrica Machupicchu, S.A.
Frente	Frente de Defensa de los Intereses de Machu Picchu
INC	Instituto Nacional de Cultura (currently under Ministerio de Cultura)
INRENA	Instituto Nacional de Recursos Naturales (currently Sistema Nacional de Áreas Naturales Protegidas por el Estado [SINANPE])
MDDE	Maryland and Delaware Railroad
PMP	Programa Machu Picchu
PROFONANPE	Fondo Nacional para Áreas Naturales Protegidas por el Estado
PromPeru	Comisión de Promoción del Perú
UGM	Unidad Gestión Machu Picchu

Acknowledgments

My most profound debt is to the people of Machu Picchu for receiving me so warmly and for their patience and tolerance while I conducted my research among them. I especially thank Teresa and Luis Callañaupa, Emilio Callañaupa and Raul Sanchez for their assistance in getting me situated during the early phases of the fieldwork. I am no less indebted to the members of Frente de Defensa de los Intereses de Machu Picchu, Oscar Valencia Aucca, Margarita Kaiser, Charo Castillo, Corina Condori Quispe, Regina Zapata and Marina Arias. I also thank Graciela Fernandez and Héctor Alegria for their kindness during my stay. I hope that those who are not mentioned by name will also accept my thanks for taking the time to teach me and to make me feel welcome in Machu Picchu. Conscious of all the kindness they have shown me, I wish them all the best, and personally have only the kindest regards for them.

I am indebted to many people who contributed directly and indirectly to making this project possible, and to whom I wish to express my eternal gratitude. I gratefully acknowledge the wise counsel and warm encouragement of Shirley Lindenbaum, Maria Lagos and Michael Blim who have guided this project from its inception, and for pushing me to develop my thoughts further. I also wish to thank Patricia Mathews Salazar for taking the time to help complete the project and for her suggestions on improving my manuscript for publication.

My handling of the topics dealt with in this research has benefited greatly from discussion with fellow colleagues and friends, particularly Martha Kebalo and Maria Gutierrez.

Special thanks go to Dr. John Beatty for his advice and comments. Since my days as an undergraduate, both he and Dr. Edgar Gregersen have given me tireless encouragement to pursue anthropology. From them I learned how to appreciate the intricacies of language and culture in social interactions without the reductionist tendencies so commonplace in anthropology's linguistic turn.

A large gratitude goes to Martin H. Meisel for his help and concern and for giving me the confidence to continue my work. I am grateful to Sonia Marcela Alvarez, Silvia Palomares, and Nayruth Yanez for their meticulous work transcribing videos and cassettes. I thank colleagues at the University of San Antonio Abad in Cuzco, particularly Zelmira Flores Ampuero, Walter Aguilar Ancori for their friendship and valuable discussions.

I would like to pay special thanks to my field assistant and fellow anthropologist Maria del Carmen Olivera Silva for her truly indispensable help and advice. This project would have never been possible if it were not for her knowledge of the Andes and ethnographic expertise. I am eternally indebted to her.

I am also indebted to several institutions that gave me help and support along the way. I thank the Instituto de Estudios Peruanos in Lima for granting me research affiliation. I thank the Unidad Gestion de Machu Picchu for graciously granting me permission to conduct research in the Sanctuary of Machu Picchu. I thank Dr. Jose de Soto and the members of the Municipio of Machu Picchu for their administrative assistance.

Many others have contributed to this project through the sharing of information, lively conversation, friendship and encouragement. In this regard, space does not permit me to mention them all. However, I would like mention for their interest in my progress: Ruth Santana, David Catacora Gonzales, Larry Testa, Ramiro Campos, Yenny Atahulluco, Linda and Blanca Serrano, Susana Huaman, Quintina Huaman, and Mario Herrera.

Finally, I would like to thank my family, especially my wife, Catuska Sissi, for believing in me and for pushing me to complete this book.

Introduction

Living Under the Hen

Privatization is when the government comes in and takes away your property. (Privatización es cuando el gobierno viene y se apodera de tu propiedad.)
—Victor, Huayllabamba, Machu Picchu

It was February 2002, also the low tourist season, when I spotted Rosa dashing across the plaza and towards Av. Pachacutec. She called out to inform me that an important town meeting was taking place at the cultural center. Rosa said that a demonstration, a tourism stoppage, or both was being planned. The purpose of the meeting was to organize a challenge against state property regulations in the protected areas of the Sanctuary of Machu Picchu that overlaps the district of Machu Picchu; the political district of Machu Picchu, comprised of a town and various communities, overlays the national park and protected area almost entirely. Rosa was straightforward about the problem: "We are not property owners here" (No somos propietarios acá).

I was confused by Rosa's statement at first. Sanctuary laws prohibiting property had been imposed for some twenty years before my arrival and people were aware of them. When I got to the town hall (cultural center) I found some one hundred townsfolk fuming and talking over a barrage of concerns about privatization. I had gone to Machu Picchu to do my doctoral fieldwork, initially focused on memory and landscape meanings in the Andes. Rosa herself would tell me about how as a child she played by the Incan stones of the Citadel. However, it is not uncommon during fieldwork to shift the direction of research in accordance with the realities and concerns of the people one is supposed to represent. On my mind was Orin Starn's (1991) critique of how ethnographies of the southern Peruvian highlands in the 1970s failed to anticipate the rise of the Shining Path and the brutal protracted civil war that resulted. Starn claimed that the anthropology of the time generally ignored signs of discontent and growing conflict because of an ethnographic framework that described Peruvian rural life as static, stressing the local ritual or ecological aspects of communities as isolated units (ibid.: 4). Regardless of the merits or shortcomings of Starn's argument, I was aware of the need to refocus my ethnographic attention to the pressing realities of the people of Machu Picchu and became engrossed in describing their mobilization. The Machupiccheños had banded together to form a challenge against conservation agencies and the privatization of the train system. The meeting resulted in people taking an active role by electing a "Front" that would organize a challenge that would ultimately lead to the remaking of their own town. Throughout this book, I describe the trials faced by people who live in the district of Machu Picchu, a community, a heritage site and touristic destination, as well as the nation's preeminent symbol—the Sanctuary of Machu Picchu. The national revenue the Sanctuary generates leads to the common expression that it's "the hen that lays the golden egg" for Peru. The main part of the fieldwork discussed here was conducted in July 2001–2002 and captures a pivotal moment in the transition towards Peru's neoliberal economy that led to the remodeling of Machupicchu Pueblo.[1] The transformation took place over the course of years beyond my initial fieldwork—I returned to the field in 2007 and briefly in 2016—but the initial fieldwork marks a historical moment that began the complexities of actors negotiating two overlapping political spaces—district and Sanctuary in a neoliberal shift towards privatization in Peru.[2] The ethnography is an account of residents who came to believe that land possession rights as opposed to property rights under neoliberal reform was not sufficient to protect their district autonomy, and the right to make a life in their community. I describe how neoliberalism entered the lives of everyday people in the interactions with agents that push its policies. It is about "the politics of small things," to quote Jeffery Goldfarb, as "people make history in their social interactions" (2007: 1). I focus on the intricate set of relationships involving tourism and heritage as experienced in local context under a shift towards free-market policies and privatization (Silverman 2002; Breglia 2006). What I analyze is a tumbling set of positions stretching across a range of global relations entangled in market liberalization. I have two central aims. As an ethnographer, the first is to bring to life the actions and struggles of the people involved in this account, and to provide a case study of identity in the Andes drawn into a process of dispossession under state and market forces; it is about people who challenged, negotiated and attempted to create a new direction for themselves. In that respect, the second goal is to make sense of the performative nature of the social interactions of the Machupiccheños and authorities as they challenge and negotiate neoliberal politics. The performances are not focused on the "touristic" but on the policies and ideologies people grappled with under a privatization regime that threatened belonging and livelihoods. What I intend to analyze is the moment neoliberalism incorporated the lives of a group of people as a concept and a cultural object, and how it became the proverbial "elephant in the room" guiding and shaping possibilities. I organize the ethnography around people's social interactions and strategic engagements that were articulated and enacted and analyzed for persuasiveness as Machu Picchu was fused into a "new spatial economy" involving racial identities during a key moment in Peru's economic history (Silverman 2002: 882). Relevant to understanding neoliberalism is an examination of how people's social identities undergo a "mortification" process. In *Asylums* (1961) Erving Goffman was astutely aware of how control over people's lives involves "dispossession of name, property and identity" (19). During my fieldwork, I often wondered how living inside the protected area of Machu Picchu was just a focused example of the kinds of relationships produced under neoliberalism, and how economies fused with the state are now global and perhaps have become our total institution. I found Goffman's work insightful in grounding everyday life for the Machupiccheños as well as in making sense of their interactions with the people and entities they challenged, especially bureaucratic encounters. Goffman's work remains underused in anthropology and yet as I hope to show is useful in theorizing the "Kafkaesque" restructuring of everyday life brought on by neoliberalism (Kravel-Tovi 2012; Bonhomme 2012: 227). I engage Erving Goffman's work and connect it to a political economy approach to show how neoliberalism frames social interaction, and how actors negotiate or attempt to break them.

The proliferation of anthropological works invoking neoliberalism has potentially rendered it hackneyed and "polysemic" in that it has multiple meanings (Ganti 2014: 91). Indeed, as Tejaswini Ganti notes, members of anthropological groups such as GDAT (Group for Debates in Anthropological Theory) at the University of Manchester argued that the concept

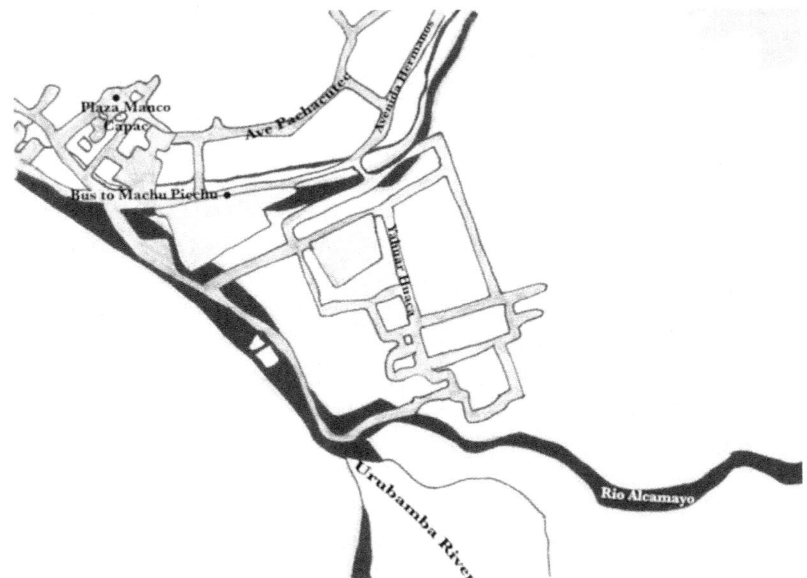

Figure I.1. Map of Machupicchu Pueblo (Drawing by Hanzada A. Kurdi)

Figure I.2. Map of Sanctuary of Machu Picchu and district of Machu Picchu. Dark line indicates the boundary of the Sanctuary with the principal district sectors including the Pueblo. Note the broken line that shows the area of Ccollpani falls within the district but outside the Sanctuary. (Drawing by Hanzada A. Kurdi)

of "neoliberalism" was more of a hindrance to "anthropological understanding of the twenty-first century" (ibid.: 90). How did anthropology go from emphasizing globalization, or for that matter using the earlier term "late capitalism," to a focus on the concept of neoliberalism (Ortner 2011)? While, as Ortner notes, no rigid dichotomy should be made with neoliberalism, the concept of late capitalism as described by Lash and Urry (1987) and David Harvey (1989) as well as others marks a historical shift from "organized capitalism" or "Fordist economy" that revolved around a negotiated stance between capital and labor in the U.S. in the 1940s–1970s to a post-Fordist "flexible labor" economy (2011). Both late capitalism and neoliberalism reflect developments in Latin American nation-states. Neoliberalism became late capitalism's ideological justification just as liberalism was the intellectual foundation for capitalism. As I discuss further below, liberalism was, as neoliberalism is today, not just an economic ideology of the market, but a philosophical movement by those who identified themselves as "free thinkers," *pensadores liberales,* and saw themselves as progressives, espousing notions of citizenship, individual liberty and private property (Mayer 2002: 292). Yet neoliberalism has a distinct 20th-century context in how its ideas were politically pushed first on Latin American countries (Ganti 2014). As Ganti notes, the current ideas of neoliberalism can be most directly traced to the post-WWII gathering of intellectuals and economists such as Friedrich August von Hayak in Switzerland in 1947 to form what was to be called the "Mont Pelerin Society" (2014: 92). As a capitalist reaction to organized labor and Keynesian state regulations, the Society assumed that any government interference in the economy or help for the poor was a slippery slope towards Soviet-style state socialism; even the idea of a "commons" or public goods was dismissed. Through a network of European and North American institutions they asserted the primacy of private property as the basis of a good economy as a well as a good society (ibid.: 92). In the subsequent decades, neoliberalism was promoted in Latin America by economists such as Milton Friedman at the University of Chicago's School of Economics that trained numerous economists throughout the region, sometimes referred to as the "Chicago Boys" (ibid.: 93); in 1973 those neoliberal ideas became the basis of the brutal Pinochet regime in Chile and their overthrow of Salvador Allende's socialist government and his subsequent murder. Neoliberalism became the "unyielding conviction that the market economy is both the most proficient and moral means for distributing goods in society" and provided the theoretical framework supporting a capitalist form of production (Loker 1999: 11).

Yet early anthropological works on neoliberalism in Latin America such as Hojman (1994) and Gill (2000) linked global capitalism to the use of state force and coercive practices involving the state apparatus, as well as vigilante "justice" as a response to state policy (Goldstein 2004). Others showed a trend to consolidate governance with free-market ideology (Sanabria 1999), and documented how corporations investing in Latin America wield a great deal of political power in negotiating contracts with governments (Vilas 2004). Despite the neoliberal emphasis on free-market dynamics over state intervention, these ethnographically informed studies pointed to the fact that neoliberalism requires strong state efforts for its facilitation (Blim 2000).

Indeed, one of David Harvey's distinguishing observations about neoliberalism is how capital investments often dispossess by dissolving rights or by imposing juridical and cultural barriers that make it difficult for anyone other than the very wealthy to survive in the economy (2003). This "taking from Peter to give to Paul" involves investment opportunities that may "lie idle," blocked for investment by property titles, land rights and many other juridical entanglements.[3] Dispossession strategies in the form of seizures and expulsions can free assets cheaply, releasing them for use (ibid.). Harvey defines neoliberalism as "the cutting edge of accumulation by dispossession," and argues that "the state, with its monopoly of violence and definitions of legality, plays a crucial role in both backing and promoting these processes" (ibid.: 157).

During my fieldwork in Machu Picchu, the Peruvian government maintained the preservation rationale for control that restricted property rights. Simultaneously though, the state privatized services in the Sanctuary to large-scale corporations that made competition in the tourism economy difficult for residents. People lived under the constant menace of eviction either because their presence was said to create ecological damage or for safety because the town is in an area prone to landslides, both leading to plans for their relocation. What we see in the case of Machu Picchu is how deregulation, privatization, market solutions, and cutting expenditures for social services were advanced under the concept of heritage (patrimony) and nature conservation. Neoliberal ideology redefines not the meaning of heritage sites per se but what public goods mean in order to facilitate capital. The narratives of "national identity" represented in heritage areas such as Machu Picchu are integrated into the language of neoliberalism as a profit-making resource (Breglia 2006). The Machupiccheños encountered and confronted a concert of economy and state that tied capital accumulation strategies with the logic of displacement. They challenged the "takings" of rights, civil status and resources meant to accommodate larger capital investments under the guise of heritage and nature conservation. Racialized identities are stigmatized or criminalized so that property claims can be avoided or dismissed. I found there was an intimate connection between capital accumulation and racialized identities (Harvey 2014: 37–38).

The facilitation of economic liberalization is shaped by local cultural and historical "assemblages" that combine to form a hegemonic process, not simply as the attainment of consent, but as a process around which people of differing power positions struggle over how the changing economy should be defined (Roseberry 1994: 366; Ong 2006). This connection of capital accumulation and identity is evident throughout Latin American history, as Roger Batra (1974) showed how the contradiction between the necessity of peasant production and the penetration of capitalism into the Mexican countryside makes for an ongoing and irresolvable process of primitive accumulation. Different identities were implicated differently through early liberal reforms. In the Andes, neoliberal reforms concurrently reproduce subordinate racial and gender categories through market interactions (Seligmann 2004; Colloredo-Mansfeld 2009; Scarritt 2015). Dispossession in Latin America has a history that reaches back to the conquest of the Americas. Indeed, the emergence of liberalism also had its share of aspirations for repossession. Mallon (1995) showed that liberalism was not always the discourse of the elites, describing how in mid-19th-century Mexico, indigenous people frequently interpreted and fought for their own versions of liberal reform. Under colonial relations in Peru, some indigenous communities initially embraced the ideals of a free market in view of breaking free from landed aristocratic relationships (Nugent 1997). However, despite participation by subaltern groups giving their own shape to liberalism, the practical consequences of liberal history increased dispossession along the lines of racial and ethnic identities. Policies were put into action through preexisting inequalities with power relations skewed against Indians. In the Andes, the rise of liberalism in the mid- to late 19th century tied issues of race and Indian identity via the struggle to create modern nation-states. While liberal ideology led to the fall of the reviled Indian tribute system, it also meant that indigenous peoples were no longer entitled to "communal lands, local self-rule, and state protection" (Larson 2004: 7). In some areas of Peru, the undermining of such rights played a crucial role of converting ethnic affiliations into what Larson calls a "racialized laboring underclass" (ibid.: 164). In other areas, people nevertheless found ways of preserving communal ownership of land by turning it over to the authority of their municipality, hence bypassing liberal reforms that promoted the privatization of land de-legitimizing indigenous claims (ibid.: 12; Mayer 2002: 300). The history of liberalism drew a cultural and legal connection between identity, land and property (Scaritt 2015: 6). Indeed, in Peru discontent among the former hacienda families after the 1969 agrarian reform fed into the rise of neoliberal ideology, although its strongest support came from a new politics of the political right (Durand 1997). Intellectuals such as novelist Mario Vargas Llosa and economist Hernando de Soto articulated an ideological vision that called for a social and cultural restructuring of life around a market mentality (ibid.: 166). However, neoliberal ideology, as the Machupiccheños clearly understood, obscures the realities of scale with farcical notions of competition in very unequal situations. While the poor are often disciplined and excluded from participation in such an "entrepreneurial" economy, other economic actors, often at the level of family businesses, require a different attention involving consent, inclusion and incorporation via subtler forms of coercion.

MACHU PICCHU AS A MARKETING STRATEGY

In Peru, along with the debt crisis, the 1980s saw Shining Path insurgents engaged in a violent revolutionary struggle against the state. The war had devastating social repercussions. Rural inhabitants were often caught between the violence of the military and that of the Shining Path (Degregori 1990; Poole and Renique 1992). Yet, by the early nineties, the military gained the upper hand on the Shining Path with the capture of its leaders. President Fujimori made an international effort to attract direct foreign investments and to change the image of Peru as a dangerous place. A strong effort needed to be made to demonstrate to foreign investors the government's commitment to transform the economy. As the sexist comment of the U.S. Under Secretary of the Treasury for International Affairs on Latin America in 1992 shows, "The countries that do not make themselves more attractive will not get investors' attention. This is like a girl trying to get a boyfriend. She has to go out, have her hair done up, wear makeup" (Green 2003: 103–104). In response, one of President Fujimori's creations was PromPeru,[4] an organization charged with coordinating and fostering activities related to the promotion of Peru to a global audience and for attracting foreign investment. PromPeru also used foreign media to help build a tourism market by creating interest in the Peruvian pre-Columbian past by diffusing information through sources such as the *New York Times* and the Discovery Channel. Nationally, PromPeru advanced social and cultural projects meant to increase local awareness of the significance of tourism for the economy, offering workshops on improving services.[5]

As the civil war violence receded throughout the 1990s, the Sanctuary of Machu Picchu became the most important part of the burgeoning tourism industry of Peru, encapsulating the interests of small, middle and large, as well as local, national and international stakeholders. But in addition to tourism, Machu Picchu factored centrally as a strategy to address national debt and structural adjustment requirements for loans through privatization. The state-operated train system that runs from the city of Cusco to the town of Machu Picchu, along with two major formerly state-operated hotels in the Sanctuary were privatized to the multinational corporation Orient Express/Belmond. The state-operated train system was geared to local service; it was cheaper and there was more room for local market goers to transport products. The state-operated hotel kept competition with the community to a minimum and was planned around local economic development goals (Desforges 1998). The privatization of these entities created an extremely unbalanced competition with residents operating small-scale restaurants and hotels. In addition, in the mid-nineties, the Sanctuary was brought into a debt repayment program through a "debt for nature" swap with Finland; a debt-for-nature exchange is a method of providing funds for nature conservation programs in third world countries, while simultaneously reducing their international debt. In short, a country or a non-governmental organization (NGO) buys a portion of a developing country's debt from a commercial bank on the international secondary market, usually at reduced prices. As in Machu Picchu, once the exchange is worked out, an NGO carries out the selected conservation programs. The basic benefits to a recipient country include the reduction of debt and access to hard currency (Patterson 1990). In the case of Machu Picchu, the debt-for-nature exchange was based on Finland's debt forgiveness over a loan default. The agreement required that a portion of that default be directed for nature conservation purposes. As a result, the state directed approximately seven million dollars from the Finland loan towards the Sanctuary through the formation of the multinational and multi-institutional organization Programa Machu Picchu (PMP). Machu Picchu is not just an asset for tourism, but its iconic nature makes it also a marketing tool to attract direct foreign capital, and a symbol representing not just Peru's pre-Columbian past but also the new Peru as safe, secure and trustworthy for foreign investors.

In the 2000 presidential elections, Fujimori won under dubious conditions. Under the pressure of the Organization of American States (OAS), elections were held again a few months later in which Fujimori lost to Alejandro Toledo. One of the striking aspects of this election was the role race played in the campaigns. Since Toledo has what are seen as "Indian features,"[6] it seemed he could manipulate this quality to gain votes in the Andes, as his greatest support came from the sierra region. He represented himself as part of Peru's pre-Columbian past and gained popular support, especially in Cusco, the seat of the former Inca Empire. For the first time in Peruvian history, Toledo held his inauguration ceremony at the Citadel of Machu Picchu, using the site to call attention to Peru's pre-Columbian origins (Silverman 2002: 882). Unlike Fujimori, Toledo's pre-election campaign emphasized anti-privatization policies, in particular, a promise to keep the hydroelectric companies in state hands. When Toledo entered office in July 2001, there were media discussions that a new Peruvian democracy was emerging after Fujimori's ten-year authoritarian rule and the protracted war against the Shining Path.

Toledo placed a great deal of emphasis on increasing tourism in Peru. He, like his predecessor, stressed tourism as one of Peru's greatest economic options and thus began seeking avenues to further develop the industry. Despite his pre-election anti-privatization rhetoric, once in office, he continued Fujimori's neoliberal project. In less than a year in office, Toledo began losing support even in the sierra region that had been his base. Popular dissent followed in many parts of the country, and in Cusco anti-neoliberal protests often invoked Machu Picchu as a rallying flag against the privatization efforts taking place. Machu Picchu became an identity symbol for both promoters and opponents of neoliberal politics.

For the residents of Machu Picchu, living in the protected area requires constant justification. Conservation efforts bring into play a process of discrediting that attempts to dissolve rights, individually and collectively. For the inhabitants of Machu Picchu, being discounted is based on having inappropriate identities relative to the ideals of the Sanctuary. Their activities either destroy nature or they do not have the "authentic," viz. commercialized, Andean identity appropriate for the expectations of tourists. In short, their presence spoils the Sanctuary for investors, and that spoiling also provides the rationale for separating people from claims to property. Counter-maneuvers on the part of residents involved claims that attempted to discredit authorities as incapable of protecting a public good. For example, they exerted pressure on state authorities to bring legal charges against a beer company that damaged the Intihuatana (sundial) of the Citadel during the filming of a commercial for which authorities were accused of providing fraudulent authorization.[7] In addition, the mobilization I documented argued that the state was not doing enough to return artifacts said to have been illegally taken by Hiram Bingham, the "discoverer" of the Machu Picchu Citadel (taken up in the next chapter) and in the possession of Yale University.[8]

Land can also be marked to involve a dispossession of a population if places are defined as public hazards and people moved for their own welfare. In Machu Picchu, there was such a factor in that the town is in a location susceptible to landslides and flash floods. The state has plans to relocate the population for its own safety, but unsurprisingly it makes no plans to stop tourism, the PeruRail train service and major hotels from operating in those areas. Indeed, according to one disaster study, the anticipated trajectory of a flash flood from one of the rivers heads directly into the large-scale Pueblo Hotel, but no suggestion was made that they be moved.[9] When such contradictions are pointed out, disaster-prone land too gets turned back to stigmatizing residents, in that resident activities are often blamed for setting them in motion and hence authorities build greater justification for controlling people's lives.

This is not to say that what I describe in this ethnography or what the Machupiccheños experience is unique. There has been a global increase in areas deemed protected in the form of nature and heritage parks and reserves as well as scholarly attention paid to them (West, Igoe and Brockington 2006).[10] West, Igoe and Brockington have pointed out that studying the lives of people in and around protected areas offers a unique insight into understanding how people produce and reproduce their social relationships and cultural worlds (ibid.). The ethnographic and theoretical contribution of these authors speaks to the continuous need for anthropologists to balance both the cultural and discursive dimensions of life in analyzing people and protected areas. This study on Machu Picchu reflects these commitments as it closely analyzes symbolic and discursive productions of social interactions in material context. Numerous ethnographies have examined the lives of people in and around protected areas and the multiple ways they are implicated in conservation policies and laws. A central theme that emerges in the literature is the displacement and expulsion of people in and around these areas (ibid.).

GATHERINGS

As in all ethnographic writing, the untidy mixture of actual life is given order. As such, I introduce and describe the principal actors in this ethnography, and my relationship to them, through the description of a fund-raising event that occurred sometime during the middle of my fieldwork. In April 2002, the members of Frente de Defensa de los Intereses de Machu Picchu (The Front in Defense of the Interests of Machu Picchu, hereafter referred to as Frente),[11] the local watchdog front elected to protect the interests of the district, decided to hold a *pollada* to raise money to hire a lawyer. A pollada is essentially a chicken grill fest popularized in Peru during the debt crisis era of the 1980s as a fundraising strategy used by people to draw on neighborhood resources, often to help pay for personal expenses such as medical, home improvements or family debts. The organizer sells tickets for the event to his neighbors who, because of the personal relationships involved, often feel compelled to participate. They then set up a party stand in a communal location where they provide the food and beverages as well as the music. On this occasion, Frente saw raising money for a lawyer as necessary to begin the legal process to change the sanctuary law that they felt divests them of property titles; hence they thought of the pollada as an event in the interest of all Machupiccheños; as we will see others saw it differently.

The preparations began in the morning hours. I hurried down to the plaza to participate. On my way, I waved to Emilio who was busy sweeping the front of his hotel. When I first arrived, Emilio took me in at the recommendation of his niece in Cusco, Teresa, who worked as a tour guide, and whom I had interviewed on an earlier fieldwork trip. It was Teresa who first alerted me to many of the problems experienced by the residents of Machu Picchu. Her uncle, Emilio, was active in one of the barrio associations, and he played an important part in my fieldwork, as it was he who negotiated my residency with the municipality and my acceptance into the pueblo.

I reached the plaza where I found Charo preparing the grill. Charo, a woman in her mid-thirties and a hotel owner, held the office of secretary in the Frente group. She was outspoken and sharp-witted, and probably at the time the closest ally of Oscar Valencia, the president of Frente. Oscar was well suited for the task. He carefully inspected the laws and rules of the Sanctuary to form strategies against conservation authorities. Oscar was a contentious figure in that his disputes with authorities were connected to his political ambitions to be mayor. Furthermore, Oscar had a powerful communication instrument at his disposal; he was the director of Radio Machu Picchu, one of two stations broadcasting in the Pueblo, and used it often as a platform for building support for his politics.

Next to Charo was Eber with a few other men, assembling the gazebo and arranging the chairs and tables. Eber and his wife, Rosa, were steadfast supporters of Frente. While Eber made a living as a mystical tour guide, his wife belonged to one of the oldest families and perhaps one of the largest land possessors in the pueblo. Shortly, Corina arrived with her husband, Guillermo, who went over to help Eber. Corina worked for

Frente as treasurer, but was also the president of an artisan association. She owned an artisan and jewelry shop on the main street of the Pueblo. I saw Corina as having a wonderful combination of elegance and humility.

As the grill was ready, and firewood delivered, Charo pulled the marinated chicken pieces out from their basins to begin cooking. Alberto, a restaurant and hotel owner, arrived to help set up the music, and so he searched for an electrical outlet. He found one just off the plaza on a narrow street leading to the market that was occupied by small vendors. The vendors shared the outlet and the electrical costs, but Alberto wished to use it for the festivities. One of the market women protested, asking him who would pay the bill. Alberto argued that it was for a just cause and that she should allow them the use of the outlet. "The pollada is for helping the whole pueblo fight this law" he said. "You know very well that no one here owns their land." The woman quipped back, "That doesn't concern me, I have no land, I have to rent." At this Alberto became angry saying, "Damn you get out of this pueblo, what are you doing here!" They parted angry at each other. His response was telling of the kinds of class divisions one finds in the pueblo that complicate neat categories. The market woman did have a market-stand and a claim on property whereas street vendors with no market space cannot. She was, however, speaking not so much as a market vendor but as a frustrated resident with no claim to land who must rent her living space. The distinction stresses, along with wealth differences in the pueblo, the politics of belonging.

Marina walked about the plaza with the tickets, inviting people to participate. Marina is a restaurant and artisan shop owner and was also an elected member of Frente. At the cashier table, Regina and Marta exchanged the tickets for the food. They along with Marina, Charo and Corina were five of the most politically engaged women of the town; and there were many others. Marta, Alberto's wife, was leader of one of the pueblo's artisan associations, and actively managed the family restaurant and hotel business. She, like many of the women described in these pages, does most of the work in the family, domestic and business, and still makes time to be actively concerned with pueblo life and politics. Regina was an officeholder in Frente, but unlike Marta was not as economically well-off, making a living at running a small food stand in the market; she was, however, equally as hardworking as Marta. The political actions of women in the pueblo cannot generally be understood as subordinate to men, as their participation in the public sphere was often equal to men and at times dominant. However, domestically, women were burdened with greater labor demands that were often valued as something less. It illustrates how different spheres of life can bring together dominant and subordinate definitions of gender (Lagos 2002).[12] Chela, though not present at the festivities, was another distinguished woman who played a prominent role in the mobilization. Like Marta,

Chela too was the leader of an artisan association. She would provide a key leadership role in building a supportive constituency for Frente from her artisan members. Chela and her husband, Héctor, were both artisans and were often busily working their materials into crafts. Unlike most of the other participants, Chela and Héctor frequently invoked Incan identity discourses (Incanismo) in formal meetings with Sanctuary authorities.

The food was ready to be served. Margarita, the vice president of Frente, came down from her hotel "Gringo Bill's" nicely dressed, covered in a fine alpaca shawl, to eat lunch. Margarita, originally from the town of Paucartambo in the Cusco department, arrived at the Pueblo of Machu Picchu in the early 1980s shortly after marrying her American husband, Bill. Margarita was perhaps the most urbane of the pueblo residents with whom I interacted. I often thought of Margarita as a sharp businesswoman, though she credited her now estranged husband for much of their initial success. Together they invested early during the growing tourism economy of the Pueblo and as a result built one of the most successful local hotels. Margarita would often recall with amazement how the Pueblo had grown from the time she opened her business, when there were only two other local hotels in the 1980s, to approximately thirty at the time of my fieldwork.

People sat under the gazebo eating and drinking; local families gathered at the tables but left soon after eating to make room for others. Raúl drank beer with two acquaintances at the end of a row of tables. Raúl was the president of one of the barrios and had become very active in pueblo activities, organizing sports events for the children. He, like Emilio, played a crucial role in helping me get established in the town. Raúl was nevertheless a controversial figure. Though he was not part of the Frente group, he was a staunch supporter who played an important role in organizing a town mobilization. Raúl had been the lieutenant mayor in the municipality, but left under a cloud of allegations for mixing his business interests and political responsibilities in the formation of a bus company. He was one of the most vociferous of the mobilizers, and one who often added a strong nationalist tone to the protest rhetoric.

Oscar was not the only one with political aspirations. The fieldwork took place during an election year, and many, particularly those in Frente, had interests in holding office in the local government. I often found weighing the role that political ambition played in the mobilization against Sanctuary authorities and corporate interests difficult. Assessing the ultimate motives of the protest created a mix of feelings. On the one hand, the protest was clearly a response to the abuses of sanctuary authorities favoring corporate capital, but on the other hand, the protest was often embroiled in political campaigning. Local politics is an ever-present feature of life embroiled in issues of conservation and privatization pressing the community.

By evening the pollada turned festive and lively as people drank beer and danced. Alberto and Margarita danced wildly in the foot-stomping dance style (*zapatear*) of huayno music.[13] Many, including myself, were inebriated but I continued filming. Eber caught sight of me and pointed an accusatory finger, saying, "Pendejo! Eres un pendejo!" (You are a *pendejo*).[14] Eber, who was teasing me in a friendly manner, was nevertheless commenting on my taking advantage of the role I was assigned by the protestors, and one which I welcomed as an ethnographer, to visually document the interactions between the mobilizers and the authorities of the Sanctuary. Most anthropologists take cameras, video equipment, recorders and microphones to the field as a way of documenting their ethnography. The technological gadgets associated with the "consumer-crazed" North American and European countries often enter into the Serrano definition of the "gringo" and what one comes to expect of them. This can be seen in the modern renditions of the *pishtaco* (human-fat stealers) figures that are often said to be gringos who come to steal human fat to fuel the machineries of the North (Oliver-Smith 1969; Weismantal 2001). Gadgets, particularly cameras, are also often what one comes to expect a tourist to have, and as they are most often gringos, it is a short step to make an association. In one sense, the role of cameraman perhaps allowed people to keep me at a certain distance by positioning me into the more familiar behavior expected of tourists, since they understood that I, like a tourist, was not really implicated in the problems they endure.

The women gathered in a corner by the radio, singing together the sad romantic lyrics of huayno music. Corina yelled over to Eber to put on "their" song "El Mal Paso"[15] (The Bad Stumble). It had become inspirational to their mobilization, and the strength it provided represented to me the subjective and enigmatic dimensions of life that no ethnographic eye or camera could penetrate. Charo hurried Eber to find the CD, adding that the song is "our" song, a dedication to Frente de Defensa. As Eber searched, the women began singing. Rosa turned to me and said, "*Por favor* (please), put the video camera away." Eber located the CD just as Charo grabbed and swung me onto the plaza where others convened. As the song played over the radio, the evening train brought Oscar, who quickly joined the circle as we all started to dance.

There are seven chapters to this ethnographic account. Chapter 1 gives the reader a description of the district of Machu Picchu and the different historical developments behind the Sanctuary and district. It begins with an overview of the history of the Sanctuary of Machu Picchu, focusing on the role of intellectuals in the United States and Peru. I then focus on the growth of the district and town, examining the role of shifting agrarian relations and economic development efforts. The latter entails the building of the current railroad system as a means for transporting natural resources for export in the world economy, and later for the growth of tourism. Chapter 2 examines the role of race and identity in the Machu Picchu economy in terms of neoliberal developments and the creating of the protected area as well as the Cusco touristic economy. The chapter provides a framework for interpreting the value Machu Picchu has in the state's neoliberal vision for Peru. Chapter 3 introduces the reader to the salient class relationships in the district of Machu Picchu and describes in more depth the social, political, and economic changes created by neoliberalism. This chapter shows what neoliberalism means for the inhabitants, relative to their economic conditions and social positions. Here we examine the factors behind the mobilization, and the class conflicts in the way it was organized. Chapter 4 turns our attention to meetings with conservation authorities as well as corporate representatives to describe the institutional lifeworld of Machu Picchu and analyzes the interactions as bureaucratic encounters with the state to describe how law and market forces converge to create an institutional rationale to dispossess people of their rights and belongings. Chapters 5 and 6 describe how residents organized to protect their holdings and discuss the challenges they faced in encountering the governing hierarchies. If chapter 4 examines dispossession mainly in terms of property, chapter 5 highlights the role of political dispossession in facilitating corporate interests. I examine in detail the official meetings between the pueblo protestors and the state authorities, and with others. I focus on the language of neoliberalism through which actors attempt to construct a global reality most suitable to their cause. To untangle these discussions, I use a Goffman dramaturgical approach to make sense of the way players reposition each other around an imaginary audience. Here I pay a great deal of attention to the way the framework for discussions is put together in various contexts to show in Roseberry's terms (1994) why they work or fail, and what makes them fragile. I examine why changes were made on the part of the pueblo that can be considered advancing neoliberal reorganization. In chapter 7 I juxtapose the framework for official interactions with a more hidden set of developments that led to a full stoppage. In this chapter I assess the outcome of protest. I discuss how people came to different conclusions about their activities, and how residents were empowered in some ways but fragmented as well, as a reenforced Machu Picchu identity also entailed exclusionary results. I conclude with a discussion of my return to Machu Picchu years after the protest to describe the changes that took place in the town.

NOTES

1. Note to reader: I use "Pueblo" with a capital to refer to the town as in its name Machupicchu Pueblo. I use "pueblo" in lower case to mean "the people" as is commonly used in the Andes.

2. Throughout the book when referring to my fieldwork, I mean my main fieldwork conducted in 2001–2002 unless otherwise indicated in the text.

3. An example drawn from the United States is when local governments use the rationale of urban renewal to invoke the power of eminent domain and expropriate smaller holdings of private property both for larger capital investments and for generating local tax revenues lost under economic restructuring.

4. It stands for the Commission for the Promotion of Peru.

5. Interview with PromPeru representative: July 16, 1999 (Fieldnotes).

6. Racial categorization in Peru differs from that of the United States in that it is not based on conceptions of bloodline. In Peru definitions of race often allude to cultural differences such as education, dress and custom rather than biological notions (see de la Cadena 2000).

7. In September 2000 the U.S. publicity firm J. Walter Thompson filmed a commercial for a subsidiary of Backus and Johnston, Peru's largest beer company. While the film crew received permission from regional Instituto Nacional de Cultura (INC) representatives, it was not officially cleared at the central level. Also the film crew used an unauthorized 1,000-pound crane not suitable for the terrain.

8. In 2010 a Peru–Yale University Partnership was established to return artifacts excavated by Hiram Bingham back to Peru. It was agreed that the archeological collection would be kept at the Universidad Nacional de San Antonio Abad del Cusco (UNSAAC)

9. See *Plan Para la Mitigacion de Desastres del Poblado de Machu Picchu—Aguas Calientes*, 2001. Note map of security zones and escape routes.

10. According to the World Database on Protected Areas, there are an estimated 157,000 areas deemed protected that cover over 12% of the landed areas in the world. For an excellent discussion of anthropological scholarship on protected areas see West, Igoe and Brockington 2006 *Annual Review*.

11. This form of organization is not unique to Machu Picchu. Many communities throughout Peru have Frente watch dog groups.

12. There is a large body of literature discussing women as key protagonists in social change in Latin America. See Jelin 1990, Bose and Acosta-Belen 1995, and Stephen 1997.

13. See Mendoza, Zoila S. (2000) in the references for an in-depth discussion of dance styles and cultural meanings associated with dance in the Peruvian Andes.

14. "Pendejo" is a Spanish slang term that changes in meaning and intensity depending on the context and country where it is spoken; its meaning can alternate from someone who is sneaky and clever to someone who is dim-witted. Here the term refers to someone who is being sneaky or crafty.

15. "El Mal Paso" sung by Nancy Manchego, produced by "Sentimiento Peru," Lima, Peru.

ONE

Imbricated Spaces

District, Sanctuary, Landscape

> In the first place our town is not called
> Aguas Calientes, we are Machupicchu Pueblo!
> (En Primer lugar el pueblo no se llama
> Aguas Calientes, somos Machupicchu Pueblo!)
> —Eber, Machupicchu Pueblo

The summer is a wet time of year in Machu Picchu.[1] It rains heavily almost daily, and in around the months of January or February the Carnival festivities begin.[2] During *Jugar Carnaval* (to play carnival), the Machupiccheños, like many throughout the sierra region, participate in flirtatious water fights between men and women. On the day before Lent,[3] the fun reaches boisterous heights as children, adolescents and adults throw water balloons or even buckets of water at each other or at an unsuspecting passerby; no one is spared regardless of status. Pranksters playfully splash even the tourist train, wetting the passengers through open windows, and momentarily drawing them into their cultural world as the train crosses the rural landscape. People live in what has become in only recent historical time a "Sanctuary."

The process by which Machu Picchu was given new valuations under neoliberalism stems from a history of double patrimonialization. In 1981 the Peruvian government established Machu Picchu as a national trust. At that time, the state claimed most of the land comprising the district of Machu Picchu as a public good[4]—as an "intangible" national resource; an area of 32,592 hectares was thus made both a historical and natural sanctuary. The rationale for the state's expropriation of the land was the protection and conservation of both natural and cultural resources such as the Inca Trail, the Inca Citadel of Machu Picchu, native plants and fauna. Thus, people who live in the district of Machu Picchu[5] now live in a state-managed and protected zone. In 1983 the geographical area was inscribed onto the United Nations World Heritage List as both a cultural and natural monument in recognition "of the Inca Civilization" and "the beauty of the landscape." To UNESCO's World Heritage Committee this dual cultural and ecological aspect represents the ideal relationship of man to nature, symbolizing a past when man was in "harmony" with nature.

Over time, and certainly by the mid-1990s, state conservation agencies, non-governmental organizations (NGOs), international governing bodies like UNESCO, foreign governments and large-scale private corporations entered the area and encroached upon the jurisdiction of the district and took firm control on what local people considered to be their land. From the state's perspective, however, the residents that control or have access to land are defined as possessors or *posesionarios*, that is, they are granted possession or usufruct rights only and not ownership in the form of property titles. In terms of political control, many residents felt that money and power interests in the Sanctuary trampled upon the sovereignty of their district governance. Both state control and privatization efforts undermined what people saw as democratic participation at a time when, after the Shining Path war and the end of the Fujimori regime, a more meaningful democracy seemed possible.

PRELUDES AND CONTEXTS

The Quechua term *Machu Picchu* basically translates into "Old Mountain" or "Old Peak." As a place name, the term initially referred to the name of a mountain located on the eastern slope of the southern Peruvian Andes about 70 kilometers east of the city of Cusco (see figure 1.1). However, a political district, a rural town, an archeological site, and a nature reserve also came to be called Machu Picchu.

The district of Machu Picchu is located in the province of Urubamba in the department of Cusco, Peru. The district was established in 1941, some thirty years after the discovery of the Incan Citadel. The district was formed, however, forty years prior to the state's creation of a historical and natural sanctuary in 1981, and forty-two years before it was inscribed on UNESCO's World Heritage List in 1983.[6] The district is comprised of a town, Machu Picchu Pueblo, the capital of the district, and four rural campesino communities. Like the district, the town capital is also called Machupicchu (Machupicchu Pueblo), though many in Peru and even in the city of Cusco, not to mention foreigners, refer to it as Aguas Calientes, (Hot Springs). For many in the town, the term "Machupiccheño" has, since the formation of the Sanctuary, slowly evolved into a symbol of identity connoting one's right to live in the district. This identity aspect,

Figure 1.1. Map of Sacred Valley area that shows key locations from the city of Cusco to Machupicchu Pueblo. (Drawing by Hanzada A. Kurdi)

of who is or is not a Machupiccheño, as we shall see later, factored heavily into a rhetoric of defense against the intrusions by corporate and state control. Unfortunately, it was also part of a politics of exclusion whereby some residents claimed to have more right to live in the Sanctuary than other more recent arrivals. This nativist attitude that leads to an exclusionary politics involved issues of belonging and rootedness in an economy that emphasizes the circulation of capital and people (Tsing 2000: 337). But in Machupicchu Pueblo there was simultaneously a constant pressure to justify legitimacy for living in the Sanctuary to authorities by demonstrating an authentic identity, despite how the neoliberal economy in the Andes has led to migrations and the reality that where one earns a living is tied less to their own community (Colloredo-Mansfeld 2002a: 639).

In addition, Machu Picchu refers to the famous Citadel. The Citadel of Machu Picchu rests on a ridge cradled between the mountains Machu Picchu and Huayna Picchu.[7] It is not known what the Incas called their citadel or the mountains between which it is positioned. The Citadel harbors the same name as one of the mountains, but reference to these mountains can be dated only as far back as the mid-19th century (Tamayo Herrera 1981). The use of the name Machu Picchu for the Citadel became common after the historian and explorer Hiram Bingham popularized the area with the account of his "discovery" expedition. In his writings, Bingham often used the name of the mountain and the archeological ruins interchangeably, leading to the current popular usage. A *New York Times* article on Bingham's discovery provided one of the first public accounts:

> He [Bingham] has just announced that he has had the superb good fortune to discover an entire city, two thousand years old, a place of splendid palaces and temples and grim encircling walls hidden away so thoroughly on the top of a well-nigh inaccessible mountain peak of the Peruvian Andes. . . . He calls it Machu Picchu. (*NYT*, Jun. 15, 1913)

The age of the Citadel was nowhere close to what Bingham initially imagined. Bingham was a historian and not trained in archeology. He was perhaps more interested in collecting objects than in documenting context, meanings and facts (Cox Hall 2012: 294).[8]

Finally, both the Citadel and the mountain Machu Picchu are in a national park of over 32 thousand hectares that is officially called El Santuario Historico de Machu Picchu (The Historical Sanctuary of Machu Picchu). It is important to note the various intersecting spaces called "Machu Picchu" because the development of each is based on different but overlapping historical processes, leading to conflicts in administration and control among diverse governing authorities. Moreover, it connotes the different ways the Machupiccheños are implicated in conservation regulations that would otherwise be obscured by the generic use of the same name. A probe into the history that shaped the current social relationships in the district is necessary for understanding the way differently located residents deal with their specific problems.

INTELLECTUALS AND THE MAKING OF THE LANDSCAPE

Whatever it may have meant to the Inca, as knowledge of the archeological site spread throughout the world, Machu Picchu came to mean many things to many people. The Citadel of Machu Picchu has been the subject of popular myths, legends, novels and poetry, and an attraction for spiritual groups and tourists. The Chilean poet Pablo Neruda made Machu Picchu the topic of an epic poem on human suffering and aspiration. The monument's history as an icon for different ideologies and identities has often placed it at the center of regional, national and international politics.

The modern image of Machu Picchu and its surrounding landscape began with the 1911 expedition by the Yale historian Hiram Bingham,[9] who "discovered" what he believed to be Vilcabamba, the city to which the last Incas had retreated from the Spanish conquest.[10] In a series of photographs published in the *National Geographic Magazine,* Bingham's presentation of Machu Picchu captured the imagination of North American and European audiences. His vivid descriptions of the Andes combined with his description of the site helped to make Machu Picchu one of South America's most spectacular tourism destinations. The Andes, as Deborah Poole notes, had already captured the imagination of many North Americans prior to Bingham, in the romantic artistic depiction of Frederic Edwin Church's *Heart of the Andes* in 1859 which was featured in exhibitions in the Metropolitan Museum of Art and other New York locations, as well as in an Andean engraving by Ephraim George Squier in 1868 (Poole 1998: 108). Poole's subtle visual genealogy of the Andes connects visual culture to economic and political relations between the North and South by noting the way visual representations are given material shape. Just as the landscape portraits of the 19th-century American transcendental movement helped construct notions of the American nation and the "future of the country," Poole argues that they fed into government notions of "Manifest Destiny" which by Bingham's time meant a "Pan-American" control on the part of the United States (ibid.: 110).

Scientific expeditions such as Bingham's were often implicated with, or co-opted, by Euro-American imperialist projects, with negative consequences (Smith: 1994, 2003).[11] Geographical knowledge played an important role in European and American colonial expansion. The supposed objective stance of scientific expeditions often concealed specific sets of social relations that assisted in the conquest and governance of territories (ibid.: 3). As Amy Cox Hall notes, Bingham's cloak of science played an important role in building the political and cultural capital that led to the financing of expeditions (Cox Hall 2012: 295). In addition, the National Geographic Society also played a significant role in constructing an image of non-Western cultures as exotic others, and through the magazine those images became a common way many North Americans learned about other cultures (ibid.; Rothenberg 1994; Lutz and Collins 1993). In the case of Machu Picchu, tourist guidebooks for Cusco began appearing within only a few years of the *National Geographic* publication (Flores Ochoa 1996).

Bingham transformed his expedition into a "discovery and adventure narrative," common to the Western genre of "great explorers" (Said 1994). In Bingham's book *Machu Picchu: A Citadel of the Incas* (1930), we find photographs with captions entitled "The Most Inaccessible Corner of the Most Inaccessible Section of the Central Andes" (Bingham in Poole 1998: 123). Not surprisingly, his account was to become many years later the inspiration for the fictional character "Indiana Jones" in the film *Raiders of the Lost Ark* (A. Bingham 1989). The beauty of the landscape deeply inspired Bingham. He compared it with "the majestic grandeur of the Canadian Rockies" and the beauty of his native land of Hawaii (Bingham 1948). His discovery narrative was interwoven with Western romantic notions of nature as pristine, describing it with phrases like "matchless charm," and referring to "the power of its spell" (Bingham 1948). From the Citadel of Machu Picchu, he observed, "[T]here is no valley in South America that has such varied beauty" (Bingham 1913: 403).

By making constant reference to how nature defended and protected the Incas, Bingham, participated in uniting ideas of man and nature in a specific relationship. This is not uncommon, as ideas of nature have been shown to express social and material relationships (Williams 1973, 1980; Smith 1996). And although Bingham showed great respect for the ancient Incas, the indigenous population was at that time often described in a denigrating fashion.

> For centuries it has reared the sky its giant ruins half-buried in tropical vegetation, *known only to a few ignorant Indians of the neighborhood.* Where the magnificent city was three poverty stricken half naked Indian families now live: On the site of the central plaza, of its shrines and mansions and fortification, they sow their little patches of corn. (*NYT* Jun. 15, 1913, italics mine)

Bingham's narrative reinforced a pervasive discourse that helped separate the achievements of the Incas from the contemporary population of the sierra. Those accomplishments were for Bingham "achievements of a bygone race" (Bingham 1913: 403). This is a recurring theme in the way Euro–North Americans have interpreted indigenous pasts to excuse racist policies, as Robert Silverberg illustrates in his account of early American explanations for the origins of American Indian mounds in the eastern United States that were described as the achievements of a "lost prehistoric race." By detaching the history from the population, such discourses facilitated policies that uprooted people from their homes, dispossessing them of land (1968: 48). Like the English in the United States, Spain's encounters with indigenous populations were no different. In terms of dispossession, the English and Spanish had similar explanations, responses and "legitimating strategies" (Mackenthun 1997: 16).

Bingham's account, which merged archeological knowledge and Western views of nature, fed into the growth of current ecological/cultural tourism in the Andes. The collection and display of artifacts and human remains juxtaposed a racial identity to the landscape (Cox Hall 2012: 296). With the publication of Bingham's article in the *National Geographic Magazine* in April 1913, Machu Picchu became a North American version of what Deborah Poole calls "the visual economy of the Andean image world," by which she means that visual representations of the Andes, "the circulation of images, fantasies, ideas and sentiments," moved between Europe and the Andes (Poole 1997). In the latter part of the 20th century Machu Picchu became a dominant Andean symbol in a global "visual economy," one that bound conceptions of identity and history to an idea of nature (Poole 1997; Femenias 2000; de la Cadena 1995). In Bingham's case the *National Geographic* presented a fantastic collection of 250 photographs entitled "In the Wonderland of Peru" and portrayed Bingham, as he did himself, as the heroic "discoverer" of Machu Picchu. In addition to the *National Geographic*, Bingham's photos were shown in schools and to "civic groups," as well as displayed in the Museum of Natural History (Poole 1998: 124).

However, Bingham was not the only one to display Machu Picchu. There is an additional local history to the making of Machu Picchu into the tourist site it is today. Peruvian intellectuals in Cusco had long known about the existence of the Citadel, and had in fact informed Bingham of its general location (A. Bingham 1989). Although the credit given to Bingham's discovery has been criticized and modified, he is still officially acknowledged as the "scientific" discoverer of Machu Picchu. To the contrary, as has been suggested, perhaps it is more accurate to consider Bingham as the first tourist rather than its discoverer (Mould de Pease in Cox Hall 2012: 296). "Cusco Indigenismo," one of the most notable intellectual movements to emerge in defense of the "Indian" began in the Andean city of Cusco. This regional movement was led by a group of intellectuals and artists that defined what is known as "The Golden Age of Cusco Indigenismo," from 1910 to 1930. The figures behind this movement made Cusco a contested site in the battle for Peruvian national identity (Poole 1997). What these individuals did was to reclaim Inca history and geography as their own by valorizing Indian culture in their art, national heritage and state policy (ibid.). The key figures behind this movement played an important role in the spatial and cultural politics of nation making. They advocated regionalism and promoted a special autonomous status for the Andes that sought to thwart state intrusions and the influence of Creole culture. Second, through artistic and literary productions they rescaled the geography of the nation to make the Andean landscape the central feature in defining the nation of Peru. Finally, many of these intellectuals played a decisive role in the shaping of important cultural institutions such as the Museo Peruano de Arqueología that accentuated pre-Columbian achievements in Peruvian national history (Femenías 2000). One figure, Jose Luis Valcárcel, took issue with Bingham's claim.[12] As an ethnologist and archeologist, Valcárcel played a key role in the development of a number of Peruvian museums, and was also very active in the collecting, categorizing and documenting of Indian artifacts, past and present (Femenias 2000). In 1915 when Bingham returned to Peru for follow-up research on Machu Picchu, he was to engage in a debate with Valcárcel that concluded with Valcárcel accusing Bingham of stealing Peru's national treasures (Zapata Velasco 1999).[13] Fourteen years after Bingham's *National Geographic* issue was published, Valcárcel wrote[14] *Tempestad en los Andes* (1927), his own powerful polemic romanticizing the Andes and the unbroken Indian purity of Andean people (Valcárcel 1927). With fiery energy and colorful language, Valcárcel demanded justice for Indians, declaring, "From the Andes will flow, like rivers, the currents of renovation that will transform Peru. . . . All of the timeless virtues of the Indian still pulse through his blood" (ibid.: 103–104). "Peru is Indian!" declared Valcárcel (ibid.: 112). Valcárcel's works on Machu Picchu declare it the most famous archeological monument of Peru.

Like Bingham, Valcárcel created an ideal Andean man and bound him to an ideal concept of nature. Bingham's discourse and visual depictions influenced a different network of institutions which helped commercialize Machu Picchu for the West; Bingham's was crucial in understanding how, as Poole states, "North Americans would come to perceive, imagine, dream about, and act on that part of Latin America known as 'the Andes'" (1998: 131). Valcárcel's connections, on the other hand, were with the Peruvian national museums that also shaped the site into a national icon. Both played a role in informing the views of such current institutional players as the UN World Heritage Committee, the Peruvian State and others whose views have helped construct the Machu Picchu Citadel and landscape into a world heritage site and a tourist commodity for Peru. Finally, both had the effect of encouraging state ownership and control of the land.

DISTRICT AND PUEBLO

Haciendas and the Struggle for Land

In Peru, the agrarian reform of 1969 under Juan Velasco's government promised to redistribute land among the tenants. Despite the state's expropriation of land from the hacendados, the legal redistribution of land in Peru did not occur evenly throughout the country or at the same time (Seligmann 1995). There was considerable variation across the country in the way the new system of land tenure was put into effect, as there were differences in the intensity of peasant struggles in diverse locations (Guillet 1979; Smith 1989; Seligmann 1995; Mayer 2009). In addition, we are witness to the history of different peasant revolts, uprisings, and strategies indigenous people employed to negotiate on their behalf during colonialism and leading up to the reforms of the 1960s (Mallon 1983; Stern 1987). In fact, Velasco was not the first to implement agrarian reforms in Peru. Prior to Velasco's coup, President Fernando Belaúnde (1963–1968), in response to land invasions and violent uprisings in 1964 made small gestures toward legislative reforms in favor of the campesino struggles (Seligmann 1995: 57). There were differential responses to the agrarian reform by different social actors. Mayer (2009) warns that one should not interpret ensuing conflict in terms of simple dualities such as differences between urban/rural and traditional/modern. However, the tensions and turmoil after the 1969 reforms played an important role in the rise of the Shining Path (ibid.; Seligmann 1995: 154). Not long after agrarian reform laws swept across Latin America were counter-reforms enacted to reverse the benefits by privatizing credit agencies, technical assistance and other features of the agrarian industry (Kay 2002). In Peru, Belaúnde, the same man who was initially acquiescent towards the campesino land struggles, initiated counter-reform laws upon his return as president in 1980 (Seligmann 1995: 73). His second regime took a much more liberal stance towards private ownership, allowing for individual property titles of land parcels. The breakup of the peasant cooperatives created conflicts of wealth among campesinos. In many cases the wealthier peasants reemerged as mini hacendados (Hunefeldt 1997: 112). In addition, it was under the Belaúnde regime that Machu Picchu was designated a national trust and world heritage site.[15]

However, it was not until Fujimori's neoliberal agenda that the final rupture with the ideals of the agrarian reform occurred. In 1991 and then more systematically in 1995, new land laws further encouraged individual ownership (Crabtree 2002: 141). Following the advice of economist Hernando de Soto, Fujimori implemented a plan that in theory would give small rural producers the opportunity, through private ownership, to better profit from market liberalization. In promoting the legal titling of property, it was expected that campesinos (farmers) would have the security to obtain loans and mortgages; but this did not happen as expected (ibid.: 143). Moreover, liberalization signaled the end of the Agrarian Bank, a significant no-interest credit reserve for campesinos. Fujimori cut agrarian services considerably, and privatized state assets such as forests (ibid.; Seligmann 1995: 73). What compromised the efforts of campesinos to benefit from loans were the very neoliberal policies that on the one hand sought to make rural inhabitants more competitive, but on the other hand undermined their ability to compete by allowing for "cheaper food imports" to enter local markets (ibid.). Yet one legacy of these efforts, for both rural and urban inhabitants, is the concern to obtain property titles as imperative to survive in the new economy. This is evident in the case of Machu Picchu.

In Machu Picchu, the rural communities were formed out of different haciendas, and the campesinos within the district organized themselves according to these boundaries. The area now considered a sanctuary (El Santuario Historico de Machu Picchu) was formed by the state out of four separate family-owned haciendas: San Antonio de Torontoy, Quente, Santa Rita de Q'ente and Mandorpampa.[16] The redistribution of land took different paths according to the different haciendas in question (Maxwell 2004: 319).[17]

First, the hacienda of Mandorpampa was never expropriated in accordance with the agrarian reform law, but rather remained in the control of the hacendado family, and campesinos lived as tenants (ibid.). Tourism developers eventually purchased some of the land from this hacienda (ibid.). In the mid-1970s the campesinos in the former hacienda of San Antonio de Torontoy received land parcels from the state. By 1978, the beneficiaries repaid their agrarian loans for their land but did not receive property titles, nor were they officially recognized in the public registry (ibid.). Nevertheless, the residents here have a degree of security since they paid for their land and are recognized as beneficiaries of the agrarian reform (ibid.). However, in Quente and Santa Rita de Quente there was a different process. As in Torontoy, the state also expropriated the land from these two haciendas and distributed it to the campesinos, with the old hacendado of Quente receiving four hectares of land (ibid.: 320). In fact, the former hacendados are allegedly still listed as owners in the public registry, although some conservation authorities maintain that ownership was registered on fraudulent grounds. Concurrent with these events, the state pushed to define heritage areas. In 1981, the state defined the existing boundaries of the Sanctuary of Machu Picchu and declared it to be a national trust. Prior to this, only the archeological ruins fell under conservation laws, and it was not clear as to how much land surrounding the sites could be expropriated.[18] Shortly thereafter, in 1983, UNESCO declared the Sanctuary of Machu Picchu to be a World Heritage Site that represented universal values of man in harmony with nature. In 1991 a law invalidated the expropriation of agrarian reform land, and placed it under the control of the Instituto Nacional de Cultura (INC), the state archeological conservation agency (ibid.: 321). Those who were to receive land from the agrarian reform were now greatly restricted in the use of that land. As a result, the campesinos were never given property titles nor recognized as property holders; the state would recognize neither the permanence nor the antiquity of the population. Moreover, according to the 1991 law, the INC superseded the authority of the Instituto Nacional de Recursos Naturales (INRENA), the agency in charge of conserving the natural resources (ibid.). What made matters more complicated is that the former hacendados have used the invalidation of the agrarian reform laws to try and regain possession of the land, arguing that the 1991 law gives the INC control but not ownership (ibid.). The state agencies, the hacendados and the campesinos have thus been in a long-drawn-out legal battle. The problem is that laws and arguments are constantly used in contradictory fashion according to the expediency of the situation. Keely Maxwell describes the clashes succinctly:

> The claims of particular stakeholders are sometimes internally inconsistent from one court case to another. State agencies reject any legality of the agrarian reform process in Machu Picchu in one court case. The same agencies depend on certain aspects of agrarian reform having occurred in Machu Picchu in another case to justify their own claims to land. Similarly, hacienda owners accept nullification of agrarian reform because Machu Picchu is historic patrimony in one case. They reject both this nullification and claims to Machu Picchu being historic patrimony in another case. (ibid.: 322)

RURAL LIFE

The life ways and problems of the people in the rural areas differ from those in the town and among each other. Since Machu Picchu is on the eastern slope of the Andes, it borders the jungle—the area often referred to as "*ceja de selva*," meaning the "eyebrow of the jungle" and translated into English as "the high jungle" or "cloud forest." The ecology can vary greatly in just a short distance, and so the rural communities can differ in what they cultivate. Up through the 1990s agricultural production was largely for subsistence because of conservation restrictions and transportation difficulties, but by the turn of the 21st century commercial activity for local and provincial markets showed some signs of increasing growth, most likely based on demands of the food industry for the tourism economy.[19] As mentioned above, a more important aspect involves the different histories each former hacienda had after the agrarian reform—that is, whether or not they managed to get some kind of recognition for their land. Economically, another factor is whether the rural communities are located along the Inca Trail. If they are located along the Inca Trail, the residents have the possibility of drawing on the tourism economy by selling water, chicha, candy, and crackers to tourists and porters, *porteadores*. However, it is in these locations that state conservation agencies most stringently enforce the conservation laws. In these areas, I found a sort of cat-and-mouse game being played between the state and the campesinos. For the purposes of this discussion, I will focus on only two rural sectors with different histories: Corihuayrachina and Huayllabamba.[20]

The communities of Huayllabamba and Corihuayrachina are located about five kilometers apart, on opposite sides of the Vilcanota River. Huayllabamba, part of the old hacienda of Q'ente and Santa Rita de Q'ente, is located on the border of both the Sanctuary and the district of Machu Picchu. Just opposite Huayllabamba, across the narrow Cusichaca River that runs perpendicular to the main Vilcanota River, is the district of Ollantaytambo. In this borderland, one could note most vividly the contrast between living in or outside of the Machu Picchu Sanctuary. The residents in Huayllabamba do not hold property titles as do those of Ollantaytambo.[21]

Nevertheless, during my fieldwork tourism was a variable in the rural economy and men did take advantage of it when opportunities arose, such as if a tour group needed extra porters to carry baggage. Women made and sold chicha,[22] mainly to the large number of local porters that passed through the area.[23] As Susana, a resident of Huayllabamba, explained, making chicha requires a lot of cooking and hence a large amount of firewood. Yet, conservation enforcements prohibited the use of gas stoves and restricted her from obtaining firewood for her stove; people were not allowed to cut wood from surrounding native trees.

Although there was a commons specified by INRENA where tree branches from non-indigenous trees could be cut for the collection of firewood, it could be a good distance away from where many residents live. The opportunity existed for people to cross the river to obtain firewood outside of the Sanctuary, but that also created intercommunity tensions with residents of the district of Ollantay. The point is that opportunities for exploiting the tourism economy depended on the location of the community. Huayllabamba is situated on a main artery of the picturesque Inca Trail through which thousands of tour groups hike annually. Therefore, unlike in Corihuayrachina and other communities, tourism played a more direct role in the economy.

The community of Corihuayrachina is located at kilometer 88 on the Cusco–Machu Picchu train line. It is a core campesino sector of the old hacienda called San Antonio de Torontoy (see figure 1.2). This hacienda extended from a place called Choqellusco at kilometer 82 up to part of the current Pueblo of Machu Picchu at kilometer 110 on one side of the Vilcanota River. After the national agrarian reform of 1968/69, the people who worked this hacienda, unlike those from Huayllabamba, became the beneficiaries of the land. As such, they sought to legalize the status of their community. According to Francisco Bacahuaman, who was the president of the campesino organization of San Antonio de Torontoy at the time, the campesinos had paid their agrarian debts to the state in the mid-1970s. Later, the state created INRENA as a state conservation agency. The apparent goal of the state bureaucracy was, as Bingham had portrayed, to re-create the image of a pristine state of nature that supposedly only the Incas lived with in harmony. As one INRENA ranger explained in an effort to tie an idea of nature with the Incas, "Could you imagine if Machu Picchu [the archeological Citadel] were built in the middle of the Sahara desert? Machu Picchu without [this] nature would not be Machu Picchu," meaning, that there is an intrinsic fit between the constructions of the Incas and the surrounding ecology.

MACHUPICCHU PUEBLO

In contrast to the growth of the rural communities and the formation of the Sanctuary boundaries, the town of Machu Picchu grew out of a different process; it was established neither out of the agricultural economy nor tourism. Although the town was formed out of pieces of the haciendas Mandorpampa and San Antonio de Torontoy, the urban development is one of progressive growth based on state modernization and industrialization. In the late 1940s the town began to grow because of the building of the train line along the Urubamba River (also called Vilcanota), as a location for train workers (*brequeros*) and their families (Tamayo Herrera 1981). It was sometimes locally referred to as "Maquinachay-

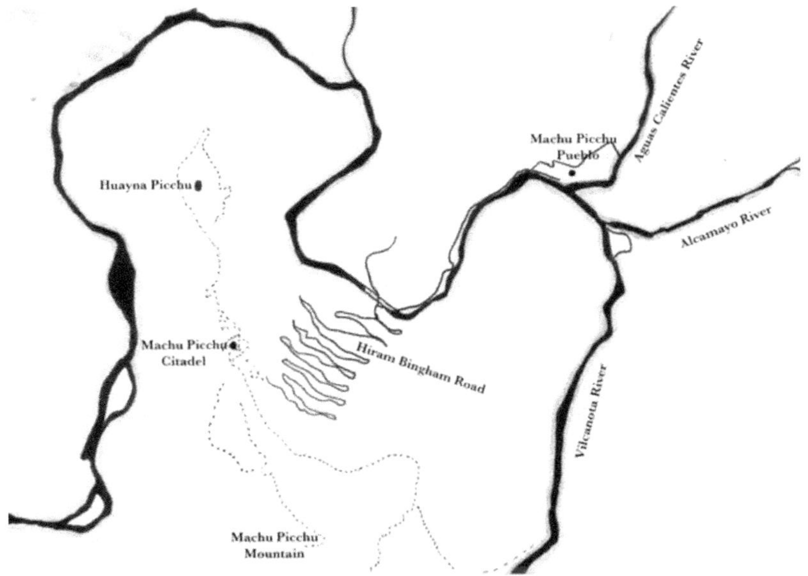

Figure 1.2. Map shows the location of the Machupicchu Pueblo relative to the Citadel and mountain of Machu Picchu. Note the location of the Hiram Bingham Road that takes passengers up to the Citadel. (Drawing by Hanzada A. Kurdi)

oc,"[24] Quechua for "the place where the engine is located." However, this is not to say that prior to the railroad developments no campesino families lived in the pueblo area. Chela recalls her parents speaking of the location of what is now the tourist train station and sports stadium as used for her family's cattle grazing. This areas of where the town is currently located were as noted part of the hacienda of San Antonio de Torontoy.

From a North American perspective, the town seemed like a "frontier town."[25] The first train ran from Cusco to Machupicchu Pueblo. The station was then moved down about a kilometer away to Puente Ruinas (Ruins Bridge), just opposite the path now leading up to the Citadel on the Hiram Bingham Road. Eventually, the rail was extended all the way to the city of Quillabamba located at the verge of the low jungle, which was the state's primary goal for the extraction and transportation of natural resources. As some older members of the town, like Don Teofilo who came to the town in the mid-1950s and was the owner of one of the first hotels, recall, the train line had benefits. It allowed campesinos to transport agricultural products to Cusco markets cheaper and faster than by road. Men worked on the trains and rails and women sold food and produce to people who came from Cusco or Quillabamba. However, it was not for farm produce that the train was built, but to carry raw materials, mainly rubber but also timber and other products, from the jungle to factories and for export (ibid.).

According to local accounts, initially, the train station was named Puente Ruinas after the bridge that crosses the Vilcanota River. From Don Teofilo's account, the name of the station did not appeal to the station chief because it implied it was in ruins and did not connote a modern image. As a result, the station chief changed the name of the station to Machu Picchu and then it became customary among the train workers to distinguish the town from the station by referring to the town as Aguas Calientes (hot springs) after the hot springs located there. However, the name of the town had always been Machupicchu Pueblo, and legally so, even though the tourism industry as well as many Peruvians continued to popularize the name Aguas Calientes.[26]

The tourism industry was built on a series of developments dating as far back as 1924 with the formation of the Touring y Automóvil Club del Perú (Deforges 2000: 178). However, it wasn't until the 1960s that the state began playing an increasing role. With the formation of the Corporación de Turismo del Perú (COTURPERU) the government set up a chain of hotels to generate income for the state (several of these hotels including Sanctuary Lodge Hotel were eventually privatized to the corporation Orient Express/Belmond). In 1965 there was the Plan Turístico y Cultural de la Comisión Especial (COPESCO plan), a cooperative effort between the state's COTURPERU and UNESCO to restore the archeological ruins and particularly the ruins of Machu Picchu (ibid.: 182; Peña Berna 2001: 36). The state funded approximately 70% of the plan, which it used for the "construction of roads, airports, transport and energy links as well as the development of tourist sites" (ibid.: 183). One such development was the construction of a road connecting the town to the Hiram Bingham Road that encircles the steep mountain to the Citadel. These initiatives of the 1960s and 1970s was one of Peru's most successful state-led investments, as the income generated by tourism went from $44 million U.S. to $201.6 million U.S. from 1970 to 1979 (ibid.). It also laid the infrastructural foundation for the burgeoning tourism economy of Cusco in the 1990s.

In the 1940s tourism in Machu Picchu was only in its nascent stages, with less than half a dozen daily visitors during the high season. The railroad and many of the laborers who built it settled in the town, turning what was largely a rural area into a small town, an urban zone in a largely rural district. The entire district has a long history of being a place of intense movement and activity. Today, thousands of tourists come and go daily. Rural inhabitants from the district as well as neighboring Santa Teresa come to the town to sell their agricultural goods. Additionally, hundreds of young men and women from all over Peru come annually to the town looking for jobs in the restaurants and hotels. Tour guides and large numbers of porteadores[27] working in the Cusco tourism industry take groups of tourists on a 3–4 day hike through the Inca Trail on a trip that ends in the town.

Since the district attracts many people who take up temporary residence throughout the year, it is difficult to discern the actual total population. However, according to the national census conducted in 1993, which was the last during my fieldwork, the district population was officially at 2,298 residents, divided into 1,141 living in the Pueblo and 1,157 in the rural areas.[28] A local census taken of only the Pueblo in 1999 counted 1,601 inhabitants (Peña Berna 2001: 28). During my fieldwork in 2002, town officials estimated that the total population of the district was about 5,000 inhabitants, but according to some approximations only about 3,000 are permanent residents, 1,200 in the Pueblo and 1,800 in the rural communities.

The municipal building is in the town, as is a well-supplied medical station. There is also a cultural center, built by the INC, which contains a small library and an auditorium for use by the townsfolk. Although a church was built in 1984, a priest makes only a few visits a year, largely during festivals. In 2002 the residents did not have potable water and there were numerous complaints about parasitic infections. However, most residents but not all had running water at the time of my fieldwork, though certain sections or *barrios* had frequent outages.

The town is comprised of four barrios (neighborhoods) settled in the following order: Huiñay Huayna,[29] Imperio de los Incas, Las Orquideas and El Mirador. In brief, Huiñay Huayna is the first settlement that grew alongside the principal Avenue Pachacútec, which leads to the hot springs. In general, the older, more established Machupiccheños live in this location; this area also contains many of the town's restaurants and hostels. The second settlement, Imperio de los Incas, developed around the local train station and so includes hotels and dining establishments that parallel the train tracks, but the distinguishing feature in this section is the location of a somewhat haphazard artisan market constructed out of basic wood frames and plastic tarp coverings. The Aguas Calientes River divides Las Orquideas from the other two barrios. Even though this barrio holds the tourist train station, Las Orquideas is mainly a residential area, and contains the town cemetery and a sports stadium. In 2002, most of the establishments in this location were grocery stores or other shops that sell goods for local consumption; this was to change considerably in subsequent years. In addition, this barrio held many of the newer residents and migrant workers who rented their living quarters, and where some attempted land invasions to establish a more permanent living claim. Finally, the most recent barrio, El Mirador, was developed out of a land invasion on the slope of a mountain that perched above Las Orquideas. Eventually, the occupants won legal status and the municipal authorities organized them as a barrio. Mostly recent migrants live in El Mirador, which is also undoubtedly the poorest section of the town.

As expected, livelihoods in the town vary. The municipality employs a number of people on a permanent basis to carry out different tasks such as administrative, construction, sanitation, and the enforcement of municipal codes. Some residents work in state conservation agencies doing archeological restorations and manual labor. There is a central food market where women operate small stands selling meat and agricultural produce, while others run lunch counters. In 2002 there were some twelve family-owned grocery shops selling a variety of packaged goods. Also, bread is produced daily in a local bakery.

However, since tourism is the mainstay of the town, economic activity is comprised mostly of domestic enterprises such as restaurants, hostels and artisans/merchants who sell ceramics, textile products and memorabilia tailored for tourist consumption. These establishments are centered either along the train tracks or Pachacutec Avenue, areas most frequented by tourists. In 2002 there were only forty-five family-owned restaurants[30] and twenty-eight hostels, excluding the four large-scale first-class hotels: Hotel Machu Picchu and Sanctuary Lodge (both owned by Orient Express), Pueblo Hotel and Hatuchay Towers. The locally owned hostels were relatively small, averaging around nine rooms each with the largest containing twenty-eight and the smallest, four rooms. Compare this to the Pueblo Hotel at eighty-five rooms and the other major hotels, respectively, at around forty (Peña Berna 2001: 201–203). In addition to hotels and restaurants, there were four artisan/merchant associations comprised of about 215 members.[31]

A major source of revenue for the municipality and residents comes from the bus transportation service that brings tourists to and from the Inca Citadel. The service is administered by CONSETTUR, Consorcio de Empresas de Transporte Turístico, a consortium made up of six companies. The bus service was initially a state-run company but was decentralized to be operated by the regional government, and then in 1995 it was privatized to form CONSETTUR. The two largest of these companies, owning six buses each, are a company made up of ex-employees of the regional government service and a company owned and operated by the municipality of Machu Picchu; in total there were twenty buses (ibid.: 55). Many residents who own hotels and restaurants also own shares in the bus company TRAMUSA, making it a local capital venture and a growing generator of wealth, which was threatened by plans to build a cable car (*teleferico*) directly to the Citadel.

One of the more colorful livelihoods revolving around tourism during my fieldwork was that of the *chasqui boys*.[32] Some boys, generally between the ages of 9 and 12, dressed up as "chasquis," who served as the message runners during the time of the Inca Empire. These boys waited at the Citadel entrance for departing buses to bring tourists back to the Pueblo. As the bus traveled down the winding mountain road, the chasqui boys dashed down a more direct footpath, beating the bus to the next road level. As the busload of tourists passed, the boy would cry out a hearty "goodbye" and then dash down to the next level and do it again all the way down; at the bottom the driver allowed him to get on the bus to collect tips from tourists. Since the boys depended on the drivers to take them up to the Citadel and to stop for them to collect their tips, the boys would repay the drivers by doing chores for them, such as washing and cleaning the bus. However, the chasqui boys were not without controversy. Many Machupiccheños felt that the boys should be in school rather than working. Many children throughout Peru work out of economic necessity, and some accommodations are made for them through night school programs. Nevertheless, when I returned in 2007 the municipality had prohibited kids from working as chasquis.

Finally, no examination of the Machu Picchu tourism economy is complete without a discussion of the hundreds of men and women who come from all over Peru to work in restaurants and hotels. Although most local restaurants and hotels were domestic enterprises in the sense that they drew mainly on family labor, many hired at least one person during the low tourist season and two or three during the high tourist season.[33] A migrant labor force of people from all over Peru were employed to wait on tables, clean rooms and as *jaladores* that pull in customers from the train station or when they pass the restaurants. Typically, the workload was seven days a week, twelve hours a day (sometimes Saturdays and Sundays are a few hours less). While pay varies, a waiter, for instance, generally received 10% of the customer's check. In 2002, during the high tourist season, workers could make between 400 and 600 soles or about 115–170 U.S. dollars a month. Hotel employees were generally given room and board, but restaurant employees had to find a room to rent, an additional cost. Rent was a great economic burden for many workers. Thus, workers would share a room with two or three other people. Workers could stay on for years, bouncing from job to job within the town as the tourist seasons reshuffled labor needs. Many supplemented their income as *ambulantes,* walking about selling trinkets and food directly to tourists.

Many came to work in the town to escape conditions of extreme poverty. Nancy, who was a 23-year-old woman at the time with a four-year-old daughter, came to Machu Picchu from rural Quillabamba, where her family cultivated coffee for a cooperative. The family produced about 400 kilos of coffee beans per year, which sold for 200 soles ($60 U.S.). However, in the town, Nancy earned approximately 400 soles ($120) a month working as a waitress in a popular restaurant. Others came to work in the town during their school vacation as a way of earning money to help pay for tuition. Lily, a young woman who was in her early twenties, came to Machupicchu Pueblo from Cusco where she studied nursing. She found a job in a restaurant where she worked 12 hours a day at 10%. The day I spoke to her she made only 10 soles ($3 U.S.) for those long hours. A good day for her was making 30 soles or higher.

Despite the long hours, many workers I spoke to would tell me they preferred the tourism economy of Machu Picchu rather than in the city of Cusco, where the economy was saturated with people looking for work; the competition in Cusco was greater, and the pay was generally less. However, not all people working in the town worked for local businesses. At fifteen, Carmencita came to the town from Cusco to sell ice cream for a company. Her arrival was for work, but as is often the case for many young men and women, also for fun and adventure. Carmencita loved to dance. In the evenings, she and her teenage friends would "chase" each other from club to club. In the morning, however, she would be ready to pick up the batches of ice cream arriving from Cusco on the local train, and walk through the plaza selling cones and cups. Businesses in Cusco did send employees by train to sell merchandise, but there was a point of diminishing returns. During the low tourism season, when sales are down, it is no longer profitable to pay for transportation fees. Carmencita eventually lost her job but stayed on in the town looking for work in the local establishments.

The train itself was a source of livelihood in the town. When the incoming train sounded its horn, there was a rush of people running through the plaza and to the station. Some of these people, aside from passengers, were *cargadores*. Cargadores, unlike porteadores who make their living carrying tourist bags on the Inca Trail, carried loads for people from the train to their homes, hotels or places of business. There were about 20 cargadores in the pueblo, waiting for train passengers, merchants and market vendors to arrive. When I met Florentino, 45 years old, he had been working as a cargador for about a month and a half, arriving from his rural community where he cultivated potatoes, corn, barley and wheat for consumption. In Machupicchu Pueblo he unloaded concrete blocks and wood planks from the train cargo compartment. On a good day, he could make as much as 20 soles ($5 U.S.).

For many, Machupicchu Pueblo offered economic opportunities not found elsewhere, though those opportunities were not always realized as imagined or at all. Miguel, thirty years old, came to the Pueblo from Lima, but first stayed in Cusco looking for work. He told me the story of how in Cusco he was robbed of all his belongings. "How ironic," he said, "that a person from Lima gets robbed in Cusco when the stereotype is that of a Serrano[34] taken advantage of in the big cosmopolitan City of Lima." Once in Machupicchu Pueblo, Miguel, who had the advantage of speaking some English, quickly got a job in a restaurant. The proprietor had promised to pay for his room, but during the low season the boss reneged and Miguel ended up sleeping on the restaurant floor. At times Miguel complained to me that he was not receiving his 10% and was constantly badgered by the owner for not doing enough to bring people into the restaurant. Eventually, he left for another restaurant; replacing him was Carmencita. This was not uncommon. There is a constant reallocating of employees, especially when tourism is down. Workers are fired or let go for not bringing in enough business and others are hired, while the former search for new jobs. So, when the tourists descended from their visit to the Citadel, and perhaps a chasqui boy was getting ready to wash a bus, jaladores surrounded the visitors with menus in hand, trying to "pull" customers into their restaurant. For the jaladores, each day the same is more or less repeated; perhaps what changed was the menu of the restaurant they carried. Guido, a man in his mid-thirties, had been living in town for over 5 years and had worked in many local commercial establishments; during my fieldwork alone, he had moved to three separate restaurants. Guido, born and raised in a town in the *selva* (jungle area), was tough, kindhearted and intelligent. I once approached him sitting by the banks of the Vilcanota River, watching it move swiftly, a short pause from his busy day. "I never get tired of looking at the flow of water," he said. Despite my ethnographic focus on middle-class entrepreneurs in a neoliberal economy, my conversations with Guido were a constant reminder of class divisions and exploitation. As Guido once said to me about the townsfolk, "For the people of the town, we're just a necessary evil. . . . [T]hey refer to us as a bad influence or call us drunks . . . but if it weren't for us, they would die of hunger."

The district of Machu Picchu was not created in a decade or simply with the designation of the Sanctuary in 1981. Rather, there were many social and historical factors that went into its creation. However, during the 1980s, changes associated with globalization and later the implementation of neoliberal policies in Peru created significant alterations in Machu Picchu.

Throughout the 1980s the government agencies were preoccupied with civil war. Fujimori seized dictatorial power shortly after being elected in 1990, through an *autogolpe* (self-coup), claiming that it was necessary to defeat the Shining Path insurgents. Although he promised to re-establish a democracy, he continued to concentrate power in the executive office and gave the national intelligence service extraordinary powers. In 1992, Fujimori dissolved the congress, suspended the constitution, and dismissed many judges and half of the Supreme Court justices. In 1993 Fujimori reformed the constitution, permitting him to stay in office for a third term, and expelled a tribunal opposed to this constitutional change (Bowen 2000).

Even though the Shining Path did not occupy the area of Machu Picchu, it was presumed both by residents and the military that the iconic nature of the Citadel would make it a prime target for the insurgents. In fact, at one point in 1986 a bomb exploded on the train bound for Machu Picchu just as it was about to leave the Cusco train station. The bomb exploded in the last car of the train, killing seven people and injuring thirty-eight. Most of those killed and injured were foreign tourists.[35] Margarita remembers the period as being some of the most difficult times for the Pueblo, saying, "Everyone was scared, the terrorists were said to be hiding in the Jungle and there were rumors they wanted to take over Machu Picchu." According to Margarita, tourism came to a halt and the Pueblo emptied as many left it to take up safer residency in Cusco.

However, throughout the 1990s, tourism in Cusco had grown more rapidly than the development of an infrastructure to support the increase. Hotels and restaurants were simply not able to provide the services the tourists expected, such as a regular flow of hot water, or even enough space to accommodate them. Restaurants struggled to provide food and a dining atmosphere akin to a European experience that tourists often sought. In Cusco, those short on capital either got bank loans (often based on land titles) or simply lost out to larger capital holders often from Lima or abroad (Silverman 2002: 887; McTigue 1997).

In 2000 a law regulating space in Cusco prohibited street vendors from selling artisan crafts, postcards, and food, as well as shoeshine boys from the Plaza de Armas (the central plaza of Cusco), thereby excluding from the tourism market those who struggle on a daily basis to survive. Particularly in the case of itinerant street sellers (ambulantes), governing authorities generally argue that enforcement is necessary to stop tax evasion. In fact, promises are regularly made that collected revenues would go to building a market place for them and hence have them benefit from the economic growth (Seligmann 2004: 100–102). However, a look back at the history of the economic transformation of space in Cusco since the mid-1990s shows that market-building projects often ensconce sellers in uncompetitive locations where they are unable to reach profit margins or even maintain overhead costs; this is especially true for artisan dealers in the tourism economy, as I show in this ethnography (ibid.). Belmond/Orient Express made large investments throughout the Cusco region, purchasing two of the most expensive hotels, El Monasterio Hotel and Hotel Plaza de Armas, with prime access to the flow of tourism money. Neoliberal governance, far from freeing the market from state control, favors large capital interests. Street selling and street work were strategies of survival in the urban Andes even prior to neoliberalism but mushroomed under Fujimori's 1990 "Fujishock," a policy that curtailed hyperinflation but resulted in a recession and a devaluing of the currency as people turned to "home productions" in the informal economy to make a living (Valderrama and Escalante 1996; Mayer 2002: 314). Itinerant sellers form part of a long-standing flexible street economy where people need to endlessly work in multiple venues to survive, often serving as provisional labor (Harvey 1990). This is not to say that privatization had only detrimental results in Machupicchu Pueblo or even elsewhere in Cusco. In Machu Picchu, the growth of tourism created wealth unequally and with the formation of new classes in the town. Conversely, the policy trends that created these new classes also jeopardized their status; it is this subject we will turn to next.

NOTES

1. I am referring to the summer season of the southern hemisphere from December through March.
2. Carnival observances fluctuate yearly. I am referring specifically to the arrival of Carnival for 2002.
3. Also the last day of Carnival, this was in the year 2002 on February 10.
4. The term "public goods" is used here similarly to Charles Taylor's notion of "irreducibly social goods," defined as things valued not for the economic benefit of individuals, but something shared. As Taylor says, they are things acknowledged to be "not just for me and for you, but for us" (1995: 139). This is not to maintain that social goods are to be treated as ahistorical or viewed homogenously by people, but rather as the product of culture around which collective responsibilities are engaged and notions of the public good recognized and even manipulated (see Craig Calhoun 1998).
5. Sometimes also written as one word, Machupicchu.
6. The district was established October 1, 1941, by law 9396. The Sanctuary was established by National Law 001-81 AA on January 12, 1981.
7. Huayna Picchu is also a Quechua term, generally translated into English as "Young Mountain" or "Young Peak."
8. See Cox Hall 2012 for a full discussion on the role of "collecting technologies" by Bingham and the Yale Peruvian Expedition to Machu Picchu.
9. For a biography on the life of Hiram Bingham see Daniel Cohen 1984.
10. For a discussion of Bingham's archeological interpretations see James Norman 1968. For an autobiographical account of Bingham's expedition see Hiram Bingham 1930 and 1981 [1948].
11. For further reading on the imperialistic relationship between images of the Andean landscape and the United States, see Poole, "Landscape and the Imperial Subject."
12. Martin Chambi was another very interesting intellectual and artist in this movement. He was very influential in idealizing the Andean landscape through photography. Further research is needed to explore his influences, but here I will focus on Valcárcel.
13. According to Zapata Velasco, in Valcárcel's 1964 publication of *Machu Picchu: el Mas Famoso Monumento Arqueologico del Peru*, he eventually reconciled his differences with Bingham.
14. This is not to imply that Valcárcel was only responding to Bingham.
15. For an excellent discussion on the history and consequences of land invasions, the agrarian reform and the rise and fall of peasant cooperatives in Peru see Mayer 2009.
16. *Diagnostico Participativo del Sector Rural del Santuario Historico Machu Picchu*. Centro Bartolome de las Casas/Pacifica, S.A., Lima, Peru 2001 [115–118].
17. A full discussion of the land tenure system in Machu Picchu is not within the scope of this study. For a thorough discussion see Maxwell 2004.
18. Based on Law 6634 of 1929, Art. 5 gives the state the right to expropriate property around which the archeological ruins are situated. However, this law was many years prior to the formation and conceptualization of the current Sanctuary boundaries, and does not state how much area around unmovable human remains should be expropriated to be sufficient for their protection.

19. According to one study published in 2001, approximately 12% of the yield was sold commercially. See *Diagnostico Participativo del Sector Rural del Santuario Historico Machu Picchu*. Centro Bartolome de las Casas/Pacifica, S.A., Lima, Peru 2001: page iv.

20. Corihuayrachina is part of San Antonio de Torontoy. Huayllabamba is sometimes spelled Wayllabamba. See figure I.1.

21. Ollantay is often used locally as the diminutive for Ollantaytambo.

22. Chicha is a fermented corn drink popular thoroughout the Andes.

23. Tourism also plays a role in Corihuayrachina, but since the year 2000 tourists are no longer allowed to hike the Inca Trail without a tour agency and without being accompanied by a tour guide. Since tour agencies start the Inca Trail at kilometer 82 on the opposite side of the Vilcanota River, tourists no longer get a chance to pass through Corihuayrachina on their way to the Inca Trail.

24. The Quechua diminutive *-ayoc* glosses in English as a place where something is located.

25. I use the term "frontier" here in the sense of the mythology of the American western frontier, as opposed to the Latin American notion of "frontier" as a border.

26. Based on the law 9396 that founded the district of Machu Picchu in 1941, art. 2 states that the capital of the district (the Pueblo) takes the same name as the district.

27. Porteadores are porters that carry equipment such as portable stoves, gas canisters and food for tourists hiking the Inca Trail.

28. Instituto Nacional de Estadisticas Informatica (INEI) .

29. Huiñya Huayna is a Quechua phrase that roughly translates into English as "Forever Young."

30. This number pertains only to those restaurants tailored for tourism and does not include the eateries used by the townsfolk.

31. Sindicato de Artesanos y Pequeños Artesanos, Asociación de Artesanos y Pequeños Productores Joyitas, Asociación de Ambulantes de venta de Polos Turísticos, and Asociación Korichaska.

32. Referred to locally by the exact term.

33. The low tourist season is from October to May and the high season is from June to September.

34. Serrano is a person from the Sierra region, the Andean communities.

35. *New York Times* newspaper article, June 26, 1986.

TWO

Public Goods, Private Interests, and Stigmatized Identities

We are the only pueblo in Peru that has no identity.
(Somos el único pueblo en Perú que no tiene identidad.)
—Raúl, Machupicchu Pueblo

When I first arrived in Machupicchu Pueblo, the townsfolk were in the midst of preparing for its big festival—the 60th anniversary of the founding of their political district.[1] As part of the festivities, a dance competition was planned. I was asked to lend a hand with the preparations by Raúl and Emilio, two of the prominent members of the Barrio Huiñay Huayna (neighborhood association) and the organizers of one of the dance groups. Raúl had spent the last few weeks preparing his dance group for the evening contest. In designing the dance he called "Rite to the Sun God" (Rito al Dios Sol), Raúl wanted to create a dance to represent Machupicchu Pueblo.[2] For that reason this dance differed from those of the other contestants who mainly copied the dance, dress and music from diverse locales of the sierra. Héctor and Chela were to lead the troupe performance dressed as Incan. Although Raúl knew little about dance or choreography, he took it upon himself as the president of the Huiñay Huayna Association to organize some of the local children and a few adults. Raúl explained, "The Pueblo does not have an identity and creating its own dance would offer something unique to Machu Picchu. . . . We are the only pueblo in Peru that has no identity."

In the afternoon, we gathered in a shed just off Avenida Pachacútec, the principal street of the town. Raúl, along with Regina and Irma, and with the help of several kids were busy preparing the costumes. The lively children spray-painted their sandals gold, while the women carefully cut and styled an assortment of colorful fabric into dance garb. The

Figure 2.1. Photo of Héctor and Chela dressed as Incas during the dance competition celebrating the district anniversary (October 2001). (Photo taken by Pellegrino Luciano)

bamboo staffs they had painted the previous day were now dry and decorated with adornments that for Raúl symbolized the Incan past. His aspiration was to create a dance expressive of pre-Columbian times at Machu Picchu.

That evening, spectators crowded the plaza waiting for the competition to begin. All other participants were residents of the town except for those dancing for the Instituto Nacional de Cultura (INC).[3] Commotion ensued as some spectators voiced objection to the participation of the INC, because the dancers, like the agency, were outsiders. Since the winner would receive a prize of one thousand soles (approx. $300 U.S.), some argued that the INC didn't need the money. Still others asserted INC involvement was unfair because it had contracted professional dancers from the city of Cusco. When it was time for Raúl's group to dance, he entered the stage to explain to a largely residential audience that this was their new dance created to represent their identity in Machu Picchu. He stressed to the pueblo that they should accept this dance as theirs because "our pueblo does not have its own dance."

At last, all the dance groups performed. The judges decided that the INC had won. The crowd scorned the decision as an affront to the meaning of the anniversary. Raúl and his group began shouting, "fraud"; Regina cried out, "It's unfair, they're not from the pueblo. . . . [T]hey're professional [dancers], why didn't the old fat archeologists do the dancing." She turned to me to justify her rationale. "That money could have gone to the school, the INC already has plenty of money and it is not fair to the pueblo if they could bring in outsiders to compete in our local event." Raúl was furious, insulting the panel of judges, all of whom were officials from the municipality. "Incompetents," he cried, and expressed the feeling that the municipality, "their" *municipio*, had betrayed the pueblo. "They don't represent us, but rather the powerful," he said as he marched his group through the plaza as they chanted "The festival is for the pueblo and not for the Mayor," and also verbally blasted the INC as they returned home.

The anniversary is a special event for the people of Machu Picchu. It is perhaps their most important festival, a time when the district asserts its jurisdictional autonomy over the sanctuary designation. Celebration of the district is an encounter with the intersecting spaces of district and Sanctuary. In 2001, I noticed how festival activities were more about emphasizing the existence of the district prior to the formation of the Sanctuary. "When was the district of Machu Picchu founded?" the master of ceremonies asked a young contestant of a beauty pageant held during anniversary festivities. "1941," she replied, and the crowd cheered. The need felt by many, such as Raúl, to create a community identity raised the question of what was considered an appropriate identity for Machu Picchu, and why having one had become urgent at the time.

TANGIBLE LIVES IN AN INTANGIBLE PLACE

The people of Machu Picchu live in a landscape promoted and defined by the tourism industry, state institutions, and international bodies like UNESCO to be an idyllic landscape. Conservation laws maintain and enforce this idyllic image. The Machu Picchu landscape is designated to be an "intangible zone," whereby biodiversity and cultural heritage are a quality and existing people are treated as a quantity by conservation agencies. It is part of a constellation of World Heritage Sites that represent heritage for all humanity a *patrimonio de la humanidad*.[4] The Sanctuary is a place where anyone's given strip of land holds the potential for being defined as ecologically or archeologically significant, not just to the nation, but also to the world.[5] In one sense, the commercial image dictates the kinds of identities that are permissible to live in the Sanctuary. For the conservation agencies, humans had no place in their conception of nature, unless it conformed to the commoditized meanings of the landscape that would require campesinos to adopt a sort of commercialized Andean identity fit for the tourism industry. Campesinos are not "Indian" enough. As a park official once explained, the campesinos should substitute their cows with llamas because they are smaller and more attractive to tourists; "cows are a danger to tourists and they dirty the Inca Trail with dung." On the other hand, campesinos I spoke to retorted that tending livestock had been a part of their lives for generations, not to mention that the ecological zone is not adequate for llamas. No one knew of any documented cases of a cow attacking a tourist and manure, as they pointed out, was a reality of nature. Conservation authorities expressed that they would prefer the campesinos give up agricultural production altogether and, like the townsfolk, enter wholly into the tourism economy. Tensions between park rangers and campesinos was analogous to the problems faced by many people who live in and around national parks across the world in that there is an effort to articulate nature to a tourism economy. Edward Brunner (2001) and Jim Igoe, for instance, both describe the way the Maasai around Tarangire and Serengeti National Parks in Tanzania create "Disneyfied" performances that cater to the fantasies of Western tourists, even importing animals the visitors expect to see (Igoe 2006: 15–18).

However, in another sense, neoliberal identity in Machu Picchu, and as I will argue outside of it as well, is also implicated by laws that residents felt methodically promoted certain economic interests over others. Jorge, an artisan seller, explained to me what he thought is meant when conservation authorities invoke the notion that Machu Picchu is "intangible" to justify restrictions.

> They say the Historic Sanctuary of Machu Picchu is intangible—everything that you see [points to the landscape] is intangible. But this intangibility is only for the poor, it's not intangible for them [points to Sanctuary Lodge]. [T]hey say it's prohibited to construct buildings with concrete but in truth, they [the state authorities] don't care. They can violate the rule [pertaining to intangibility] but for the campesinos that have been living here for years, and understand the ecology, only they are [said to be] destroying the environment. We see this hypocrisy with our own eyes and feel it in our hearts.

Ideally, intangibility in Machu Picchu is supposed to express how the inherent beauty of the Sanctuary exemplifies shared universal values that are inherently greater than the landscape's physical properties. Intangibility blends into a world heritage discourse that certain social goods convey value not just to the nation but to the world. This would imply that the Sanctuary is or should be excluded from the politics of privatization or the demarcation of property ownership; property ownership is prohibited. However, as Peru sought to attract direct foreign investment, the notion of "intangible" was used to structure relationships of wealth in terms of access and use of land. Governing agencies systematically manipulated the concept of intangibility to limit the local population but facilitate foreign investors with market opportunities. Intangibility was strategically used to serve neoliberal policies via stigmatizing the identities of locals as detrimental to the ideals that give Machu Picchu universal value. Economic outcomes were not the product of market forces but an example of how governance and the market economy work jointly to blame residents for disturbing the intangible value of the Sanctuary. What I wish to call attention to here is the degree to which government and economic elites invoked notions of a collective social good generally contrary to the politics of private ownership normally associated with neoliberal economies. Whether it be via the concept of intangibility or public safety, neoliberalism rested on a background of meanings about what is in the "public interest" that make policy intelligible enough to facilitate capital accumulation.[6] While heritage sites like Machu Picchu make this more apparent, it is also revealing to note how even outside such sites, dispossession efforts that facilitate capital accumulation needs are often in ideological contradiction, justified through laws that appeal to notions of social rights and public goods and welfare.

In Machu Picchu intangibility coincided with a politics of blame, and with a control of activities. Restrictions on rural activities in the Sanctuary became particularly stringent after 1997 when campesinos were blamed for a forest fire; campesinos denied it was their fault and claimed it could have easily been a tourist's cigarette. Unrelated to the fire incident, in 2002, thirty-three campesinos were charged with various ecological violations, such as cutting tree branches or cultivating in restricted spaces, that could have been punishable by eviction from Sanctuary grounds. INRENA's drive to conserve an ideal nature continues to force many restrictions and difficulties on farmers, though over the course of a decade after my fieldwork changes have been made. But at the time the rural areas of the Sanctuary were not allowed to have electricity because lights disrupted the idyllic image of nature. Access to electricity was sometimes a point of conflict between campesinos and park rangers because despite the restrictions the latter could use solar-powered electricity for their barracks.[7] In addition, campesinos were restricted from obtaining firewood for their wood-burning fireplaces. They were permitted to build domiciles only with adobe earth material, whereas park rangers used concrete blocks for their station houses, which was pointed out by many rural and urban folk alike to be hypocritical.

The townsfolk faced different but nonetheless equally problematic restrictions as those in the rural communities. For them, the year 2000 was a particularly intensive year of change. That year a Finnish-funded study conducted by PMP (Programa Machu Picchu) called "The Urban Plan" (Plan de Ordenamiento Urbano) cited the social, economic and demographic impact of Pueblo life in the Sanctuary. Like the Master Plan of 1998, this plan reiterated the notion that the Pueblo was the quintessence of disorder, a visual eyesore and responsible for ecological damage (Plan Urbano: 16). It also noted that the population was "without collective identity," claiming that the community did not hold traditional festivals, such as those for patron saints, asserting that "the [population does not participate in the] Festival of the Cross in May and the [Festival] of the

Virgin of Carmen in July" (Plan Urbano: ibid., 31). The report further claimed that there was little social life, asserting that the only interest Pueblo residents had in Machu Picchu was economic (ibid.). The objective of the Urban Plan was to implement a strategy to prevent further urban growth, create order, and make the Pueblo an attractive place for tourism. Yet a conversation with a few Machupiccheños might have clarified some of the ahistorical distortions. Since the town's formation in 1941 there were years when practices reflective of expressive culture such as religious festivals, or symbolic displays taken by outsiders to be representative of a common identity, were more prominent than in other years. Don Teofilo spoke of how the brequeros (train and rail workers) celebrated their significant saints festivals. While in other years, such as in the 1980s during the civil war, as Margarita noted (chapter 1), many took up temporary residency elsewhere, and I would speculate people who remained were less inclined to perform festivals. Nevertheless, I do suspect that the Urban Plan report may have encouraged a more active effort at creating a "Pueblo identity" to reform town image. During my fieldwork, I noted the collective importance of the three-day "Festival of the Cross" as one of the most significant religious celebrations in the Pueblo, beginning with religious dancers dressed in elaborate costumes and with cross-bearers leading processions throughout the town. The cargo holders were organized around the different barrios of the town; the crosses were kept on public display, marking the four different barrios. Cargo holders fulfilled their obligations using their own money to give away large quantities of food and alcohol to the Pueblo (see figure 2.2). There were communal activities such as a puppet theatre and a nighttime fireworks show. The cross-markings are often a source of religious expression that constitutes part of the social memory of the community. One cross-marking was said to identify the location of an alleged miracle that occurred in the Pueblo. During a 1995 flood of the Aguas Calientes River, a large boulder stationed just above the riverbank blocked alluvial debris from crashing into homes when the river overflowed. The organizational complexity and the attention to detail shows that people were quite embedded in their cultural practices, regardless of whether they performed them according to the desired expectations of urban planners. The assertion that the Pueblo did not have an identity, just when economic reforms were being implemented, worked to discredit the population, and by extension advocate that the Machupiccheños had no cultural claim to their land.

The criteria for belonging in the Sanctuary involved having the right identity for the landscape, in the town as well as the rural areas. A high-ranking INRENA park official emphasized to me that the campesinos were not "traditional." To him "traditional" meant Quechua-speaking descendent of the Incas. In his words, "All others [in the sanctuary] are migrants" and did not form communities, but were from his perspective

Figure 2.2. Photo of participants carrying out cargo duties during the festival of the cross in Machupicchu Pueblo (May 2002). (Photo taken by Pellegrino Luciano)

a disorganized horde of people. It was common for conservation officials to refer to campesinos as *grupos humanos*, or human groups. To belong to a community, and by extension to a jurisdictional polis means to have legal claim to live there; this is exactly why the district is so important to the residents. By avoiding the term "community" and by extension district, it helped to erase from discussions the campesinos' right to live in the Sanctuary. The state institutions and their plans constructed an identity-based rationale to de-legitimize the right of the inhabitants to live in the Sanctuary. The idea of intangibility and a manipulative notion of the "social good" were skewed against the Machupiccheños. If the discredited identity were not enough, the 2000 urban plan further argues for the relocation of the entire Pueblo to a place outside of the Sanctuary on the grounds. Such a move, according to the plan, would avert the risk of natural disaster; hence expulsion would be for their protection. The problem of natural disasters in the area is not necessarily a specious concern; I am not questioning here the risks of landslides and flash floods that threaten residents. Rather it is the way the discourse was used, or rather what was not included in the plan that was revealing. The larger capital investments in the Sanctuary were not burdened with either identity prerequisites or the relocation for their own protection; hence both aspects became a way of clearing the landscape of those who stand in the way of large capital such as Orient Express Inc., a multimillion-dollar private enterprise. It exemplifies the dialectic, as David Harvey notes, between state processes involved in control of territory and economic ones involved in capitalism (2003: 183). Public goods reorganized as a capital accumulation strategy set the stage for dispossessing inhabitants of the Sanctuary.

SOCIAL INTERACTION IN A NEOLIBERAL ECONOMY

One of the questions I was drawn to during my fieldwork concerned the way neoliberal policies set parameters on social action and shape behavior at a micro level, normalized but observable in terms of everyday life. Understanding the neoliberal restructuring of everyday life in this Andean context necessitates knowledge of history but nevertheless requires a conceptual framing of social interaction to put what are apparently different acts under a single domain of analysis. Here I find the ideas of Michel de Certeau, James C. Scott and Erving Goffman insightful into how neoliberalism frames possibilities in terms of resistance or accommodation to power. It might stretch the imagination to think of the residents of Machu Picchu as "inmates," living in a "total institution" (Goffman 1961), because the conservation institutions of the state are not designed for the management of people in the same sense as is a prison or mental hospital, but rather that of a heritage and nature area. Moreover, people are not confined behind physical walls and cut off definitively from the wider society, as are people in a Goffmanesque "total institution." Residents of Machu Picchu are not so brutally "stripped" and "leveled," in Goffman's depiction of a mental hospital, of status and identity, as they would be in the context of incarceration. And of course, the residents of the district don't quite live in "batches" where all activities are carried out in the constant presence of others (Goffman 1961: 4–28).

Nevertheless, Sanctuary life shares similarities with life in a "total institution," primarily the case for the campesinos in the rural communities as opposed to the town residents. For instance, while people there are not confined, exit and entry into the Sanctuary is indeed highly controlled for the rural inhabitants, and it is difficult for a resident to receive a family member or friend without the guest paying exorbitant tourist entrance fees or getting special permission. Furthermore, the privatization of the railroad has meant that residents are subject to high fare hikes that in effect limit their movement. While residents of the rural communities do not live in "batches," INRENA rangers constantly watch their movements, and from the operational perspective, the status of community identity is denied to the campesinos. As mentioned above, residents, from one official's perspective, are nothing more than a chaotic mass of people that must be moved around in orderly fashion.

The greater semblance of a total institution arises when governing institutions assimilate neoliberal trends into the management of the Sanctuary. Corporate and governmental interests come together to impose an intensified order of spatial inclusion and exclusion. Residents are now "stripped" in the sense of having their land possessions taken or constrained for the financial benefit of others, and "leveled" in the sense of having a new commercialized identity imposed on them as a qualification to live in the Sanctuary. Equally important, people must respond to the strict rules and regulations of the Sanctuary, and adaptation responds to a mortification process. What we see is something akin to what Goffman referred to as "secondary adjustment," where people adapt to an institutional order often through secretive and deceptive practices. These are "practices that do not directly challenge staff but allow inmates to obtain forbidden satisfactions or to obtain permitted ones by forbidden means" (Goffman 1961: 54).

The concept of secondary adjustment bears striking similarity to Michel de Certeau's (1984) view of "tactics" and James C. Scott's (1985) well-known notion of "weapons of the weak." De Certeau was concerned with the practices by which ordinary people subvert the hegemonic order from within. Likewise, Scott examines these subversive everyday tactics, but to critique the commonly viewed definition of resistance as possible only through collective and organized action. As Scott famously wrote, everyday forms of resistance such as "foot dragging . . . feigned ignorance" or small acts of sabotage have been overlooked in favor of holding outright revolution as the prototype for resistance (Scott 1985: 29). Both authors see tactics as uncoordinated, improvisational and idiosyncratic. Unlike Scott, however, de Certeau places a great deal of emphasis on the force of "tactics" in subverting a hegemonic order. On this note Scott and Goffman coincide. Secondary adjustments, like weapons of the weak, are not attempts at subverting social hierarchies, but rather mitigations to harsh circumstances. Goffman saw secondary adjustments in the setting of a total institution as modes of adaptation to power, and likewise, for Scott, those mitigations, though considered forms of resistance, are done secretly to avoid confrontations with power.

As Machu Picchu is part of a configuration of "tourism icons" in Cusco, and the city of Cusco is a kind of tourist "gateway" to the Sanctuary (van den Berghe and Flores Ochoa 2000: 8), I anticipated that investment interests would generate similar types of relationships that would result in comparable forms of adaptation on the part of local people. A cursory examination of these adaptations in neighboring areas outside of the district of Machu Picchu links enforcement to the implementation of neoliberal privatization policies, and to show a process of producing stigmatized identities to capital investments in the tourism economy.

Up until 1999 the Plaza de Armas (central plaza) in the city of Cusco was teeming with small-scale outdoor vendors selling artisan goods arranged on the pavement, along the portals, and under the balconies that encompass the plaza. *Ambulantes* (itinerant street sellers), men and women often without the resources to rent pavement space, ambled around the plaza as they carried their goods, such as clothing, jewelry or food, to sell. Shoeshine boys scurried from bench to bench looking for customers among the city dwellers and tourists. Boys and girls sold postcards or posed in traditional Cusco garb with a llama or a lamb, and for a small fee offered tourists a photo opportunity. Street comics attracted some tourists, but mainly local people of all social classes gathered around to watch the slapstick comedians perform their skits of mockery. And of course, the plaza area was also filled with tourist establishments such as tour agencies, artisan shops, restaurants and bars. At the turn of the millennium there were major changes. As Helaine Silverman notes, the government of Cusco sought to redesign the city as an "open-air museum" that included artwork and stonework reflective of Incan times (2002: 884). The Plaza de Armas was a vital space for its economic plan. The wealthier establishments were left untouched, but the merchants selling their wares on the portal pavements were sent off to a newly built artisan market located about a mile away from the plaza where most foreigners rarely went. The rationale was that the sellers were unsightly and that they posed a hazard to tourists by attracting criminal elements. In contradictory fashion, another artisan market was constructed for them near the central market, an area where many tourists were specifically told not to go because it was considered dangerous and unsightly. These markets were also not well advertised at the time, and tourists tended to make their purchases in the establishments in or around the plaza. The displaced small merchants thus suffered great economic loss. At the turn of the millennium, foreign tourists were still generally "plaza-centric." The pedestrian activities of North American or European tourists rarely went beyond the peripheries of the Plaza de Armas, and when they visited the sights in and outside the city, a bus usually picked them up at their hotel. Hence, just as the Orient Express/Belmond train and hotel businesses captured the high-end tourist market in Machu Picchu, plaza space was regulated to capture the dollars of wealthier Western tourists by removing competition and the temptation for customers purchasing cheaper goods or memorabilia that are, for many tourists, an equally sufficient way of consuming local culture. In fact, when I revisited my fieldwork in 2007 I found many more tourists purchasing cheaper items in the main San Pedro market. Though just a few years earlier it was common for tour guides to instruct people not to go there because it was supposed to be dangerous.

Back in 2001, however, a more dramatic alteration of plaza space in Cusco was seen in the laws that prohibited street sellers of any sort from entering the Plaza de Armas. Whereas once poorer families could reasonably benefit from the tourism economy by selling goods without having any overhead costs, now they could not. Furthermore, this kind of spatial control was not only in the Cusco Plaza de Armas. Spaces such as plazas, which are predominantly social and public spaces, where many kinds of economic interactions occur, were not only converted into "tourist spaces" but organized according to the interests of wealthier propertied classes (Urry 1990; Low 2000).[8] The way Peru applied the ideas of what was in 2000 the new economy, influenced by economists such as Hernando de Soto (1989), was implemented in an ahistorical fashion that assumed the market place to be a smoothly regulated equal playing field with no prior history of racial discrimination (Seligmann 2004: 151). In the tourism economy of Cusco, the plazas were in effect "cleaned up" of poorer people who did not look well educated or cosmopolitan, and thus viewed as "cholo" or "racially" different.[9] Even successful market women, as Seligmann notes in her ethnographic study of open-air markets and street vendors in Cusco, become prosperous more because of their own informal networks and "bonds of solidarity" with other "cholas" than from the reduction of bureaucratic interference promised by neoliberal reform (ibid.).

Nevertheless, people do adjust to the laws governing their built environment. People even currently sneak goods into the plaza hidden in bags, under vests and the like. They make their products visible only when they approach potential buyers. However, now with the change of laws there is a need for vigilance. On one occasion, a child of about 10 years tried to sell me postcards, but when a police officer passed by, he shoved his package of cards under his shirt. Police can confiscate a person's goods if they are caught in the act; hence, special tactics are necessary to avoid suspicion.[10] Those who sell food are often faced with the problem of arousing police attention because customers tend to eat purchased food openly. A popular option for the sellers is to camouflage the economic transaction as a personal exchange between friends. Once in 2002 while I was sitting in the Cusco Plaza de Armas, a food seller sat down beside me, feigning a personal relationship by pretending to be engaged in a conversation. While this might work when dealing with the denizens of Cusco, or a curious anthropologist, it is often much harder with foreign tourists because of language barriers and because tourists are likely to interpret such behavior with distrust. Certainly, tourists can be hassled or even robbed and they do lodge legitimate complaints with the police that in turn influence enforcement. But in addition, Western tourists also do often come to Peru with preconceptions that it is a dangerous "third-world" country. Tourists may thus mistake such action as an attempt at being swindled, or perhaps being offered contraband or stolen goods. In the nearby community of Fortaleza above the city of Cusco similar problems occurred around the archeological site and park of Sacsayhuaman, a popular tourism destination, and the place where the Inti Raymi winter solstice ritual is held annually. Most of the residents there were not granted permits by the INC to sell artisan goods to tourists, even though they live next to the ruins. As one woman explained, "We have to [quietly] chase after tourists as if we were delinquents [trying to rob them]." For in performing their otherwise benign economic activities they are in fact breaking laws. In one incident in the Plaza de Armas three police officers chased a man and grabbed and beat him. A crowd of street sellers gathered as they came to the man's assistance. One woman cried out to the officers, "Why don't you hit me," as another handed the arrested man a napkin for his bloody nose gained in a scuffle with the police officers. The middle-aged man had been selling cigarettes in the plaza when he was told by police to leave. He refused, arguing he was on the periphery of the plaza only and not in the plaza itself.

In contrast to the city of Cusco, in Machu Picchu the boundaries of the Sanctuary not only define the market space, but also an entire protected area, and the very commodity sold in the sense that a tourist must pay to enter the park to have a "heritage experience." In Machu Picchu, the changes in Sanctuary laws in 2000 affected the interactions between tourists and residents with profound economic consequences. Here, great effort was now made to separate tourists from rural residents. For example, tourists were once allowed to hike the Inca Trail alone, crafting their own kind of "authentic" experience through interactions with inhabitants. Residents could also make some extra money by renting a bed to a hiker. At that time tourists were far more likely to attempt to engage in conversation and to receive local interpretations of Inca monuments. Also, before the privatization of the train, tourists could, if they chose to, take the local train to the point from where they would start their hike on the Inca Trail, or they could go directly to Machupicchu Pueblo to visit the citadel. They also purchased local goods not generally marketed for the tourism economy, such as fresh agricultural produce and locally baked foods from merchants boarding the train at different stops along the route. While it was crowded and not the most comfortable ride, many tourists chose the local train not just because of lower cost, but also to be engaged with the realities of a contemporary population of the sierra. With a shortage of seats, a tourist might be asked to share a seat with a child on their lap to lighten a mother's load. From a resident's perspective, these interactions were also opportune moments to make connections with foreigners that can also lead to economically significant relationships.

Afterwards, tourists were no longer allowed to use the local train. Tourists were also no longer allowed to hike the Inca Trail alone, but must go through tour agencies that provide a tour guide; historical and contemporary life is now interpreted by a professional tour guide who echoes official versions of the past.[11] Tour companies provide all the food, and there is much less interaction between the Machupiccheños and tourists. Tourists no longer rent beds in a local adobe house or spend the evening with local people talking about anything from local myths about the *machus*[12] or *sirenas*[13] to the agricultural cycle or the political situation in Peru. Tour groups have designated campsites that, while often located near homes, offer few opportunities for interaction with rural inhabitants. During my fieldwork in 2002 the interactions I noted taking place between the rural residents and tourists were largely confined to the purchase of a bottle of water or a candy bar as tourists packed their gear to leave; for tourists, gone are the days of *choclo* and *chicha.*[14] Residents must pick other moments and places to sell to tourists directly, often tagging behind them as they walk. Hence, conservation goals became synonymous with elite economic interests leading to greater policing efforts and more stringent laws.

What we find in the situations described above is that people's actions are closer to Goffman's and Scott's views as being forms of adaptation. Contrary to de Certeau, it is difficult in this example to see how tactics undermine hegemony. As the police event in the Plaza de Armas shows, a challenge to hegemony occurred only when a tactic was uncovered, and the challenge was not from within as de Certeau would have it, but by direct confrontation on the part of the plaza street sellers. In fact, Goffman's emphasis on the importance of "appearances" clarifies some of de Certeau's framing of behavior. Hegemonic groups and those who enforce their rules may be concerned only with appearances, as in cases when police do "look the other way" if infractions are not done too openly and the proper image of order is maintained. Dominant groups may not be concerned with the small-change earnings of a few subordinates, only that the relations of dominance are not challenged. Upholding the proper image of order may already encompass all the concrete concerns of dominant groups. Effectively, a covert "tactic" may be so intricately woven into a credible performance of compliance so that if one were to perform an insubordinate act, it would nevertheless uphold the hegemonic order. The Cusco street seller who was arrested in the plaza challenged the officer's definition of the plaza boundaries instead of appearing to comply with the order and simply return later, as do many street sellers; hence the man's covert selling tactic can be seen as a mode of adaptation, while his open challenge to the officer can be seen as an act of resistance.

In addition, Goffman also shows how, as laws become more rigidly enforced, secondary adjustments or tactics can backfire and be made to serve the interests of dominant groups. This dialectical aspect is not captured quite as well by de Certeau. Goffman's notion of "looping" in prisons describes how the secondary adjustments inmates need to make to survive the rigors of the institutional order can then be used by the staff to further justify the rationale for their incarceration. Rather than forms of resistance, the use of covert tactics responds to the level and need of subordinate groups to appear as credible subjects.

Often overlooked is that people too are personally affected by the kinds of tactics, weapons and secondary adjustment they need to carry out. Perhaps what is most interesting is the possibility that subordinated people can create narratives that provide for them a sense of historical awareness about their own actions and behaviors and are missing from neoliberal ideas of the free market. Contrary to the criticism of Goffman's role theory of the self as being one that lacks an "inner story,"[15] the notion of secondary adjustment shows how people can create personal narratives to draw on "inner resources" as a way to adapt to rigid institutional conditions (Manning 2000). On this question, Goffman and de Certeau complement each other. De Certeau's forte is in illustrating how spatial practices such as walking inspire narratives that can appropriate a built environment to meet one's own ends (1984: xiv). Regardless of whether we call such practices "tactics" or "secondary adjustments," the narratives that unfold can help organize common experiences in a way that unifies participants and fosters larger collective forms of action. In Machu Picchu, local people created narratives about their own actions and behaviors that differed from conservation framings. The constant making of "secondary adjustments," in the residents' repeated encounters with the conservation logic of dispossession, encouraged social memories that offered greater possibilities for effective action when narratives recast the ahistorical and naturalized notions of neoliberal market talk that was being given to them into historically specific power relationships, as the following event illustrates.

THE HACIENDA, OLD AND NEW

One Sunday morning in May 2002 during an extended stay in the community of Huayllabamba in the District and Sanctuary of Machu Picchu, I stopped at a house along the Inca Trail where the previous day I had helped harvest corn from the fields. I planned to talk to one of the older members about how life had changed in the community since the agrarian reform. It was with that idea that I first approached "Don Marcos."

When I arrived, Don Marcos was chatting with the two park rangers. It was sunny and warm so the three sat in the shade drinking large glasses of chicha.[16] It seemed like a friendly conversation; they joked and spoke about the weather and the fields.[17] What was not initially apparent was the "cat and mouse game" they were playing. The rangers were apparently inspecting the house for signs of ecological violations. Once the park rangers left, Don Marcos apologized for keeping me waiting. He handed me a glass of chicha with some *mote*[18] and asked me to wait some more because he wanted the INRENA rangers to clear the area. It was not plain to me why he was so apprehensive. I was going to help him cut fodder for the animals, and he was going to tell me about his life in the old hacienda. After a half an hour, we departed. Don Marcos had an axe in hand, partially hidden under his poncho. He was wearing a blue-colored wool *chullo*[19] on his head, blue sweat pants and, as is common for campesinos, sandals on his feet. For me the real attention grabber of his dress was that Don Marcos wore a purple long-sleeved shirt that, appropriate to the situation of insubordination, read: "The King and I Performance."[20]

We crossed the cornfields and continued down the slope to a meadow adjacent to a river. There, we approached a capuli tree he had singled out the day before. He turned to me and said, "I'm not really going to cut grass for fodder but a tree branch instead"—an act prohibited by INRENA.[21] From his perspective, it was his neighbor's tree from whom he had secured permission to cut a branch the previous day. Nevertheless, he knew he still had to conceal his intentions and actions from the rangers. Don Marcos climbed to a branch. He wrapped one arm around the tree trunk while using the other to begin chopping. We took turns chopping the branch until it fell. Once it was on the ground, we carefully dragged the log to an area where Don Marcos began to trim off the leaves and smaller twigs.

As Don Marcos stripped the limb, I inquired about the old hacienda. Only paying half attention to my question Don Marcos provided his own more interesting reflection saying: "Peru [the state] is like the hacendado, it's as if we live in a hacienda." "Why?" I asked. "Those from UGM and INRENA prohibit everything, they don't want us to work, they don't want us to cut trees, work the fields, they don't want us to do anything, yeah just like the hacendados they watch everything and prohibit everything, and yeah those from UGM and INRENA are just another [hacendado]." Don Marcos described the hacendado-peasant relationship in his community: "The hacendado would come to see how many animals we had, how we worked. He watched our families, each week a different family. Sometimes everybody, women and children, had to work. That's the way the condition was, by week and by turn."

We were ready to go. We lifted the tree trunk; he took the front and I the rear. It was heavy, but we walked quickly in a coordinated fashion as if performing a military log drill. We took a short rest midway. Then, Don Marcos continued talking about the hacienda, but again for him the past and the present were not so different. As he remembered it, just prior to the agrarian reform there were about 30 families living in the hacienda of Huayllabamba, working as tenants cultivating corn in the valley and tubers (*olluco* and *occa*) in the higher altitudes. They would cultivate additional crops like potatoes, barley, beans for the hacendado in "la casa grande" (the big house)[22]—the hacendado's house on kilometer 88 along the railroad. He explained that the work done for the hacendado was referred to as *la condición,* or "the condition," referring to the contract that allowed campesinos to cultivate the hacendado's fields.

Don Marcos explained in a sarcastic tone: "People say it's a Sanctuary, at least that's what INRENA tells us all the time." For Don Marcos the campesinos shifted from living by the conditions of the hacendado to those of INRENA, explaining how now they conduct garbage collection duties for the state. That is, park rangers organize local people for unpaid garbage collection assignments on the Inca Trail. Don Marcos said, "We collect two or three sacks, that's the condition to continue here, we have to carry the garbage to kilometer 88, always kilometer 88 just like with the old hacendado. It's the same, I mean we didn't use the name 'Sanctuary' then, but now that's what they call it, a name given by INRENA and the INC."

The neoliberal changes leading to the mammoth growth of the tourism industry in Peru at the turn of the millennium transformed Machu Picchu into a commodity that commercializes an image of the past. That image dictates the kinds of identities acceptable within the Sanctuary boundaries. Both rural and urban residents are forced to find ways to contend with this image, not just in the sense of marketing to the tourism economy and profiting from it, but also in the sense of belonging and making a life in the Sanctuary. It is in the question of belonging that history of race and Indian identity in the above-mentioned dance festival are directly embedded in the development of a tourism economy and the subsequent incursions of state institutions of conservation. For the conservation authorities of the state, under the pressures of UNESCO, and the expectations of the tourism industry, an idealized nature must be populated by nothing short of an idealized Indian. The current population is out of place, because they do not fit well with the romanticized notion of an Incan past, symbolized by the Citadel. This politics of identity underscores the dispossession effort that takes place between residents and the governing authorities, and the rationale to make or reject claims.

THE POLITICS OF NATURE NATURALIZED

Once past the veneer of nature as harmonious, peaceful and tranquil, maintained by the tourism industry and national and international institutions, local experiences with nature evoke sentiments of fear, risk and distrust that were intimately tied to their political struggle. For many, particularly those involved in the mobilization in 2002 against the changes that were taking place, their feelings of fear and uncertainty crystallized into observations about the violent unpredictability of nature, the economy and the state.

Back in February of 2002 when that first protest meeting held in the cultural center ended, the exact details of what the proposed demonstration would entail had not taken shape. Would they shut down the town, and stop all commercial activity? One sure way to gain attention would be to block the PeruRail train from entering the town, thereby preventing tourists from visiting the Citadel. This possibility concerned some of the townsfolk, since it would threaten the Cusco tourism industry, and could stop tourism altogether, and damage their own economy. As one can imagine, residents' feelings were mixed. The tendency was for people who were more directly involved in the tourism economy to be against blocking the train. A restaurant owner like Juan, for example, was against blocking the train, but Regina, a Frente leader with no direct business interest in tourism, was not. Equally important were the legal risks that would be incurred if they were to block the train. In part, due to the frequent attacks on the train, PeruRail had announced that it would take legal action leading to criminal prosecution for sabotage against anyone or any group placing anything on the tracks. To block the train, protestors would thus have had to risk their own safety by standing in front of it. The leaders of the protest were worried about legal repercussions. In fact, when the date of the demonstration drew near, a party of the mobilization went to Cusco to inform the department authorities of their intentions. However, the day before the demonstration was to take place, a series of landslides isolated the participants, leaving the group in Cusco. The landslides occurred on the perimeter of the town, so no one was injured. Nevertheless, the train was blocked from service and the tracks needed repair, which would take a few days for clean-up crews to accomplish. Thus, it was a natural event and not a planned demonstration that prevented tourists from arriving. To go ahead with the demonstration under those conditions would be pointless, as it would have had no political or economic impact. It was decided to postpone the event until the landslides were cleared and normal train service resumed.

For a couple of days after the landslides though, I found the town unusually quiet from the lack of normal tourist activity. Electrical services were severed, and the town had a different social atmosphere, as people were somewhat free from the routines of daily life. Even the central market could not receive its daily supply of produce. The landslide deposits of mud, trees and boulders just outside the town became something of a local attraction (see figure 2.3). Many saw in such events premonitions of a more serious disaster that would lead to the destruction of the town. It was common, especially during the rainy season, for people to start their mornings by discussing their nightly fears of landslides and flash floods. It was not difficult for me to see how nighttime makes some people nervous throughout the rainy season. During this period, there is hardly a horizon in the canyon, and under the cover of darkness, one can only make out the mountain silhouettes looming over the town as ominous mists of clouds roll down from their tops. The hard rain pattering on tin roofs, along with thunderclaps, can leave one anticipating the roar of falling landmass or rushing water.

"I couldn't sleep all night," a market woman living by the river said to me. "I kept hearing the grinding sound of rocks being dragged by the river." Many, who had experienced flash floods, or more specifically, *huaycos,*[23] often recalled the strong smell of vegetation torn and carried forward by mud and water. With these latter landslides, the context was set for the townsfolk to give nature politically relevant meanings. Throughout the pueblo, conversations and commentaries about the landslides abounded. Nature was the talk of the town, and one could see how narratives of the environment could take shape in the telling of local history, as well as political expressions about life in the Sanctuary. In the plaza, one man said, "Even nature is protesting against the abuses of the 'big' people." "Yes, nature too is supporting our cause, but just as it screws up business for them, it screws up business for us, too," responded another. For one woman, the landslides meant only more abuse, this time by nature. She declared, "If it's not the powerful screwing with us, not letting us live and work in peace, it's another, even more powerful [force] that screws with us—nature, the *Pachamama*." For some, especially the women of the market, the landslides brought forth harrowing tales of the Santa Teresa and Ccollpani floods of 1998. Both communities lie adjacent to but outside the Sanctuary boundaries some 12–15 km from Machupicchu Pueblo, but whereas Ccollpani falls under the district of Machu Picchu, Santa Teresa does not. Some people mentioned the possibility of a similar event happening to the town. "There are lagoons high up in the mountains," said a woman cooking and selling *anticuchos*[24] by the train tracks. "And a landslide up there could bring all that water tumbling down on us."

Even in the absence of the landslide, everyday talk about nature, its danger and the inability to control it when a disaster occurs was often discoursed as caused by the greed of others in town in a way that reflected class tension. "That's why I say no one owns this land," said Nayruth, a young woman from Cusco working as a waitress in one of the Pueblo restaurants, about her friend Liliana's narrow escape from a rising river. "Only the mountains truly own this land," she concluded. Neither of the women had possession rights to land, but Liliana, a survivor of the 1998 flood in the town of Santa Teresa, was one of many residents resettling in the town on land adjacent to the River Alcamayo, known as dangerous for flash floods.[25] Liliana abandoned her squatter claim and rented a room for her family after her squatter tent was nearly washed away one night when the river rose high.[26] She left on her own for her safety. But two days later, park rangers and the police evicted the remaining squatters on the grounds that they were violating conservation rules by building and clearing brush and trees on prohibited land. "The people of the pueblo are bad (*son malos*) and if a disaster occurs, it's because of their malevolence," said Maria, a market woman also originally from Santa Teresa. She implied that the more established townsfolk do not

Figure 2.3. Photo of Machupiccheños examining the destructive aftermath of a nighttime landslide on the outskirts of the Pueblo (March 2002). (Photo taken by Pellegrino Luciano)

accept her as a member of the pueblo. Tying nature, property and the Sanctuary together in one sentence, Maria said: "Because they have houses they believe themselves to be the owners of the Sanctuary."

To understand how the neoliberal shift challenged the Machupiccheños in the Sanctuary and threatened dispossession, one needs to distinguish between the commoditization of identity from the governance of identity. The commoditization of identity is a much more direct response to market forces such as the supply and demand of the tourism industry (i.e., what images connect to the expectations of tourists and by extension sell). On the other hand, the state's manipulation of identity as a means of social control was more akin to the effort to build an institutional framework that facilitated the movement of capital as a capital accumulation strategy. Noting the inflection that shapes identities allows one to better see how the tourism economy is politically organized to favor elites, whereas a focus only on identity as a commodity opens the door for blaming market failures on local peoples' inability to create a competitive product for tourists. What may at first appear from Raúl's defiance during the dance competition described at the beginning of this chapter as an all too common attempt to commoditize an identity for tourists, can now be more completely understood as a defeated address to the state's method of disqualifying the population's right to belong in the Sanctuary. On one hand, for both the conservation authorities of the state and the expectations of the tourism industry, an idealized nature

Figure 2.4. Photo of Machupicchu Pueblo viewed from Mt. Putucusi (April 2002). (Photo taken by Pellegrino Luciano)

must be populated by nothing short of an idealized Indian. The current population is out of place, because they do not fit well with the commercial and romanticized notion of an Incan past symbolized by the Citadel. In another sense, race and Indian identity were not merely implicated in the dance festival for commercial reasons, but were also more directly embedded in an effort to open areas to attract direct foreign investments.

The concept of secondary adjustment here is a tool for understanding how people respond to economic conditions designed to favor more powerful interests. Secondary adjustments may be categorized according to degree, so that certain activities that occur outside the formal context of what Goffman called a "total institution" can also be thought of as adjustments (Goffman 1961: 197). I found it useful to apply that reasoning to situations in the market economy. Market interactions are loaded with secondary adjustments organized around dominant economic relationships. Framing social action in this way calls attention to how laws given the rationale for protecting public goods or public spaces are then geared to the "cleaning up" of the market place for larger investors. Many low-level secondary adjustments resemble de Certeau's description of "*poaching* in countless ways on the property of others" (1984: xii). As long as the adjustments do not go beyond a certain point, they are accepted. From the "injured" party, one might, at most, receive scowling stares, or as the saying goes, "a piece of one's mind," for conducting activities that might be considered crude and inappropriate. Michel Foucault's similar term for such secondary adjustments is "necessary illegality."[27] Foucault explains how from the age of monarchy through the 18th century, people of lower strata found a "space of tolerance" for certain kinds of thievery and other infractions needed for continued existence. Those "necessary illegalities" changed after the downfall of the feudal system and the emergence of new propertied classes. With the emergence of capitalism came an increase in crime, and what were once considered tolerated practices were afterwards defined as crimes against property (Foucault 1977: 82–85). Thus, one can conclude that serious attempts to thwart secondary adjustments by using force imply that one party is no longer willing to tolerate the informal survival strategies of the others and furthermore may use it against them.

In Machu Picchu, the introduction of a neoliberal economy changed the relationship between social interaction and forms of economic adaptation. When it came to economic discipline, those who controlled greater capital defined significant spaces so as to exclude some people from participating in a segment of the market. Efforts were made to criminalize the more fuzzy infractions of secondary adjustments. Secondary adjustments became much more of a gamble at the same time as they became more crucial for survival. Now people incur greater risk for arrest, expulsion or property confiscation by authorities. Such disciplinary measures that dispossess can then be incorporated into a "capital accumulation strategy" (Harvey: 2003: 145). In effect, the more pervasive secondary adjustments became, the more those governing institutions turned to documenting ecological violations or damages to a public resource (as in the case of the thirty-three campesinos mentioned above). This situation led to increasing justification by governing agencies for the further dispossession of Sanctuary inhabitants, and the subsequent turning over of that space to larger capital holders in the form of contracts and concessions for tourist transportation and lodging. If Machu Picchu is an intangible good then perhaps equally intangible are its institutional walls.

As David Harvey notes, there are many contingencies involved in the way dispossession can occur, as was the case with the occurrence of a natural disaster. When this unpredicted event happened, people scrambled to impose meanings that took the shape of conflict over belonging. For the locals, I saw internal struggles for the right to make a living.

However, the governing authorities also used the danger of natural disaster to threaten residents with removal, ostensibly "for their own welfare," without similar threats made to larger investors.

As a national symbol, Machu Picchu represents Peru to the rest of the world, and it receives a lot of media attention. To retain its value as a commodity, Machu Picchu must retain its image of man and nature in harmony. Overt violence on the part of the state to remove the population would have likely undermined its value as a tourist commodity and attracted negative media attention. Consequently, the right use of the media and the control of information played an important role in the battle between authorities and the Machupiccheños; forms of communication used thus warrant closer examination, a topic to be taken up later. Looking back on the initial protest meeting, however, Frente and the leaders of the mobilization were still faced with the challenge of building a wider district consensus. For the time being, the landslides prevented the protestors from proceeding with the demonstration. This had a positive outcome in that the delay gave them time to open formal channels of communication between the local activists and the conservation authorities. Finally, the landslides also gave the leaders of the mobilization, specifically the president, Oscar, more time to gather and disseminate information, as well as to develop a strategy and a detailed plan of action he would call a platform of struggle (*plataforma de lucha*).

NOTES

1. The District Anniversary date is October 1.
2. Dance and dress are highly symbolic in the Andes. They are strong markers of community and region, but the Pueblo of Machu Picchu does not have a specific dance or dress of its own. See Mendoza, Zoila S. (2000) in the bibliography.
3. The National Institute of Culture is currently the Ministry of Culture. They are charged with preserving the archeological heritage of Peru.
4. According to UNESCO Legislative Resolution 23349, Peru is required "to identify, protect, conserve, restore and transmit to future generations" its world heritage sites.
5. Article law 24047 maintains that the state has the obligation to protect cultural patrimony from all attempts to alter its intangible nature. Peruvian national law has expressly declared the Machu Picchu archeological park as cultural patrimony of the nation in article law 23765 under article 21, and biodiversity and protected natural areas under article 68 of the Peruvian Constitution. Crimes committed against heritage sites are defined under article law 27244 under articles 228, 230, and 231 of the penal code, which states that destroying or altering a cultural asset constitutes a crime.
6. This is in a somewhat similar fashion to the "too big to fail" mantra in the United States during the 2007–08 world financial crises.
7. Though no access to electricity was the case at the time of this fieldwork, under pressure from the district government but resistance from INRENA, electricity lines were built in some areas in around 2012.
8. For an in-depth discussion on the public significance of the plaza in Latin America see Setha Low, *On the Plaza: The Politics of Public Space and Culture*. Austin: University of Texas Press, 2000.

9. For an excellent discussion of race in Cusco, see Marisol de la Cadena 2000.

10. These enforcements primarily come from the municipal police as opposed to the national police.

11. The exception is found in agencies that specialize in mystical tourism. The explanations of the past offered by such tour guides vary, but it is often a highly romanticized narrative that caters to the Western imagination commonly reflective of a popular "New Age" syncretism. Hence it is not surprising that many Cuzqueños refer to these tour guides as "chisticos," which is comprised of two words condensed into one: *chiste* meaning joke and *místico* meaning mystic.

12. Machu or the plural Machus refers to the "ancients," usually pre-Incan people who are said to be of a different bodily form. It is popularly believed that they inhabit caves or smaller natural openings along mountains. There is a gender component to the beliefs in that Machus are male and are dangerous to women, whom they try and kidnap.

13. Sirena translates to mermaid. Popular belief among many campesinos in the Andes is that mermaids inhabit rivers and streams, and as females they lure fishermen into the water where they drown. For an in-depth discussion see Stobart, H. (2006) in the bibliography.

14. Choclo is the local term for corn and is often eaten with a piece of locally made Andean cheese. Chicha, as mentioned in a footnote in the previous chapter, is a fermented corn drink.

15. See Jonathan Glover, *I: The Philosophy and Psychology of Personal Identity*, London: Allen Lane, The Penguin Press, 1988.

16. Chicha is a drink made from fermented corn.

17. While the rangers do superintend the actions of the campesinos, it would not be fair to depict their interactions entirely as negative. Friendships do develop and cooperation does occur, but by the same token this fact should not detract from the realities of the power relationship that exists between them.

18. Mote refers to roasted kernels of corn.

19. A chullo is a traditional wool cap particularly used in the sierra.

20. The t-shirt was made for a high school play performance from Annandale High School, whereabouts unknown.

21. INRENA distinguishes plants and wildlife according to whether it is native or exotic to the zone, a distinction not generally made by rural inhabitants. Exotic trees may be cut with permission, but many residents either do not secure permission or do not know INRENA classifications of exotic.

22. The term *La Casa Grande* (the big house) is used by many campesinos in the area to refer to the hacendado's (landlord) house.

23. "Huayco" is a Quechua term that refers to flash floods caused by mudslides that dam a river until it creates enough pressure to carry forward everything in its path. Smaller rivers are more susceptible to being dammed by debris and thus are more likely to cause huaycos. Residents stay very attentive to the flow of the rivers. When a river stops flowing or slows to a trickle, it is taken as a sign that a huayco is coming. During my stay in Machu Picchu, there were false alarms that sent people running out of their homes with blankets in hand to the highest possible ground.

24. Meat skewers usually made from cow hearts.

25. It was a capillary of this river that caused two of the four landslides discussed above.

26. On April 10, 2004, a large mudslide (huayco) came down from the River Alcamayo destroying a segment of the Pueblo and killing at least 11 people, one of whom was a prominent engineer, Roberto Rossel Gutiérrez.

27. For a good discussion on the similarity and complementarity of Michel Foucault and Erving Goffman see Ian Haking 2004.

THREE

Patchwork

Money, Class, and Patronage

Neoliberalism is the new political economy in fashion.
(Neoliberalismo es la nueva política económica que está de moda.)
—Chela, Machupicchu Pueblo

From the start of 2002 much of Peru was engaged in a series of anti-privatization protests. At the center of the social turmoil was a serious disenchantment with President Toledo's government. In the city of Arequipa, the protests over the sale of the state-owned electrical company became violent. The mayor of the city backed the efforts of the protestors and even threatened to secede from the state. In the end, the protests prompted Toledo's government to alter its privatization program, at least in Arequipa. In Cusco, protests were also intense but less violent. There were rumors that even the Sanctuary of Machu Picchu would be privatized; rumors that fueled nationalist and regionalist sentiments. Protests in the city were a regular occurrence and it was common to hear people chant the slogan that Machu Picchu was not for sale.

For the Machupiccheños, a group of mobilizers in town organized as a Frente de Defensa (defense front) or Frente connected their struggle against capital intrusions and conservation biases to the wave of anti-privatization demonstrations and protests against neoliberal developments that were taking place across Peru. However, people's willingness to organize against foreign capital investments has much to do with their class conditions and social positions. The politics of belonging is a material and cultural entanglement (Smith 1989). Lesley Gill noted, for example, that recipients of NGO services in El Alto, Bolivia, are often involved in their own factional struggles for power and wealth, aligning themselves with NGOs for resources rather than being passively constituted by NGO discourses. "Factional cleavages come to characterize the struggle for resources. These cleavages are not based on horizontal class alliances but turn on ties of patronage and dependence that people use to forge shifting alliances tinged with partisan politics or imbued with the discourse of NGOs" (2000: 83). Similarly, in Machu Picchu one also found international organizations drawn into the struggles among different local factions. While privatization under neoliberalism is often depicted in terms of a broad economic realism, the value of ethnography is that it highlights the subjectively specific portrayals given to the class relationships involved at the local level, and shows how these facets shape political positions around social problems (ibid.).

In addition to the greater enforcement of Sanctuary regulations and the bureaucratization of life, possession rights as opposed to property titles further disadvantaged residents economically in this moment of change. More stringent conservation efforts made people hesitant to make costly investments to upgrade their services without the legal assurance of property titles; there was a pervasive sense that people could be evicted from the Sanctuary at any time, making all business investments high-risk ventures. While the degree varied, the sense of risk ran from the more established restaurant or hotel owner to the newer residents "invading" a terrain. Possession status rather than a property title meant getting a bank loan for a business was difficult for residents because they had no secure form of collateral. In addition, there were higher interest rates charged on loans not only because of insufficient collateral but also for the high risk of living in a zone prone to natural disasters. Possession status entails restrictions on the sale of buildings, although it is not prohibited. In Machu Picchu, possession status means that an individual must offer the state first-bid at government prices, and only if the state turns down the offer to purchase can people then sell privately to obtain the best market price. Many residents expressed the feeling that possession status disadvantaged their businesses and left them more susceptible to the encroachments of larger capital investors such as Orient Express/Belmond. This was particularly true for hotel and restaurant owners and to a lesser extent the artisans as they sought to expand their own operations to accommodate the increasing number of tourists; these were folks who had possession rights to land. The poorer residents on the other hand, mainly migrants from nearby communities, did not possess land. The measure for deciding who was from the pueblo was usually ascertained simply by the amount of time one had lived there and whether they had access to land. Most residents in the town originally came from somewhere else, but some have longer family histories in the Pueblo. Those who have possession rights to the land where they built local hotels and restaurants tended to be more from "here." Possession rights and territorial claims converge to form a special kind of propertied class. It is common for people who claim that they are from Machu Picchu but born elsewhere to qualify their claim with phrases like "but I've been here for 20 years or more." In other words, they establish a lineage that connects them to land possession entitlement. Indeed, much of Pueblo life was defined by the politics of belonging and about deciding who can or cannot claim possession rights to land. Many of the older residents resented the building on invaded land.[1] As noted in the last chapter, park officials had forcibly removed two land invaders on the grounds of ecological violations. A significant number of the landless came to the town after a natural disaster in the nearby communities of Santa Teresa and Ccollpani destroyed their homes and fields. As Ana, originally from Santa Teresa, recalled, when she arrived in the Pueblo some of the older residents began linking the floods that displaced people with the people that "flooded" the town. Many of the women who worked in the central market fell into the category of newer residents. Many of these newer residents often expressed resentment against the older landholding groups, claiming that the "old guard" saw themselves as the only ones who had the right to make a living in the town. As one market woman put it, echoing what Nayruth had said to me after the landslide (described in the last chapter), "Because they own houses they believe themselves to be the owners of the Sanctuary." This central division in the Pueblo posed a serious challenge to uniting people in the mobilization against state laws, and large-scale private enterprise.

By contrast to the poorer townsfolk, many of the poorer campesinos in the rural areas did have possession status but with fewer opportunities to economically benefit from tourism or agriculture because of the farming restrictions. Class formation and divisions in Machu Picchu and particularly in the town was based on land possession rights and access to the tourism economy. Since the formation of the Sanctuary, the state was relatively lenient about what town residents could do with possession rights. With little state supervision, some Machupiccheños even managed to negotiate with local and provincial bureaucracies to record their holdings in the public registry. However, vast political and economic events soon accelerated a process of conservation changes in 1995 that a few years later led to concerted enforcement of the existing law and the voiding of all registered property on the grounds of the 1981 sanctuary designation. In addition, in 1995, a debt-for-nature exchange with Finland was put into action leading to the creation of Programa Machu Picchu (PMP), as I noted previously, an organization charged with closely monitoring conservation in the Sanctuary.[2] The efforts of this organization concentrated on environmental studies that residents felt either ignored their existence or accused them of environmental degradation.[3] As noted in the introduction, a debt-for-nature program offers funds for nature conservation programs in exchange for international debt. The Finland-Peru agreement meant debt forgiveness over a loan default, and approximately seven million dollars applied towards Sanctuary conservation. In 1998, a study conducted by the Instituto Nacional de Recursos Naturales (INRENA), the PMP and the Instituto Nacional de Cultura (INC) resulted in the implementation of a "Master Plan" (different from the Urban Plan mentioned in the previous chapter). Like the Urban Plan, however, the Master Plan describes the residents in terms of "chaos" and "disorder." Nor did the plan receive input by the Machupiccheños, and thus allowed vested interests to circumvent resident scrutiny. One of the most important outcomes of the Master Plan was to support the building of a cable car (*teleférico*) that would stretch from the train station to the Citadel. The plan maintained that it was a more ecologically sound mode of transportation (Plan Maestro: 70–73). In addition, in 2000 the residents witnessed the privatization of the train service and began to experience the implementation of this 1998 Master Plan that cleared the way for the cable car project proposal from yet another subsidiary of the company Belmond, also formerly known as Orient Express. The cable car project would have undercut the local bus company TRAMUSA, as well as the municipal bus service transporting tourists to the Citadel; both bus services are a major source of income for local investors and the municipality. The project sparked immediate protests from residents who had an investment stake in TRAMUSA. The cable car plan was ultimately put on hold when UNESCO intervened and threatened to terminate the World Heritage status, maintaining that the cable car would create a greater risk of causing landslides. UNESCO also argued that it would do damage to the environment, although the proponents of the project held that the cable car would be more ecologically sound than the current buses because of exhaust pollution, and the effect of vehicle weight on the mountain terrain.[4]

Furthermore, in 2000 a new state institution, the Unidad Gestión Machu Picchu (UGM), was created in the Sanctuary to mediate the squabbles between INRENA and the INC over the control of funds, as well as the Sanctuary itself. However, the UGM became embroiled in the same issues of control, only leading to a greater bureaucratization of life for the Machupiccheños, not to mention unnecessarily wasting away part of the debt-for-nature funds granted by Finland. Finally, that same year, the law #001-2000 was passed reaffirming state ownership of all land and clarifying the possession rights status of the residents.[5] This law created great concern among the Machupiccheños, not because they finally became aware that they only had possession rights, but rather they understood possession status had different consequences now under privatization efforts. The consequences not only made competition difficult, it threatened outright dispossession. Generally, dispossession is understood as either the taking away of tangible property such as land or the removal of people from land or access to resources. Residents felt insecure that the more stringent conservation enforcements might lead to their expulsion from the Sanctuary. Property titles, they felt, would give them greater legal leverage to hold on to their belongings. Property titles might give people greater security and legal recognition, as Hernando de Soto argued in *The Other Path* (1989), but this would only be part of what "capital accumulation by dispossession" could entail. He seems to only be addressing the threat and fear nested in everyday life in Peru affecting business activities without considering the role of the state in facilitating class interests or its involvement in creating the threat and fear. Rather, dispossession in this case and throughout much of Latin America can be thought of as an inbuilt part of neoliberal policies (Harvey 2003). The state, in privatizing the transportation services to Orient Express/Belmond, created such crass inequalities in competition between corporate capital and locals as to risk the livelihoods of the latter without taking responsibility for actual expropriation or eviction. Privatization led the Machupiccheños to distrust the motives of all state agencies operating in the district.

When some one hundred Machupiccheños gathered at the cultural center to discuss a plan for a district-wide protest against a list of state institutions and NGOs such as PROFONANPE[6] and the PMP in addition to Belmond/Orient Express in February of 2002, Oscar led the event. The discussion centered on state law 001-2000 that annulled all land titles that were recorded in the public registry after the 1981 sanctuary declaration. However, to reaffirm, the regulations that govern restrictions on property are not recent. Rosa had explained to me the property restrictions in an interview some five months earlier. Residents had been living with property restrictions since the declaration of the sanctuary, but never had there been an attempt to organize a protest against the regulations. The Machupiccheños were now connecting their struggle over land rights to consequences stemming from privatization and neoliberal policy changes. Yet organized dissent had to contend with a hierarchy of class interests. Middle-class hotel and restaurant owners that possessed land initiated the challenge to privatization and conservation policies in the district. In order sustain a wider form of dissent against privatization, at least in the town if not the district, class gaps had to be bridged with smaller artisan dealers and sellers as well as market women. One reason for why people and factions came together had to do with the mutual problems they shared with the privatization of transportation. An analysis of the role of the train in everyday life shows how Orient Express/ Belmond has a great deal control over the space/time elements of the local economy.

TRANSPORTATION AND MOVEMENT

The train is an important reality of life in the district of Machu Picchu. There is no other viable form of transportation; there are no roads for motor vehicles. The movement of the train marks daily life. The rhythm of activity in both the town and the rural communities is rooted in the time schedule of the train.[7] For example, early each morning during my fieldwork, as the first rays of light broke into the canyon above the town, traveling residents and departing tourists gathered at the train tracks to wait for the Cusco-bound train. As they lined up at the ticket window or waited around the platform, local women stood by ready to sell cakes, sandwiches and hot drinks (see figure 3.1). *Cargadores* (cargo carriers) walked through the Pueblo or met in Plaza Manco Capac searching for people who needed help carrying baggage.[8] There was at the time only one morning Cusco-bound train for locals. Once it departed, the local buses were then ready for their first trip up to the Citadel, and the women moved over to the waiting buses to sell their morning snacks to overnight tourists.[9]

One day riding the local train service from Cusco to Machupicchu Pueblo, I braced myself for the usual experience—a trip jam-packed with passengers transporting goods and produce. I arrived at the PeruRail train station early to avoid struggling through a bottleneck of passengers boarding the train. Surprisingly, things were proceeding rather smoothly and there were fewer cargo-carrying passengers than expected. As I took my seat I spotted some familiar faces; Doña Marta waved to me from the

Figure 3.1. Photo of local women selling food and snacks to tourists by the train ticket window (November 2001). (Photo taken by Pellegrino Luciano)

other end of the car. Soon the train departed and we climbed out of the Cusco Valley in zigzag motions. It takes about four hours to reach Machupicchu Pueblo directly from Cusco; the train stops at many communities in the countryside. During the rainy season the landscape turns into a lush green and is dotted with yellow and purple flowers. The snows on the mountains melt, exposing the jagged peaks. The Vilcanota River turns earth red and is swollen to the edges of its banks as it travels fiercely down the eastern slope of the Andes into the Montaña, the jungle.

At the first stop, it became clear why there were so few cargo-carrying passengers. As people tried to board the train with their goods, they were forcefully directed by security to the cargo compartment, a new and relatively costly procedure for poorer inhabitants. Prior to these new regulations, people just packed their goods onto the wagon rather than pay the cargo fees. This was a tolerated practice when the train service was run by ENEFER,[10] the state-operated agency. Orient Express/Belmond, an English company, purchased the state train route in 2000 under the name PeruRail, and purchased the Sanctuary Lodge, the five-star hotel located next to the Citadel, as well as Hotel Machu Picchu located in the town. The governance structures of global corporations are often difficult to trace because of international mergers. Corporate entities are often deceptively presented as national or even of specific cultural origin. On varied occasions I heard foreign tourists complain about the management inefficiencies of PeruRail, perceiving that because of the name it was state operated. Perhaps likewise as a result, anti-privatization movements are often nationalist in orientation. PeruRail was a joint venture between Peruval, a Peruvian company, and Orient Express/Belmond, Ltd. Orient Express, Ltd., was the "leisure division" of Sea Containers, Ltd., that owns 47% of the equity of Orient Express. While Orient Express is seen as an English company, Sea Containers is registered in Bermuda with operating headquarters in London, England, but is nevertheless, owned primarily by U.S. shareholders.[11]

Under President Fujimori's economic policies, PeruRail was given a 30-year tax exemption, plus an extra 5-year grace period to recuperate any losses incurred during that time. Many residents, especially the poorer ones, could not afford the PeruRail train system. Town and rural residents complained that PeruRail did not put much effort into their local service; PeruRail is in the tourism business and not geared to transporting local people as was the train service when it was state operated. Furthermore, PeruRail was in 2002, as it is currently, in the business of selling "romantic" landscape views. While such a specialty makes PeruRail locally useless, it allowed them to justify the exorbitant rates charged to tourists for such a short distance of travel. Since the service was privatized, residents had little opportunity for recourse. Machupiccheños of the entire district thus had little control over their only form of transportation. PeruRail offered residents a "social service," and used it to argue that they fulfilled a moral obligation towards residents. But for the Machupiccheños and frequent local riders, the train was a necessity that up until privatization was thought of as something akin to a public transportation system.

A major issue between PeruRail and residents concerned the quality of transportation service they offered them. For instance, many town residents expressed discontent at the uncomfortable conditions the *porteadores* created for them; porteadores or porters carry baggage for tourists hiking the Inca Trail. Once the Inca Trail ends in Machu Picchu, the porters take the local train back to Cusco, making it overcrowded. Residents had asked PeruRail to add an additional car to make more room for everyone. However, they refused, citing the costs. Porters generally carry backpacks, portable stoves and gas canisters. The gas canisters on the train created a dangerous situation. PeruRail insisted that the problem was that the porters did not want to use the baggage compartment for cultural rather than economic reasons, in that they were unable to abide by "rational" rules. However, because of PeruRail's time pressures, the porters were only being given a couple of minutes to board, making it virtually impossible to do anything else but storm onto the train. Even if the porters had had the time to place their cargo in the baggage compartment, the train would have still been brutally overcrowded. Had PeruRail run such a service in England or the United States they would have possibly been indicted for creating hazardous travel conditions, and yet the implication on the part of the company was that the Machupiccheños should be thankful for the service "handouts" they were given, an example of how commonly held goods and services are recast in terms of humiliation once privatized. Residents often pointed out to PeruRail that as ticket-paying customers, the porters were entitled to a seat and therefore PeruRail should provide the appropriate accommodations by adding an extra train wagon. At the time, PeruRail refused to add an extra wagon. They cited the cost, and maintained that the "social service" was already a profit loss to them.

One evening, local business owners and artisans gathered to discuss PeruRail and the Sanctuary Lodge's new joint promotional package that included a meal in the price of the train ticket. The sister companies of Orient Express/Belmond had leased out artisan concessions on their tourist train and around the hotel. By capturing the artisan, hotel and restaurant markets, they could capture a significant portion of the local tourism economy such as food, transportation and artisan memorabilia—the mainstay of the townsfolk.[12] Spatially, the privilege of operating in a location adjacent to the Citadel already gave Sanctuary Lodge the advantage of exploiting a picturesque landscape view from high above the valley. By contrast, the Machupiccheños were prohibited from engaging in commercial activity around the Citadel.

The bulk of tourists arrived at Machu Picchu by train, and Orient Express/Belmond had a monopoly over the control of transportation. Tourists generally arrived in the late morning and at the time of my fieldwork were forced to catch the only train back to Cusco in the late afternoon—that is, if they did not want to stay in town for the night.[13] Therefore, after touring the Citadel for five or six hours, tourists descended to the town to wait for the return train. In the interim, they might purchase a meal and shop in the local artisan market. However, with the joint promotion the company had initiated, the townsfolk were worried that Orient Express would capture what little time tourists had left before boarding the return train since, again, Sanctuary Lodge is the only hotel and restaurant privileged to be situated on the mountain precipice just outside the Citadel entrance.

In addition, PeruRail began selling memorabilia directly on their trains, and Sanctuary Lodge Hotel had subcontracted part of their space to two large chains: Ilaria, which sells fine jewelry, and Alpaca 101, fine alpaca wool products. Sanctuary Lodge argued in a meeting with the townsfolk that these expensive artisan items were of a higher quality than the merchandise being sold in the town, and thus not in competition with them. However, the issue they failed to mention was how choice was being taken away from the consumer. Under time pressure, tourists were more likely to make the convenient purchases offered by the expensive companies. I assume tourists do tend to extend their economic means by purchasing items they normally would not buy at home, especially if they are visiting a place construed as "exotic." At the time, what exacerbated the tough market environment for the townsfolk was the fact that it was already the low tourism season, and the September 11 attack on the World Trade Center resulted in a further drop in tourism. Adding to the concerns of the townsfolk was another joint proposal by Sanctuary Lodge and PeruRail to reconstruct the old train station about a kilometer from the town in a place known as Puente Ruinas that would allow them to transport tourists to the foot of the Machu Picchu mountain where they would then sell their own arts and crafts before and after visits to the Citadel; in effect, they would bypass the town altogether. This possibility fueled a sense of outrage and insecurity, and made Orient Express' control of the tourism economy more apparent. As Margarita once said to me, "With a thirty-year contract, if PeruRail and Sanctuary Lodge are not challenged they will destroy the pueblo."

Consequently, for the townsfolk, the privatizing of the train led to an enormous loss of control over their economy. For residents of the town, the privileges granted PeruRail and Sanctuary Lodge became the standard by which they measured the "marriage" between conservation and privatization policies throughout the Sanctuary. Chela, the president of one of the artisan associations, organized what she called a "commercial" protest against Sanctuary Lodge by selling goods adjacent to the Citadel, saying, "After all, why don't we have the right to locate our commercial activities [by the Citadel] if Sanctuary Lodge can?" Hence, in response, to Sanctuary Lodge leasing commercial space to two major chains, the artisans of the town along with small merchants[14] went up to the Citadel to sell their own products even though it was prohibited. As the leader or Secretaria General of the principle artisan association Sindicato de Artesanos y Pequeños Comerciantes, Chela played a vital role in organizing her group of mostly women for protest and, ultimately under her leadership, in supporting Frente's challenge against corporate capital and state control by helping to build a greater pueblo backing from a large sector of the town.

The artisans and sellers expected to do better business by the Citadel, but many were surprised at the dramatic increase in sales by comparison to their normal commercial activity in town. Chela showed the artisans what they lost economically because of restrictions. She demonstrated that the position maintained by Sanctuary Lodge was incorrect and that even high-end tourists would indeed purchase more local products rather than, or along with, expensive name brands, when available. Nevertheless, the Machupiccheños were prohibited from conducting commercial activity near the Citadel. They had been warned by the police, most probably at the urging of Sanctuary Lodge, not to attempt another "commercial" protest, as it was called, because they would be arrested.[15] Jorge nicely expressed his resentment of this double standard, as he did when I spoke to him about the meaning of intangibility. He questioned the rationale for prohibiting residents from doing business there:

> If they say this is a free market and there should be competition then why can't we come here to sell and compete equally with them [Sanctuary Lodge] here—if they are allowed to sell their products then why can't we? Why is it not equal? There are people in Machu Picchu that need to bring home "the bread" on a daily basis to cover their costs. If no one is allowed here, then no one should be allowed here, otherwise what kind of competition are we talking about in neoliberalism or in this globalized world, as they call it? Give us something consistent! It's only a free market for the rich. If you have money you can grab the market but if you don't have money, you don't have possibilities. . . . This competition is not legal. This is not competition!

Jorge's comment on the need to "bring home the bread" evokes Gavin Smith's observation of how "political struggle must be reintegrated into the parallel experience of each participant in trying to keep bread on the table" (1989: 170). As Smith showed in his analysis of the struggle to undermine the hacienda system among the Huasicanchinos in Central Peru, it was precisely the threat to livelihood that united different groups and interests for political action (ibid.). Likewise, in Machu Picchu, the less wealthy artisans/sellers and other micro-entrepreneurs directly connected to the tourism economy began seeing it in their interest to join the restaurant and hotel owners in the protest. Such alliances, while generally not long-lasting, are not uncommon in Latin America, since neoliberal reforms have also posed difficult circumstances for small businesses as many find themselves unable to compete with direct foreign investments (Shadlen 2000: 101; Durand 1998: 276). Typically, small family and even middle-sized businesses often lack resources and expertise, information and technology compared to large corporations, making it difficult to protect their interests separately (Shadlen 2000: 74). However, this alliance, as Maria Lagos points out in her study on peasants and merchants in Cochabamba, Bolivia, does not suggest that class differences are overshadowed by common political ground, nor that their efforts in collective action will bring the comparable returns (1994: 132). In Machu Picchu, others who were less directly involved in the tourism economy, such as the women of the central market or those who did not possess land, proved more difficult to organize. The issue of class and wealth differences was evident when several people attempted to form a train company that would compete against PeruRail. Creating the train company required that a large number of Machupiccheños make the initial capital investment. Even if that were possible, they would still need a major investor at the level of PeruRail. They needed to partner with a company that had the necessary capital; in some respects, the latter was easier than the former, as the following meeting illustrates.

MOBILIZING LOCAL CAPITAL

The townsfolk fought back against the transportation monopoly of PeruRail and the power they had over the district economy. A group of Machupiccheños, mostly members of Frente, proposed a plan to create a train company to compete with PeruRail. Oscar, the president of Frente, summarized his rationale to me as follows:

> We believe that Fujimori created total corruption in Peru. Companies [like PeruRail] were given special contracts and preferential treatment. In Peru, there should not be monopolies! With this in mind, the people of the Pueblo decided to create a company.

After the plan was developed, the directors went house to house throughout the town asking for interested investors. To their credit, they did not discriminate in the asking. However, the price of membership was too steep for many households, about $1,200 U.S. In addition, while the directors kept participation open to everyone who had money for the investment, class tensions between older and newer residents created problems of trust. Ana, for example, one of the more recent and poorer residents, told me that she rejected the offer because she distrusted the motives and would lose her money. Personal relations of trust are fundamental to organizing capital ventures at the local level, especially in the Andes. Short on capital, one of the main dilemmas for the fledgling company was whether it should be open to outside investors. A meeting was held led by Oscar and Margarita, two interested investors, to reinforce confidence in the plan and increase the list of willing participants. Originally, the formation of the company began with 250 participants, but that number quickly dwindled to about 100; understandably, the lower the number of participants the higher the financial burden for each investor. Therefore, it was imperative for them to alleviate fears of losing money to thwart what would eventually happen—a further withdrawal of participation.

After passing out the information, Oscar quickly turned his attention to the abstainers who had promised participation. He vigorously emphasized that no additional money was required at that time, only signatures. Many were confused because they did not understand the procedures involved in such an investment and thus expressed concern about losing their money. Neither did they trust the board; I noticed a perceptible element of distrust in the room. Oscar pressured them—"There are people in Cusco waiting [to invest], so all must sign!" He explained the procedures as well as the function of the board of directors to alleviate fears of people losing their money. "The money is placed in a bank account where all transactions are visible on monthly statements. Money can only be removed with the authorization and signature of the directors, so it can't simply be stolen by anyone, and they can still remove their money via the directors, if they wanted their money back," he said. There was only silence. Margarita went into a homily on the importance of this business venture, and she said:

> You should think about the future of the Pueblo, PeruRail is a monster.[16] They have six pages on the Internet, when most only have one or two. [She spoke about how PeruRail bullied other business owners in the past, using metaphorical terms] they broke their arms . . . but as a pueblo, PeruRail would have to go house to house to break our arms. We should continue our struggle because it is not only for our future but the future of our children.

As the meeting ended it was decided that everyone had a week's time to submit the full investment money. Margarita herself turned to me and said, "That's most of the group"; she made a face to express disbelief in the possibility of people coming up with the 2.5-million-dollar capital needed in conjunction with a foreign company that would be willing to form a partnership with them.[17]

The attempt to establish the company was full of criticism among the townsfolk. The feeling by many was that it simply would not be economically sustainable; people would lose their money. Emilio, a hotel owner and also an interested participant, privately expressed serious doubts about the plan saying, "I don't think it's possible." From his perspective, the cost was too great; even if everyone did contribute the full initial capital it would not nearly be enough to operate a train company. As a hotel owner and knowledgeable businessman, he pointed out the many hidden costs in maintenance and insurance, not to mention hiring engineers, conductors and mechanics. No one had that capital. In addition, he even questioned whether it was politically feasible. Emilio believed that state officials in Lima were financially tied to Orient Express and had a personal stake in the monopoly. The sweetheart deals given to them by the state sounded suspicious to Emilio. He supposed corruption and buttressed his sentiments with a contemptuous smile: "This would not be new, that's the way Peru is," as he doubted the state would ever grant permission to rent out the rail system.[18] Emilio backed out from participation but while he was a sympathetic critic, others were more strongly against the attempt. "What a pity!" (*que lastima*), blasted Juan Carlos, an elderly restaurant owner and lifetime resident of Machu Picchu. We sat outside his farmhouse eating freshly caught trout as we spoke about the efforts to form a train company. "These people are going to lose their investment. . . . They can never generate the money needed. . . . What they're doing is a rip-off—to each his own kind of craziness." Nonetheless, while the formation of the company was never realized, the active search for an international investor on the part of the pueblo was impressive in that it showed that people are not hapless victims to corporate capital. In fact, the bid from such small-level capital holders to attract international investors illustrates how people seek out new global alignments on their own terms and may intertwine global corporate capital with local capital (Nash 2005).

PATRONAGE AND MONEY IN MUNICIPAL POLITICS

Another factor leading to organized protest was the growing dissatisfaction among the older, more established land possessors with the incumbent mayor (*alcalde*). He had accommodated newcomers by allocating what little land there was or offered those individuals posts in the central market. Allocating both land and market space in Machu Picchu and throughout Peru is commonly understood as a political practice connected to patronage. The feeling, mainly amid the restaurant and hotel owners, was that the mayor was favoring large capital interests over the interests of local businesses, but built his constituency by attending to people who were relatively new to the town and had no access to land. This antagonized class relationships in a "divide and conquer" manner and led many, such as Margarita and the leaders of the Frente mobilization, to feel excluded from major decisions, especially on the spending of municipal money. When they found out that the mayor used municipal money to invest in the building of a Cusco-based hotel, allegedly to increase income for the district, they expressed anger that there was no public meeting to discuss the issue; it was too late for the municipality to pull back from the investment.

Some of the older residents, concerned about the way the mayor was using municipal funds, accused him of misappropriation. Municipal employees had not been paid for two months. Many, like Emilio, could not believe that the municipal government would be short funds to pay the construction workers. The municipality was swimming in money, and from Emilio's perspective it was outrageous that it should default on paying the workers' wages. The accusations that district funds were unaccounted for was further compounded by the fact that it was also the start of a local election year. Many members involved in the mobilization had political aspirations of their own, and the mayor seemed already to be involved in campaign efforts. His opponents claimed that he was allegedly dipping into municipal funds for his own campaign efforts. The problem arose in part from the fact that a great deal of capital passed into the hands of the municipal authorities, yet the town was in such disrepair. The following conversation I had with Emilio during my fieldwork gives perspective to the amount of money that goes into the municipal government of Machu Picchu.

As I was passing by Hotel Pachacútec, early during my fieldwork around October of 2001, Don Emilio, the owner, waved to me to come in and take a seat. He informed me that one of the district councilmen (*regidores*) had come around looking for me; members of the municipal administration were taking an official trip to the district communities, and they wanted to see if I as an anthropologist would be interested in going with them. Emilio explained that elections were approaching and that I should be cautious. He spoke openly about the politics of the Pueblo. The trip to the communities was all about campaigning and promises to win votes for the mayor. "The mayor is worried," Emilio said, making clear by his tone of voice that he was against him. Pre-election estimates had indicated that close to half of the district residents wanted to revoke his status in recall elections *(revocatoria)*. Emilio focused his eyes on me as if concentrating on an idea. "The mayor does nothing for the Pueblo. He's from Cusco, not from here." From Emilio's perspective, the invasions of outsiders were caused by the mayor; he claimed that the mayor sought to attract new residents to add them to his constituency. "Three hundred new people are now residents, where did they come from," he said. Inhabitants must officially change where they are registered to vote to be officially considered residents. This requires paying a fee, and Emilio charged that the mayor used his authority to waive the fee for many. Emilio stressed that the workers who come to the town are not residents, but he believed that they were the ones who had been able to change their residency status through the mayor's efforts. Emilio's accusations came on the heels of media allegations that PeruRail allegedly paid its employees to change their residency status in order to throw votes toward favorable candidates.[19] These people were referred to as *golondrinas,* after the swallow, which is considered a bird of passing, with no real fixed residence. I don't know whether PeruRail was guilty of this seduction or whether the mayor was responsible, for certainly, he would not have been alone in attempting to win patrons. Nevertheless, it became a concern among the older established townsfolk and Oscar used it to call attention to the strategic importance of controlling the municipal government if they were to survive the onslaught of Orient Express/Belmond.

The mayor was now going to concentrate his political efforts in the communities to promise the campesinos development projects. When I asked Emilio where the municipality would get the money to fund projects, he laughed. "You think the municipality doesn't have any money?" In 2002, the municipality had six buses that transported tourists up to Machu Picchu. Each bus held up to thirty tourists, and each tourist paid at the time $9 U.S. round-trip; the buses made at least three or four trips per day. The municipal government made an average of $3,000 U.S. per day on that alone. In addition, the municipality also collected the entrance fee (approx. $1.50 per tourist at the time) for the use of the hot-water springs in town. Finally, the Instituto Nacional de Cultura had agreed to set aside an escrow account of $2 for every $10 entrance fee to the Citadel of Machu Picchu; that amounted to half a million U.S. dollars per year in 2002. Considering the size of the district, that intake of money made it one of the wealthiest rural communities in Peru. Emilio's point was that despite the money that "flows" through the municipality, the district has little to show for it. The mystery for Emilio was, "Where's the money?" (*Donde esta la plata*?).

Furthermore, there was a growing dissatisfaction with the mayor's handling of NGO-designed projects for the town. Major, potentially life-altering projects were funded through the Finland-Peru debt-for-nature exchange. The most important of these projects entailed the building of a reservoir for potable water. Also, two other projects were planned: the construction of a new artisan market and the channeling of a small river (Rio Aguas Calientes) that cuts through the town and is noted for flash floods. Planning for these projects did not include any public consultation or pueblo participation. Many of the older, prominent members of the town were angry and alarmed over the fact that their advice had not been sought. In part this was because many of the them had dealt with natural disasters in the past, having endured forest fires, landslides, and flash floods, and some, who had a great deal of experience with their natural environment, saw the lack of consultation as an affront to their knowledge. Moreover, concerns about natural disasters cut across class lines and political affiliations. Many, even those who did not participate in the mobilization, worried about the precarious location of the reservoir. The reservoir was planned to be built above the town on a slope noted for landslides. This added to a vague aura of fear among some residents that state authorities, Orient Express and the PMP were bent on clearing the Sanctuary of Machupiccheños, either through expulsion or disaster. The mayor was characterized as incapable of protecting the town from outside institutional intrusion.

The mayor though was not without support. As a medical doctor and a practitioner at the local health station before his election, he was thought of kindly by many in the town and in the rural areas, as one who has extended his services generously. Also, many of the poorer, newer inhabitants were grateful for his help in gaining residency status and expressed loyalty. He competently managed the disaster relief after a 1998 flood of the Aobamba River that destroyed the homes of many in the district communities of Ccollpani and Intiwatana, as well as communities in other districts on the opposite side of the flooding river, such as Santa Teresa in the province of Quillabamba. A sizable number of these disaster victims settled in the Pueblo of Machu Picchu, and, under the auspices of the mayor, many found jobs and were allotted market stands. Many of the market women I spoke to expressed allegiance to the mayor, as it was under his administration that the central market was built. Furthermore, as already mentioned, many of these residents, particularly the women in the central market, felt some contempt toward the older, more established townsfolk. One market woman, "Micaela," rebuked previous municipal authorities for their false promises of giving her a piece of land, only to reject her because she was new to the Pueblo. She spoke kindly of the incumbent mayor:

> He listened to me . . . when I told him about the games they played with me about not being from this pueblo [and not giving her a piece of land] . . . I know that if some land would be available this mayor would offer it to me.

I assume that the mayor apparently felt secure in his constituency, and brushed off the mobilization as nothing more than party opposition in an election year. In meetings with state authorities during the early phases of the protest movement, he publicly mentioned that the actions expressed the complaints of only a handful of troublemakers, his opponents, largely the members of Frente. No doubt the political ambitions of some of the leaders in the mobilization, particularly Oscar, played a role in organizing protests. The fact that election-year politics played a role in the forming of the mobilization cannot be underestimated, but it can be misunderstood. The mayor, detached from the malaise in district life brought about by economic changes, did not see how the ranks of the mobilization grew around him even though many who joined the ranks were not necessarily political opponents. I observed, for instance, moments when the protestors had asked him to join them in helping communicate their problems when they had to meet state representatives; he had participated with reservation at first but in an unassuming manner. Had he claimed a greater leadership role, he may have won back popularity. The mobilization grew out of the contradictory experiences the Machupiccheños had with the state's neoliberal policies. While the mayor of places like Arequipa aligned himself with the anti-privatization protests and gained political approval, the mayor of Machu Picchu appeared to be apologetic on behalf of the entities that were being challenged, constantly emphasizing the "diplomatically sensitive nature" to attenuate the vigor of the demands made by the protestors.

Ethnographic analysis uncovers the many contradictions of real life that complicate the well-ordered depictions of social movements or collective action often represented from an outsider perspective (Edelman 2001: 286). The mobilization in Machu Picchu primarily grew out of the concerns and interests of small and mid-level entrepreneurs, mainly restaurant and hotel owners, who were doubly threatened by the corporate intrusions into their economy and the possibility of losing land-possession status; most, but not all, of the leaders were from this group. Many other stakeholders like micro- and small-scale merchants gradually joined. The newer residents such as the poorer market women were more reluctant to get involved. In part, the lack of participation from these latter groups had to do with their loyalty to the mayor, as he was blamed by the older residents for many of their problems with large-scale corporate capital.

I was sometimes asked by the leaders of Frente and others to film their formal encounters with the authorities, seeing me as a person who could help legitimize their cause. On many occasions, the protestors would tell authorities who were reluctant to allow me into their meetings that I was their "CNN man," often lightheartedly tacking on an additional *N* (CNNN . . .). In a sense, they were suggesting that I connect their problems to a larger audience, perhaps the world. Some of these expressions also refract the history of the North-South power relations that define Latin American life. For example, the authorities and some of the participating Machupiccheños would both jokingly say, "They have their own gringo on their side" (*Tienen su propio gringo a sus lado*). But, what does it mean to have a gringo at your side? Does it lend credence and prestige to a group's cause? These expressions coupled with actions such as the attempt to form a train service in order to beat PeruRail at their own game, and even the distrust people expressed amongst themselves about their investments, were attempts to negotiate and manipulate the politics and economics of a changing world they did not control. Rather than retreat, the Machupiccheños displayed in their different ways, a determination to survive in a place where corporate and governmental forces would prefer that they disappear (Nash 2005).

Although a concrete plan was still in the making, the leaders of Frente decided to challenge numerous groups, like INRENA, INC, PMP, UGM and Orient Express, not to mention the municipal government and the provincial authorities of Urubamba. Confronting one institution would have been a formidable task, but to take on all of them seemed to some, and to me, a highly ambitious project. Nevertheless, far from seeing themselves as helpless victims, they endeavored to become "the mouse that roared." The Machupiccheños were cognizant of the "global" nature of their problems, and they had their own ideas of how to confront them. They were ready to defend themselves against all "invaders."

NOTES

1. In Peru when land is invaded in large numbers it is often referred to as *invasiones*.

2. While many third world countries around the world are involved in debt-for-nature swaps, they were first implemented in South and Central America in 1987. The first agreement was in Bolivia, and then Ecuador and Costa Rica quickly followed (see Patterson 1990). Debt-for-nature agreements in Latin America have had mixed results, but have generally fallen short of greatly diminishing debt as well as meeting conservation ideals (see Edelman 1995).

3. The exclusion of local populations from involvement is a well-documented complaint about debt-for-nature agreements, and at least in the case of Bolivia helped launch a political mobilization against the government by native people in the eastern lowland city of Trinidad, see Jones 1985.

4. According to an article written by John Roach for National Geographic News, April 15, 2002, the Vice Minister of Tourism Ramiro Salas spoke publicly about the possibility of locating the cable car on the back side of the Citadel ruins. The author goes on to suggest that "pressure exerted by Belmond/Orient Express and its partners may be succeeding."

5. This law is an updated version of 001-81 that established the Sanctuary in 1981.

6. Fondo Nacional para Areas Naturales Protegidas por el Estado.

7. Another means of transportation to Machu Picchu is by helicopter, but operations for the public were suspended, and it was used only for dignitaries. When it was operating, usually in the high tourist season, it cost over $100 U.S. and is not meant for local transportation.

8. Cargadores, similar to porteadores, make a living carrying cargo on their backs. In Machu Picchu, the cargadores by and large make their living loading and unloading cargo from the train.

9. There is only one road in the pueblo permitting the use of vehicles. It connects to the Hiram Bingham Road that leads up to the ruins.

10. ENEFER stands for Empresa Nacional de Ferrocarriles.

11. See www.seacontainers.com and www.perurail.com.

12. It is not clear if the privatization of the railroad even improved the conditions of the train workers. One rail employee, "Enrique," who previously worked for ENEFER, the state-run service, and now for PeruRail, says that his life did not improve economically. One of his main complaints is that the company does not pay overtime whereas ENEFER did, even though PeruRail expects workers to work past their hours. Enrique further grumbled that at least the employees of ENEFER were once able to eat free meals from the station kitchen, but that changed with PeruRail.

13. As opposed to tourists who arrive after hiking the Inca Trail and the occasional wealthy tourist who comes by chartered helicopter service.

14. By small merchants means those who sell rather than produce artisan products, as well as t-shirts and cloth products.

15. My assumption that Sanctuary Lodge urged the police to remove the artisans from doing business outside the hotel is based on a comment made by the director of the hotel during a public meeting with the townsfolk I attended and recorded in which the director stated that the police came the following day at their request.

16. Residents often refer to PeruRail and Sanctuary Lodge with the term "monster."

17. They had initially approached the Maryland and Delaware Railroad Company as a possible partner.

18. The rail itself remains government owned. Even PeruRail rents the use of the tracks, paying $4 a kilometer per trip.

19. Although I left the field in July 2002, just before the elections some six months later in November, my field assistant informed me that it was estimated that the number of legal residents had grown to 940 extra voters.

FOUR

Knowing What to Do

This is the voice of the people, which is the voice of god.
(Este es la voz del pueblo que es la voz de Dios.)
—Cori, Machupicchu Pueblo

One rainy Saturday morning in early February 2002, INRENA rangers gathered outside their station house in the community of Corihuayrachina to start their daily forest patrols. A group of campesinos and town residents also gathered nearby. As the rangers geared up to inspect for ecological violations, the Machupiccheños were meeting to discuss the judicial proceedings against thirty-three campesinos charged by INRENA for allegedly damaging the environment and were threatened with expulsion from the Sanctuary. Among the Machupiccheños, two prominent actors in local politics, Oscar and Walter, met to help organize the campesinos for protest, but also to interpret the laws of the Sanctuary and gain support for their own political aspirations.

THE WELL-INFORMED PERUVIAN

From the perspective of the residents, governance of the Sanctuary was frequently experienced as a set of shifting contexts from one authority, event and situation into another at a national and even global level of significance. Different criteria for action were constantly merging, making what to do in terms of a governance change somewhat uncertain. From a subjective and undoubtedly an intersubjective perspective, one can find a "sociology of knowledge" unique to the neoliberal circumstance. Here I find the work of Alfred Schutz useful in understanding what kind of "life-world" neoliberal globalization creates. Dealing with bureaucracy requires a certain know-how—knowledge about government organizations and techniques of interaction (Weber 1978: 225).

Complicating matters for anyone wishing to confront state bureaucracy was the fact that the mandates governing the Sanctuary were not always easily accessible to local people, nor were they always clearly stated. Even when rules were clearly stated, in practice the activation was negotiable, leading to experiences of confusion or deception and misinformation as part of the interaction with agency personnel. The numerous studies on the communicative interactions between people and bureaucracy show a great deal of cultural variation in how people are objectified and/or how the state gains knowledge about their subjects (Herzfeld 1992; Cody 2009; Kravel-Tovi 2012). The bureaucratic ecology of the Andean world is complex. Linda Seligmann describes how Cusco market women become adept at managing and resisting bureaucracies. Part of local knowledge involves skills at negotiating with regulatory offices and dealing with legal issues, as well as handling licensing and other fees (2004: 132). I am focusing here more on how people learn or gain knowledge about a bureaucracy that is intertwined with yet exceeds the boundaries of the state, such as NGOs and international organizations. The experiences of the Machupiccheños showed how the changing configurations of institutions and interests in the decision-making process made new demands on local knowledge. State bureaucracy in Machu Picchu is intricately woven into capital interests as well as international organizations, NGOs and multinational entities in ways that require new interaction skills to deal with ever-changing bureaucracies. Different "zones" of knowledge can overlap and blend with each other. As Alfred Schutz explained:

> various realms of relevances and precision are intermingled, showing the most manifold interpenetrations and enclaves, sending their fringes into neighbor provinces and thus creating twilight zones of sliding transitions. (1970: 113)

Knowledge is partial and never complete; this is true for ethnographers as well. Many years have passed since my fieldwork, with hindsight to reflect on where the Machupiccheños were effective or not, at least according to their platform of struggle, in their efforts to challenge bureaucracy and the corporate interests of Orient Express. History and past personal experiences are often the most intrinsic sources of knowledge for acting in the world, but under intense social change there are also many impositions in which actors lack experience. The following is a fieldwork excerpt of the conversations from the gathering in Corihuayrachina.

"It's because people don't have property titles or rights otherwise these thirty [-three] campesinos wouldn't have these problems. This is revenge, how ugly," Regina said. The gathering broke into smaller groups as people turned to their neighbors to chat. It started to rain softly. Walter was concerned. "It's scary, you know, the landslides." He was referring to the fierce rainstorm that hit the area the previous day. The conversation moved fluidly from dangerous weather to Sanctuary politics. The weather concerns turned into a discussion on the tragic incident of a family that had drowned a few days earlier. A young couple and their small child were tragically killed when they fell into the swollen Vilcanota River after the hand-drawn cable car (*oroya*) snapped as they pulled themselves across. "The chain was rusted," said a man. Walter heard different stories about this incident. He spoke of rumors that the deaths were the result of foul play, allegedly implying Sanctuary authorities. The conversation moved back to the thirty-three campesinos. Oscar got excited, pulling out papers from his folder. One of his talents was a well-developed ability to interrogate law and to point to contradictions in the way it is applied. He waved a document in the air saying, "I have the law right here. Where does it say in the law that one has to [even] ask permission to cut grass?"[1]

The common narrative held by Sanctuary representatives was that the inhabitants of the Sanctuary were not the original inhabitants. To be an "original inhabitant" is a vague qualification, but it reflected the way the law granted permissions. For INRENA and the INC, "original inhabitants" meant families who had continuously lived in the area but could also directly trace their ancestry to the Incas in some sort of unadulterated way; not likely to be found in most current populations of the Andes after five hundred years of conquest and colonialism. They formed part of the racialized narratives that discounted residents as belonging in the landscape, as noted earlier. For the group, an additional problem rested on the interpretation of the laws and the ambiguousness of the definitions. Oscar, who saw a potential in using the law as an avenue for defending residents, expressed frustration over the way institutional actors use various concepts. "Now we have to define [who] is original—what is a Sanctuary? It's all so arbitrary." For Oscar, one could hardly lay down any fixed rule around which the authorities were consistent. Walter jabbed at the Programa Machu Picchu (PMP), "What have they done to improve the lives of campesinos, they're more concerned with plants, animals and stones, what about people?" Oscar rhetorically wondered about the institutional vision for Machu Picchu. "Where are the humans? How can you have such anti-human laws? It's unconstitutional," he declared. Walter reconstructed the history of the Sanctuary, placing emphasis on the sequence of events.

> First you had the haciendas and those who worked for the hacendados. After the Agrarian Reform, we had the right to the land. It was before the 1981 declaration of the Sanctuary. It's ours legally—and what about the money we paid the state for the agrarian taxes? The Sanctuary came after. Before the Sanctuary there was the agrarian reform and the state charged us. We should reclaim that money!

Walter disentangles the history of land from the Sanctuary to position the agrarian history as relevant to the campesinos, and perhaps to all in the district. The agrarian history and expected rights under the agrarian reform was what helped motivate people into collective action. But that position had been legally bypassed and hence marginal against the definitional power to not only impose the concept of "Sanctuary" on that land but to challenge how that land is now woven into the economic interests of large capital.

As the group broke into chatter over how they had been swindled by the state, Oscar pointed to the contradictions of privatization. He noted a law that prohibited taking plastic bottles into the Sanctuary, "*ley de botellas*" (the law of bottles), as he referred to it.[2] In practice the law was not enforced, he felt, because of pressure from the Coca-Cola Company. His point was not to argue against environmental protection, only noting how moneyed interests made enforcement inconsistent. "When it comes to protecting nature, the big companies can do what they want," he said. The flow of discourse consistently interrogated the alliance between corporate interests and governing authorities. Their narratives directly reflect and grapple with the established trend in the current political economy to consolidate governance with free-market ideology, meaning corporations wield a great deal of power in negotiating contracts with governments. Global capitalism has used coercive practices involving the state apparatus (Gill 2000; Goldstein 2004; Vilas 2004). Oscar shuffled through his papers and said, "Now where does it say that rural residents can't have a gas stove—this is called arbitrariness!" The conversations shifted to a 1997 forest fire blamed on campesinos. As noted in chapter 2, no evidence was ever presented that the fire was started by campesinos, although it was the argument held among the institutional actors. Indeed, authorities used the fire incident to support a plan to eject inhabitants from the Sanctuary. Oscar quipped sarcastically, "Campesinos, the cause of the fire? They're just messing with us." Walter added, "They blamed us for the fire, as if we don't know how to take care of our land, why wouldn't we take care of the animals. These animals are from the Apus[3] and we [the Machupiccheños] protect them." He concluded, "This is why we formed a committee to defend all the communities rather than each community to try to defend itself alone—out of necessity we are forming a front to take on these problems."

The conversations reflect the way the changing economic policies had affected people's lives in the Sanctuary. Packed into the discussions were many layers of experience with conservation regulations that convinced district residents the state had manipulated the rules to their own self-interest and for the interests of corporate elites. But despite the layers, these were relatively recent experiences since around the year 2000, not even since the 1981 sanctuary designation. The encounter described offers us insight into the way experiences with current secondary adjustments made by people on an individual level, such as the example of Don Marcos in chapter 2, are now directed towards collective organizing against policy restructuring. Life in the Sanctuary gave rise to "spatial stories," based on the tactics by which people must live (de Certeau 1984: 115–130). The discussions also pointed to the way many campesinos encounter laws and bureaucratic procedures of the government as often enforced in an arbitrary way (Poole 2004: 36). While the grievances of the above actors point to what may have given shape to organized dissent, finding a path through the global institutional alignments of Machu Picchu can be a perplexing task. Once the path of dialogue with authorities was decided, residents required knowledge about the jurisdictional roles the many agencies had over their lives. What they now needed was an answer to the question, *"To whom do we address our complaints?"* When confronting authorities, residents needed to know the chain of command linking subordinate and higher offices. They also needed to identify the various roles of the many agencies involved in what many considered a bureaucratic overload.

The Machupiccheños showed a great deal of astuteness when confronting and interacting with authorities in knowing where to go and whom to challenge. Nevertheless, life in the Sanctuary means that change can happen suddenly with little notification. As the most important national symbol and most popular tourism destination in Peru, Machu Picchu receives a great deal of bureaucratic and media attention. The number of bureaucrats connected to the Sanctuary seemed to mount endlessly, so that residents could not understand the hierarchy as a whole. For many Machupiccheños, especially during my fieldwork before current communication technologies were popular, important outside information often traveled slowly, making the knowledge needed to act on one's behalf incomplete and subject to manipulation by many vested interests. For example, at one point in early March of 2002 it was believed that President Toledo was making a formal visit to the Citadel. The leaders of Frente along with the artisans and others believed this to be a good opportunity to take their case right to the top of the bureaucratic "chain of command," in a sense. Oscar was hopeful that they would get an opportunity to speak with him so the president could be personally informed of district problems. For Oscar, the top priority was to ask the president to dismiss the PMP from the Sanctuary, and to ask that conservation laws be changed to permit property ownership titles. At the time, the understanding by many was that the PMP was an NGO, and therefore from their perspective, had no governing legitimacy in their district; this was an error.

As the president was not likely to stop in the town, Regina wanted to find a way to communicate with him. She suggested they place large banners along the train route requesting a meeting. Increased police presence only seemed to confirm the rumors that Toledo was in fact arriving.

However, despite their plan and efforts to acquire demonstration materials, Toledo never showed up. Again a few days later there was an increased police presence in the town. This time the police were dressed in riot gear. The president of the United States at the time, George W. Bush, was to make an official visit to Peru, and it was rumored he would go to Machu Picchu. Since neither Bush nor Toledo arrived, some people wondered whether the police presence was in fact preparations by law enforcement for the pueblo demonstration and stoppage. A similar issue had led to just such an event a few months earlier when police under INRENA supervision forcibly removed a squatter settlement from a natural protrusion in town. The large police presence in this incident was first thought by some in the town to be preparations for a visit by the queen of Spain. Despite the world attention that Machu Picchu receives, residents depended on governing groups for information, which made it easier to distort or control interests. This is part of how people in Machu Picchu contended with interpreting the signs that conveyed alarm about a changing political and economic environment. Interpreting signs of alarm was a tricky business that made it difficult to hold authorities accountable for their decisions. Consequently, there were ever-increasing opportunities for officials to shift blame and conceal responsibility. This brings to light the power differentials explicit in what Alfred Schutz refers to as "intrinsic" and "imposed" relevance (Schutz 1970: 114). As a World Heritage Site, the intrinsic nature of local knowledge is disrupted and imposed upon by a set of global possibilities that cannot be properly assessed but are easily manipulated. From the perspective of outsiders such as authorities in Lima as well as the national media reporting on events in Machu Picchu, the actions of locals appear irrational, and as their message moves through the bureaucratic hierarchy it becomes "nonsense." Schutz's theory of relevance in the form of knowledge and communication channels can help close a theoretical gap between structural accounts of larger social forces of the political economy and the subjective meanings actors are constantly constructing in order to operate within policies imposed and beyond realms of experience (Goettlich 2011: 495–499). The "good" and the "bad" in the form of lifeworld interests cannot so easily be discerned nor disentangled.

FACE AND FACELESS INTERACTIONS

The Ambassador of Finland paid a visit to the town to unveil the design of a new artisan market and tourist center. The visit occurred just a day after the expected presidential visit described above and with little notification to the townsfolk. What was supposed to be a joyous occasion for everyone turned sour when town activists who had geared up for a demonstration directed at Toledo simply modified their banners for the Ambassador. What transpired in this encounter between the Ambassador and the residents exemplifies the frustrations many Machupiccheños experienced about control and authority over their own district. Along with the Ambassador were representatives of PMP and other governing agencies. The protestors filed into the cultural center, many with posters and banners, demanding the Ambassador do something about the national law 001–2000 prohibiting the ownership of property titles of land. The assumption that the Ambassador of Finland might have had some influence in the governance of Machu Picchu was not far-fetched, considering the debt-for-nature exchange, where Finland pays a sizable portion of Peru's national debt in exchange for conservation commitments to the Sanctuary. At least that was Oscar's perspective when he insisted the Ambassador remove the PMP and stop INRENA's bullying practices against campesinos. Although formally lacking voting power, the Finnish government nevertheless had a strong operational voice in the PMP, of which INRENA was part. Not surprisingly, however, the Ambassador stated that he made no decision on these matters, leaving the authority he represented a bit of a mystery. Hence, when Machupiccheños questioned, as did one man, what right an NGO had to control the lives of people in their district, the answer typically received by representatives was that they had a contract with the state, and complaints must be directed to state agencies. State agencies told residents they could do nothing because of the debt-for-nature agreement with the government of Finland. Finally, when residents encountered the Finnish Ambassador, the representative of the Finnish government in Peru, he told the Machupiccheños that he makes no decisions on the matter.[4] "The world is now global" is thus a phrase that Margarita often used as an expression of bewilderment, as well as an indication of her desire to understand the "who," "what," and "whys" that condition life's possibilities. Uncertainty about the focus of bureaucratic responsibility was one of the main reasons the Machupiccheños experienced confusion, suspicion and frustration. Neoliberalism, as it was given experiential shape in Machu Picchu, was about the way accountability was diffused among many actors. If we examine the multi-institutional experiences associated with neoliberalism as new forms of hierarchy negotiation, we can draw a much clearer assessment of the consequences those policies had in what was an otherwise contradictory set of conservation and economic development efforts.

The Ambassador wished only to discuss the current development project, but the protestors continued their line of interruptions more in the form of a plea rather than a challenge. The Ambassador listened but remained silent. While people differed in their styles, most present brought to bear their arguments on a shared complex of concerns. Chela's question, "How can we concern ourselves with building an artisan market when we do not have the security of property titles?" aimed at the fears Machupiccheños had in trusting governing authorities. At the core of the issues was the jurisdictional right residents needed to constantly assert over their district. In fact, it was common for Machupiccheños to assert the primacy of their district when addressing agencies. This is what Corina did when she stood alongside the Ambassador in front of the audience, looking directly at whom the protestors believed to be the head of PMP sitting in the front row. She politely welcomed the agency representatives with "good evening," but unlike when addressing the Ambassador, her demeanor changed. She said, "I've lived here for 40 years, all my life and this is the first time I see the head of PMP. I don't think he has been here before and certainly has never tried to get to know us. I ask only one thing, that PMP get out of here!" (Que se vaya), and ended with the declaration, "This is the voice of the people, which is the voice of god" (Este es la voz del pueblo que es la voz de Dios). Others, too, followed in this manner. First, a speaker would state the alleged abuse against their pueblo, and then declare that the PMP leave their district. The statement that the "voice of the pueblo is the voice of god," a declarative phrase common in Andean community meetings, is a claim to a collective right of self-determination; the decisions made by the Machupiccheños were what should count as the final say on a matter; for Corina that meant those who have taken residence and livelihood in the district, and not based on indigenous identity. Her position stood in contrast to the conservation discourse on who belongs in the Sanctuary based on commercialized notions of indigenous identity. The emphasis by residents to reinforce the legitimacy of district jurisdiction is understandable. The politics of protected areas, heritage and nature conservation areas are typically created and justified under a consolidated politics of the public good (Igoe and Brockington 2007). The institutional arrangement threatens their political status. Without the legality of the municipality, residents would lose their civil status and facilitate their expulsion from what is otherwise a protected area. Dispossession in protected areas can come in many forms, but often neglected is political dispossession (Cernea 2005). As I have argued elsewhere, in Machu Picchu there is a vibrant political culture.[5] As it is a district, there are elections, candidates, campaigns and all the bombast of politics. As the number of conservation organizations and efforts increased over the years, mayoral candidates have actually increased anti-conservationist rhetoric in their campaigns in order to win votes. Defending the legitimacy of the jurisdiction had become an imperative. To have a territorial polis from which "to speak or speak back" proved to be one of their greatest strengths and one that continues to give conservationists their biggest challenge. Ironically, this challenge to their jurisdictional rights arose after the authoritarian era of the Fujimori presidency and when the media was filled with rhetoric about the possibilities of building real democracy in Peru; for the people of Machu Picchu, this rhetoric was a contrast to their experiences of governance. As long as governing agencies conducted their activities in what they define as a sanctuary first rather than a district, they could bypass the demands for resident participation, fail to inform them of project intentions, and skew conditions to favor those large capital enterprises the townsfolk felt had taken over their economy. Their experience resonates with Lisa C. Breglia's (2006) portrayal of the struggles of locals to be heard over problems of heritage conservation and development around Chichén Itzá in Yucatan, Mexico, where locals make little compared to the vast profits generated from the tourism economy. As Breglia eloquently says:

> Most notably absent are the views and opinions of local communities as they go about their workaday lives in the midst and shadows of some of the most famous and fabulous instances of heritage spaces in the world. (ibid.: 19)

The Machupiccheños showed a great deal of assertiveness in confronting authorities. In terms of knowing what to do, however, was the difficulty of understanding the PMP as a representative body for the Finland-Peru debt-for-nature exchange, whose mandate is administered by the state-NGO conglomerate called PROFONANPE. Even more confusing was the fact that the problems with the way projects were managed fell more directly into the hands of the companies subcontracted by PROFONANPE, such as Pacífico, that did the work. This misunderstanding exemplifies the kinds of institutional knowledge people needed to address their complaints appropriately. While certainly there was no great love for the PMP in general, the protestors aimed at criticizing the way PROFONANPE was administering the PMP mandate. However, by directly targeting the PMP they brought into play a much larger institutional dynamic. It illustrates how much harder it is to single out the institutions and their functions over one's life when global relationships are involved in governance.

When the Ambassador and his architect were finally able to discuss the design of the new market with the heads of the artisan associations, it became clear that the new market would accommodate only 130 posts, despite the fact the number of artisans and/or sellers of artisanal products had grown to 215. Was this just a classic "third-world" development project error because no one had bothered to stay in touch with changes in the district? Martha informed the Ambassador in a soft, concerned voice that the exclusion of so many artisans would create serious conflicts among the pueblo. His response was that the artisan market was designed only for the original artisan association that held possession rights over a strip of land alongside the Aguas Calientes River. The problem, as both the Ambassador and the architect saw it, was that there is a "natural" shortage of space in the canyon where the town is located, a definition of space that could only antagonize the townsfolk. In a trivial sense, he stated the obvious, but every town resident knew that the Pueblo

Hotel controlled as much land as the entire town and yet no one restricted their space. This oversight on the part of the Ambassador and the architect exemplifies the difference between the way space is officially represented in Machu Picchu and how it is lived (Lefebvre 1984). Therefore, some in the town like Cori, Chela and Martha claimed that the Pueblo Hotel held a property title, and that they needed one as well to survive in the Sanctuary because of the perception that a title offers more security and protection from state authorities. The Ambassador denied that possibility, insisting ardently, "No one in the Sanctuary has property titles, possession only." The Inkaterra Pueblo Hotel (not part of the Orient Express/Belmond chain) is nonetheless a multimillion-dollar investment and one of the most expensive in Machu Picchu. It is part of a Peruvian-owned company that specializes in ecological tourism, sitting on 25 acres of land that includes an orchid garden and displays of other flora, and fauna such as spectacled bears that are native to the Andes. It is organized like a nature sanctuary within a nature sanctuary. Whether the Inkaterra held a property title is beyond my knowledge, but their control of and ability to alter a protected landscape suggests the privilege of having their possession rights treated more like property ownership.

As the meeting progressed, the townsfolk were particularly upset with the plan to create a reservoir for potable water and a proper drainage system. The residents were informed of this undertaking only by posted billboards that claimed the project would take an estimated time of 60 days. In fact, the project started late and went past the estimated completion time. The streets were turned inside out with trenches dug in all quarters, and no end in sight. It made the town unattractive, a point of criticism by conservation authorities, and hard for tourists to enter local restaurants, hotels and shops. More problematic was that many businesses were left with no running water. However, large capital enterprises such as Sanctuary Lodge and the Pueblo Hotel were unaffected. The fear of disaster once again crept into the discussions of property, governance and nature. Chela and others expressed concerns over the intended location of the new market, which would be built alongside the Aguas Calientes River where people felt that a flash flood would destroy it. The Ambassador assured them that a retaining wall would be built. But the point was missed. Machupiccheños already knew what was necessary to protect them from the river; the fear was whether they could trust the authorities to properly understand their needs, and more importantly, whether they were working on their behalf.

Protestors complained that the pipes used for the "Waters Project" were not large enough and, not in accordance with construction codes, were placed too close to the surface. The leaders of Frente had confronted a PMP civil engineer about the problem. The engineer's explanation, perhaps technically correct, was that since there were no automobiles in the town, except for a section where buses take tourists to the Citadel, there was no need to place the pipes any deeper. Oscar, in a fury, demanded to know what right the engineer had to make that decision on behalf of the Machupiccheños. He declared, "What if in the future we want to bring cars to the pueblo, or get rid of the train altogether and build a road to Machu Picchu, or for that matter just change the location of the bus station." The engineer became visibly flustered, picked up his belongings and stormed out of the meeting. What the Ambassador, schooled in the graces of diplomacy, could do, the engineer could not. More precisely, the different status positions and power between the Ambassador and the engineer sets the context for different styles of interaction between themselves and residents. Put simply, the Ambassador, as a high-ranking foreigner intimately connected with the affairs of the Peruvian state, could deflect responsibility in ways the engineer could not.

While I was walking home from an outing one late evening a few days after the event with the Ambassador, I met a waiter I knew from one of the local restaurants. I found him quietly slipping leaflets under people's doors on behalf of Programa Machu Picchu. He handed me one as he somewhat shyly explained that he was paid for the work. In retaliation for the townsfolk opposition over the way the PMP was conducting projects, the PMP notified the townsfolk that they were immediately halting all projects, namely, the water project and the building of the artisan market. The PMP officials claimed their decision was due to the hostility from "certain local personalities" as well as for acts of vandalism against their equipment. Despite this accusation of vandalism, they provided no examples of acts, or for that matter evidence that the "certain local personalities" were guilty of them. The leaflet ended with, "These lamentable measures could be lifted in the next 60 days if the causes that motivated these decisions disappear." The consequences were immediately felt. Abandoning the projects already in progress meant leaving the town in complete disorder with holes and trenches dug in all major locations; it also left many local establishments such as hotels and restaurants without water.

The coercive force of the message was made to work through local social relationships that in effect get the Machupiccheños to police themselves. First, the note came from the PMP, but it was not clear from which institution—the Peruvian state government such as INRENA, UGM and the INC, the Finnish government, PROFONANPE, or all of them? One could not tell, since all formed part of the PMP directory. The same applied for who wrote it and gave the go-ahead to distribute the notice. The proliferation of multinational/multilateral organizations brought a proliferation of faceless forms of governance. Equally as "anonymous" was the referent of the message, identified only as "certain local personalities." However, considering that Oscar and the members of Frente had publicly denounced the PMP before one hundred town residents, would it really surprise anyone to learn that the "certain local personalities" referred to them? After about a week of no water the townsfolk began voicing their dissatisfaction with the condition of the town. "Frente sticks their noses in everything, and it's because of them that we're left without projects," one man said, and another responded, "This Oscar is a big mouth and he's always screwing us over. Now he screwed us again." I found Juan Carlos in the plaza upset about the condition of the town. His restaurant was left with no running water, and to stay in business he had to carry it by the bucket from a source in the market. "Every day I'm without water," he complained. Juan Carlos nonetheless had mixed feelings about the PMP decision to abandon the pueblo projects. He criticized them for their actions, but blamed Oscar and Frente for their confrontation.

In short, despite the indirectness of the message, the referent was well understood by the townsfolk. In a small face-to-face town, people could identify the intended recipients, while the governing authorities could hide their tracks. The note succeeded in creating discord in the unity of their mobilization and in exacerbating already existing class divisions. This was most particularly the case in the rural areas where the PMP now threatened to divert all the remaining funds allotted for the town projects. Rural community leaders were informed by the authorities that they might receive PMP town money for use in their areas. As one leader from the rural communities told me,

> Since the town surely doesn't need this money because they have so much, we can use it here; we need it. The town rejected this money and the projects, but here we can use all sorts of projects with the help of the PMP, UGM and INRENA who are now well disposed to collaborate with us in everything. Now they'll listen to what we have to say. Before . . . we had to beg, but now no.

The notice distributed by the PMP contained one key message: blame. The members of Frente were blamed for the PMP decision to abandon the pueblo projects. The note was a directive that something should be done about it by the Machupiccheños themselves. Different local interests and levels of inequalities among rural and town residents were thereby manipulated to control and contain dissent. Residents were coaxed into policing themselves. Later commentaries, even among the activists, devolved into expressions of fear with statements such as "Who did we get ourselves messed up with?" What I took to be a darker version of that sliding transition was made up of presidents, queens and world celebrities. In withdrawing their projects, the PMP was in effect willing to punish everyone on account of a few dissenters. By inconveniencing everyone, the PMP got other residents to put pressure on Frente to conform to project plans. The use of intermediaries in such communicative acts is often used to set status distance (Beatty and Takahashi 2001: 63). Moreover, using a written medium as a channel of communication is significant in that it provides anonymity for the sender and avoids the "unpleasant situation" of face-to-face interaction (ibid.). Taken as a whole, the ambiguous signature, the indirectness of communication and the use of intermediaries to deliver a message can be seen as a means of creating a new hierarchy of non-local authority without any notion of consensus. New political hierarchies can induce cooperation for their plans by using the preexisting uneven developments in the rural areas and the town, and the uneven possession rights of artisans and the Inkaterra Hotel. Factoring heavily in this process of inducing cooperation is a form of communicative practice used to establish new hierarchies with the help of intermediaries such as NGOs.

Anthropology has been critical of the role and influence of NGOs in underdeveloped countries. NGOs are said to discursively construct development and establish patronage relationships between themselves and the subjects of their services so as to narratively and perceptually reproduce "first-world" and "third-world" categories (Escobar 1995). Other scholars have emphasized the "non-discursive" but rather political economic factors that shape the power relationships between people and institutions like NGOs and the state (Edelman 1999; Gill 2000). The PMP, however, is a different kind of entity, made of multiple governments, NGOs and private interests all combined; it is not only well suited at discursively constructing categories such as "sanctuary" but also able to subvert local unity or antagonize existing class divisions that undermine organized political dissent. It was not that the townsfolk did not welcome projects, but the problem was that they were not allowed to participate in decision making. It was already difficult for the townsfolk to compete with large investors like Orient Express, so that when construction projects made competition harder, Sanctuary authorities appeared to assist large capital interests. We see above how privatization policies could undermine a very important sense of trust and security needed for conservation agencies to work with the resident population.

The neoliberal Peruvian economist Hernando de Soto (1989), influential as an intellectual and as advisor to restructuring Peru's economy, argued that bureaucracy plays a detrimental role in the lives of small-business interests. According to de Soto, state bureaucracy limits opportunities and the only viable route in helping the poor is to free the market of such governmental clutter. However, as we have seen in this chapter, the state is hardly the only bureaucracy in a globalized world intruding into people's lives. There is an international bureaucracy made up of NGOs and international organizations, as well as other nation-states, that play a role in structuring a local economy and the opportunities of the less wealthy. More problematic is de Soto's assumption that the state bureaucracy would simply disappear in a neoliberal economy. The promotion of the property laws de Soto argues for provides little or no solution if the state can avoid issues of ownership rights by defining people as possessors, or by simply expropriating land in the name of the "public good." In fact, de Soto says little about the state power of eminent domain and its unequal application. As the case of Machu Picchu shows, under neoliberalism, expropriation and the limitations placed on property rights are consistent with the interests of large capital investors. Bureaucrats played an important role in structuring Peru's neoliberal economy to favor large capital interests, as well as in disciplining opposition.

In addition, government bureaucracy not only helps structure the neoliberal economy, but the implementation of neoliberal policies also reorganizes the bureaucracy. While it is easy to criticize bureaucrats, one should consider how salaried men and women are also negatively implicated in budget cutbacks that place them in the position of having to recurrently demonstrate the necessity of their jobs lest they be fired. As the government scales back on services and benefits to the public, it largely leaves bureaucrats the task of demonstrating efficiency in police functions as in the increased efforts to catch ecological violations. In Machu Picchu, it fostered a kind of "culture of fear" among lower-level bureaucrats who passed their job insecurity on to their subjects in the form of inflexible interpretations of policies, as well as threats of more stringent forms of enforcement.

THE FIRST MEETING WITH THE AUTHORITIES

Frente's decision to engage in talks with the conservation authorities was not well received by all the Machupiccheños. In agreeing to open channels of communication with governing agencies as their means of effecting change, the leaders of Frente postponed shutting down the town to commercial activity. A few felt that talking to the authorities would be taken as a capitulation and that they would be giving the impression that their threats of a stoppage were just bluffs. Furthermore, it was not just the authorities that some town residents worried would perceive the activists as irresolute, but rural residents in the district as well. In fact, some involved in mobilizing rural residents were concerned that the change in plans would be taken as the townsfolk vacillating about challenging authorities due to their own economic interests. Juan Carlos, who was from Pampaccauha, one of the rural communities, felt that they would now be disillusioned due to plans to hold talks. During the anniversary festival described earlier, campesinos from Pampaccauha were the only ones to stage dissent against INRENA; they displayed banners demanding liberty and respect for their agricultural way of life as they marched through a parade of festivities (see figure 4.1). The members of Frente had composed a written agenda they called *plataforma de lucha* or platform of struggle that detailed their complaints and demands from each governing and commercial entity that operated in concert over their lives.

On an early sunny March morning in 2002, I joined the members of the protest as we boarded a train for Ollantaytambo. The members had a long day of appointments starting with the provincial mayor in Urubamba and concluding in the city of Cusco with the state conservation authorities, as well as with PeruRail. Also planned for that evening was a meeting with the Cusco tourism association (AATC). In all there were about 20 Machupiccheños; some were from Frente, while others were leaders of their craft association, and still others were just concerned residents. Cori, Regina, and Margarita were dressed in their dapper outfits as they met up with Charo, Héctor, Chela, Oscar, Marina, Raúl, and Eber, the main actors. The broad goals of the meetings on both sides were to come to agreement to avoid the protestors' planned stoppage that would bring tourism to a halt and complicate tourist itineraries across the country; hinging on the meeting on the part of the protestors was whether they would construe their demands as being met.

Our taxis arrived at the Consejo (provincial municipal building) in the central plaza of Urubamba. Young shoeshine boys quickly stepped up to the well-dressed crowd, apparently anticipating potential customers; they were not wrong in sensing our desire to put a final polish on our official look. "Dos soles, dos soles,"[6] the boys shouted. Margarita placed her ankle-high fashionable leather boots up on the lad's stool. Our appointment was for 9 AM, but we were a bit early so the group scattered to

Figure 4.1. Photo of campesinos from the district community of Pampaccahua, marching in the civil parade of the 40th anniversary festival of the district of Machu Picchu—their banners protesting INRENA control (October 2001). (Photo taken by Pellegrino Luciano)

get some breakfast. Regina and I rushed to the central market where we quickly drank some sweetened hot milk. As we gulped it down I asked her what she hoped to accomplish from all the meetings scheduled for the day. For her, the purpose of this trip was to confront the authorities and the private companies, such as PeruRail and Sanctuary Lodge, to tell them that they were committing abuses against her pueblo.

The meeting with the provincial mayor appeared to have gone well. They ostensibly won back some money for the district that had been withheld by the province. In addition, the provincial mayor supported the protestors' cause against conservation authorities and Orient Express. Later, in Cusco, we went to the INC office, where we held meetings with the state agencies and PeruRail. The bureaucrats stressed the importance of dialogue and compromise and made a few concessions, including a willingness to fund the town library, offer employment to district residents, and reduce entrance fees for national tourists; all were items on the protestors' platform of struggle. The meeting with PeruRail was also interpreted as a success. From the protestors' perspective, PeruRail had promised not to sell any artisan crafts or food on the train. In contrast, the talks with INRENA did not fare so well. The activists felt INRENA was not very cooperative on two important issues. The protestors wanted the charges dropped against 30 campesinos for violating ecological laws and threatened with eviction from the Sanctuary. In addition, they sought a modification to the law that prohibits property titles. The INRENA official refused to make any concessions and stated it was out of his control. Nevertheless, there was an overall sense that the meetings were a success and therefore there was good news to bring back home. However, whether this optimism was justified is another question. Broken promises are certainly not unheard of in Peru. *Florear* is a word commonly used to mean "to flower," or rather to flatter and placate with words. Despite the uncompromising demeanor of the INRENA official, it can be said that he was at least frank about his position.

I began this chapter by inquiring into the kinds of knowledge people needed to navigate through the bureaucracy of the Sanctuary. I described how local politics draws on and rebounds off state and international institutions, as two rival actors with political ambitions attempted to organize campesinos to fight back against charges of environmental damage. More importantly, we saw that knowledge of laws and bureaucratic functions were crucial not just to confront the governing authorities of the Sanctuary, but also to know whom to hold accountable for what. Not only did the Machupiccheños contend with the procedures of their own state officials and the arbitrary enforcement of rules, but that complexity was multiplied exponentially when international and multinational entities were added into the mix of institutions. Responsibility was now diffused beyond the state agencies. Despite the development goals of these multiple institutions, without accountability or participation, the

Machupiccheños experienced those efforts as a loss of control over their lives and control of the district. Moreover, the Sanctuary designation, however important it may be to the nation and the world, often conflicted with the sovereignty of the district, leading to a real loss of control for the residents in their local politics and jurisdiction. Nevertheless, for the people of the town, the Sanctuary provided the prestige that sustains their tourism economy. In the poorer rural areas, where tourism was less significant, the Sanctuary designation offer fewer benefits and a greater loss of control. Sanctuary authorities manipulated inequalities to coercively stifle dissent in a "divide and conquer" manner. In threatening to divert town funds to rural areas, the authorities keyed in on the antagonisms that exist because of rural and town economic differences. Also, privatization initiatives made coercion doubly effective in this case. By temporarily abandoning the water project for two months, the Sanctuary bureaucrats left the Pueblo in complete disarray, making local restaurants and hotels inhospitable and more vulnerable to the unaffected large-scale Pueblo Hotel and the hotels of Orient Express. Through economic sanction, the town residents could then be made to put pressure on the dissenters. In short, the message of who is dependent on whom was effectively communicated by state and NGO authorities. The dynamic power play in which the different participants in global hierarchies choose channels of communication as a vector of instilling fear was also seen in later negotiations between the authorities and the Machupiccheños.

NOTES

1. I do not know exactly what law Oscar is referring to in this situation.
2. Here Oscar is referring to the law 02-2000-UGM-CD which states the regulations for entering the Inca Trail. Disposable bottles are one of the items people are prohibited from bringing into the Sanctuary.
3. Apu is a Quechua term referring to a sacred place.
4. It should be noted that most of the participants I spoke to did in fact express overall gratitude for the Ambassador's efforts on the project for the building of the artisan market.
5. See Luciano 2011.
6. Meaning "two soles," which is approximately 50 cents U.S.

FIVE

Machu Picchu and the Witnessing World

> If I were a director in the government I would be embarrassed to call myself Peruvian because, sirs, we are trafficking in the heritage of our ancestors.
> (Si fuera director del gobierno hubiera tenido verguenza de llamar me peruano. Porque senores, estamos traficando con el patrimonio de nuestros antepasados.)
>
> —Eber, Machupicchu Pueblo

Proponents of economic policies, regardless of persuasion, draw on metaphors, narratives, and rhetorical strategies to promote an ideology. The question I wish to explore in examining economic process is how ideological positions are "scripted"; of interest here, is how performance shapes decision making. All aspects of social life must be performed and the manipulation of capital is no different, as we'll see in the official meetings between protestors and authorities in Machu Picchu. A new economy required a form of talk, and the language of neoliberalism examined through "dramaturgy" shows how social interactions are staged for an audience with the objective of inducing favorable actions (Goffman 1959). As Kravel-Tovi (2012) notes on conversion performances in Israel, the Goffmanian approach provides insight into the "situational mechanisms" bureaucrats and people construct with each other as objects and subjects of knowledge that moves beyond the "totalizing" picture of a Foucauldian analysis of state power (371–382). Here I am interested not just in the "theatricality" of bureaucratic encounters but also in calling attention to the significance of "role-play" as people shift talk to assume the role of an imaginary other in different contextual formalities, noting the differences between state and non-state bureaucracies (ibid.: 375).[1] The following interchanges in this chapter show how people frame issues as such to direct an audience's attention to a version of reality. Erving Goffman famously argued that "a scene is put together, by exchange of dramatically inflated actions, counteractions, and terminating replies" (1959: 72).

Kenneth Burke also explored the processes involved in persuasion, and how it functions as a tool for orienting people into an ideological position, or as he says, "the use of language as a symbolic means of inducing cooperation" (1950: 43). For Burke persuasion was not sufficient to explain cooperation between differing interests; persuasion refers to the end product of symbolic action and not its process. Burke instead posits the concept of "identification" in addition to persuasion through presupposing joint interests based on like substance ("we are really the same"). Burke's concept of "consubstantiality" refers to the bonds people establish through shared experiences or goals. According to Burke, both "identification" and "consubstantiality" work together as rhetorical maneuvers that induce human action toward specific directions (ibid.: 20–21). Combining both Goffman's notion of regions, "back and front stage," and Burke's concepts of identification and consubstantiality provides insight into the micro-sociology associated with larger political-economic forces such as neoliberalism, and the forging or rejection of new social relationships along class interests. The applicability of Goffman's approach is heightened by the fact that my analysis focuses on interest groups and their cooperative "teamwork" during which they agree on and "learn a script" (1959: 79). Goffman spatially distinguishes teams and audience in terms of "regions": "front stage" or "front region" and "back stage" or "back region" (ibid.: 107). As he notes, "In preparation for meetings and negotiations the groups learn a kind of script, rehearse and use various strategies" (ibid.: 18).[2]

Examples of "stage" distinction during my fieldwork in Machu Picchu can be seen in how Oscar frequently provided instructions to fellow protestors on how to behave in the presence of the state authorities. As the leader of Frente, he was often concerned about participants' contradicting one another during the meetings. The need to tell a coherent story and maintain the proper presentation was illustrated in a meeting with Peru's Vice Minister of Tourism in April of 2002. Oscar gathered all of us around him and explained in "back stage" manner: "When we're inside you can't have personal conversations. This *sh sh sh* won't happen. That could go on in Machu Picchu when we're talking with [one of] our associations, because if the Minister is talking while you are chatting with somebody else, this is lack of respect." Oscar instructed participants on displaying proper behavior in front of a high-ranking government bureaucrat. "Those who have to go to the bathroom go before because once we're in the meeting there is no exiting. There won't be this constant opening and closing the door." What he was most adamant about was the group staying focused on their "platform of struggle," waving it in the air as he instructed: "We don't say anything outside of the agenda. . . . [T]he task is not to talk just for talking, we can't contradict each other." The platform of struggle was in Goffmanian terms the "script," and this agenda had already been circulated to authorities and tourism associations alike. It was framed in the language of protest, justice and abuse against the district of Machu Picchu.

PRIVATE SECTOR PERFORMANCES

Typically, proponents of neoliberal policies construct economic narratives that portray the free market as a pure state of nature, not to be tampered with by human intervention. The language of neoliberalism can make opposition to it difficult (Green 2003: 17). As Green states, "A linguistic sleight-of-hand has seen U.S. politicians and policy makers emphasizing Washington's support for 'market democracies.' Democracy is clearly something no one can oppose, and Washington's push to spread market forces into every corner of the world economy wins public support on its coat-tails" (ibid.: 18). Calling "unfettered capitalism" "free trade" or a "free market" gives it a degree of legitimacy (17). Equally, terms like "enhancing efficiency," "getting the prices right," and "removing trade barriers," connote progress (ibid.). Likewise, the term *flow* (e.g., capital flows), borrowed from big business to describe the movement of global capital, evokes imagery of nature. The word implies a process without human direction, goals or intent—capital, like water, just flows. Yet to think of capital as flowing is misleading in that it obscures the social activities involved in its movement, portraying the flow as beyond human control and hence inevitable. As much scholarship has noted, this image conveys a social Darwinian message that survival depends on adaptation to the vagaries of the "flow," such as climate change or environmental variability. The term is also prescriptive in that it is a short step to the conclusion that progress, growth, and human welfare depend on, and are the result of survival through competition (Rivero 2001: 79–80).

However, under the moneyed extremes, especially as found in Peru, the ideal of competition is hardly realized. As PeruRail's control of transportation in Machu Picchu showed, neoliberal ideals can easily lead to monopoly, not competition.[3] Hence, competition here is an idea that required cooperation in maintaining it as a belief as something beneficial to the parties involved. Attaining cooperation is tightly bound to levels of trust involved in the relationships. The fine line crossed in moving from friend to foe means reading between the lines to answer the question *just whose side is this person on.* Since I had the fortunate opportunity to attend all the meetings and "hang out" with Frente and the mobilizers my goal was to see how "micro" I could possibly describe interactions, and no doubt I missed a lot but was given the opportunity to film a few of the formal meetings and so I was able to review many details expressed in conversations that are bodily. Face-to-face strategic interactions allow meanings to be communicated not only through language proper, but also as part of "being in sync" with people "co-present" in an engagement, through gesture, tone of voice, and movement of body. This is particularly important because nonverbal cues have been shown to play a role in building trust and credibility among social actors that is not well captured through discursive analysis alone (Hall 1989: 71–72; Manning 2000).

The Frente group and the town representatives, after a long day of meetings with government officials and bureaucrats discussed in the previous chapter, concluded their first round of dialogue by convening with the Association for the Tourism Agencies of Cusco (Associacion de Agencias de Turismo de Cusco or AATC) for an in-house discussion with leaders and fellow members of the Cusco tourism industry about their problems and intentions. While they were still in the city of Cusco, not far from the Plaza de Armas, the Machupiccheños though tired, climbed a final flight of stairs to the AATC office and took seats in a conference room. The day had been harried for the Machupiccheños; other than the short meal gobbled early in the morning in the city of Urubamba, the members had had no time to eat and we were hungry. The Machupiccheños had hoped to receive some support for their cause of protest from the AATC, because as tourism professionals of the same region, they worked closely together. However, that was not going to happen. As shown in the last chapter, large-scale private corporations like NGOs and multinational organizations can divide different sectors of a local economy by aggravating pre-existing class differences.

Mr. "Jorge Nieto," of the AATC, presented his view of the protest in terms of competition and adaptation. Nieto began by stating that he had had a long talk with Ms. "Yoselin Luther" of PeruRail, who was standing quietly by his side, and that he was optimistic over the results of their discussion. Nieto said, "It seems to me we have good news in general." He portrayed Yoselin as "demonstrating a tremendous amount of good will." As a private-sector leader in Cusco's tourism industry and a supposed ally to the Machupiccheños, Nieto unexpectedly took a position against the protest, and conveyed this message in more than words.

When Nieto began talking about the necessities of a tourism economy, he used a tone of voice that underscored each syllable to animate his logic. He said, "In order to protect our tourism, you, I'm not going to make up stories, but those who have traveled . . . understand that the subject of security—SE-CU-RI-TY is KEY in any tourist operation. Not one tourist goes to a location where he believes he will be unsafe." Although he did not directly mention the Shining Path and the civil war, he made implicit reference to "the ten years of suffering." "We suffered ten years of recession in tourism in great part due to bad news, not necessarily where we are [Cusco] as much as other places, but just look how much we suffered." Nieto concluded his remark, saying that his message was "a message of security for the international markets." Oscar took the pause as an opening to speak about the roundtable discussions of the day, but Nieto cut him short and asserted that the platform of struggle created distance between people.

Nieto's attempt at placing the positions of PeruRail and Frente under different shades of deference was communicated through the sequencing of his speech acts and his interjection. Also, although for Nieto, Oscar's "platform of struggle" created distance, he communicated a certain distance of his own towards Oscar. Since the seating arrangement was already established, Nieto who was standing waiting for more people to enter the room spoke down to Oscar, who was seated. Though Nieto's conversation was with Oscar, he did not give Oscar his face in typical conversational style. Rather, Nieto stood with his body semi turned away from Oscar and gazed at the audience, avoiding eye contact with him. The "good will" of Yoselin was paired with Nieto's stress over securing international investments in Peru. By contrast, the comment on "ten years of suffering" and Nieto's interruption of Oscar's speech act set a different ambience for the members of Frente. Oscar was not a person easy to interrupt. We recall when Oscar and Porfirio competed to organize campesinos in the district community of Corihuayrachina. There, Oscar raised his voice, waved documents and broadly condemned privatization as an emblem of the state privileging of multinational corporations. In the context of "home" Oscar was generally able to influence a definition of the situation among the participants. Oscar and the Frente members were also quite proficient at holding steadily to their positions when interacting with state authorities. The mobilizers in Machu Picchu polarized their conflict in terms of "the residents and the state." Nieto and the AATC, however, represented a different kind of power entity, a private sector bureaucracy with a more business set of interests than the restaurants and hotels of Machu Picchu that were economically intertwined.

When Oscar did speak, he explained to an audience of tourism professionals from Cusco what Frente had been calling their "platform of struggle," and although he depicted the earlier meetings of the day in terms of good news and many solutions, the term *struggle* seemed out of place. The association of "struggle" with civil war "suffering" made Frente's position seem like a violation of the condition that security in a tourism economy is imperative; it put Frente on the defensive. Nieto turned *security and safety* into a premise he controlled, and which could not be violated without the risk of being de-legitimized as a claimant in the Cusco tourism economy. Interacting within such premises leads us to consider how the situation is framed to produce certain outcomes. Who in their right mind could ever be against security and safety? Nieto then launched into another speech act, and the lesson now was to teach Frente about the current state of the world and its relationship to tourism in Machu Picchu. "I'm going to take a few minutes to reflect and I'm going to start with the good news." Nieto informed the Machupiccheños on the results of his talks with Peru's Vice Minister of Tourism and the achievements made in creating the new ministry of tourism that now placed the UGM, the INC and INRENA under a single bureaucratic umbrella. In a statement akin to his comment on Yoselin's "good will," Nieto praised the state's effort to promote tourism, declaring, "These are good times." He then posed a rhetorical question: "And how are we achieving this? We simply discovered that everyone has the will for change . . . we started speaking peacefully."

One may ask, for whom are these good times? Those operating in the urban sector of Cusco's tourism industry would not suffer from the monopoly of Orient Express as would the Machupiccheños. Different interests reflect the broader rural-urban economic divide between the city of Cusco and the town of Machu Picchu, and again between the townsfolk and the poorer rural communities. The Cusco tourist agencies and tour guides would probably stand to lose much more from a protest stoppage by the Machupiccheños, at least in the short term. Nevertheless, none of the Machupiccheños questioned that divide or the assertion that these are good times for all. A large component of Nieto's talk concerned descriptions of the "global situation." The idea of globalization can be spun according to interest. Here we see how the idea of "globalization" is not just "descriptive but prescriptive" (Bourdieu 2003: 85). Accepting a specific description narrows the possibilities for action and often implies a tacit agreement on which economic policies are plausible. Performing the "global" plays a role in sustaining an economic and social order, as Nieto paused for a moment, looked at the audience, and then continued his sermon with what he now intended to be the bad news:

> You know what? There are now no more countries. It's as if somebody came with a giant eraser and erased the borders, no more [borders]! You pass through Spain, France, Italy, Belgium, Holland and you know, nobody asks where you are going. Nobody asks for your passport. It is free, completely free. In the past we had to change our money for francs, for liras, for florins, for marks. Now we have one currency that is the euro. Every single country in Europe now uses the euro . . . and you know what? In this global world everyone has opportunities. The euro currency, you know where they make it? The Pueblo of "Condorito," which is a tiny Chilean pueblo connected to a mine, won the world international bid to mint the European currency. And you know why? Because this little tiny Chilean pueblo is *[raises his voice and emphasizes each syllable]* COM-PE-TI-TIVE. *[Lowers and softens his voice and repeats]* It is competitive. What are we lacking in order to be competitive?

Nieto continued his lesson on global economics, stressing limitless opportunity and the value of competition. The message was contained in the analogy that the town of "Condorito" is to the world as the Pueblo of Machu Picchu is to PeruRail.[4] Hence, the message was that those who are competitive are justly rewarded. Since, according to Nieto, opportunity knocks at every "global" door, the inability to compete is the fault of the residents of Machu Picchu. Nieto's argument is exemplary of a common way of classifying world heritage and conservation needs according to a site's value in the tourism industry (Edensor 1998: 184). He gave Machu Picchu a market value relative to other places in the world worthy of tourism destinations, like the Great Pyramids of Egypt, Stonehenge, or the Taj Mahal.

The power of Nieto's geographical rhetoric is in part based on his travel experiences and his authority as a tourism professional. But also, consider the dramaturgical elements involved in the way credibility was built. First, who played the role of "audience" in Nieto's oration? In the immediate sense the targeted audience was the people present, namely those from Machu Picchu. But there was also a sense in which Nieto positioned himself to rhetorically create an imaginary other and that the "real" audience here was the "world" at large and he is providing "back-stage" instructions to the Machupiccheños on how to properly act in a front-stage region, namely the global audience. In and of itself this is not unusual. Goffman noted that different kinds of "stage" activities are in no way fixed or literal but are rather fluid and invented, even occurring simultaneously (1959: 247). In effect, people often "stage" a back stage in order to construct more personalized relationships or to create a notion of alliance (MacCannell 1973: 596). Controlling the "stage" or "region" in Goffman's terms allowed Nieto a position to walk two sides of a conflict, and this allowed him to criticize Frente and the Machupiccheños, all the while maintaining an attitude of agreement with them; such is the power of identification. The question of trust posed above, *whose side is the person on*, cannot so easily be answered. Nieto continued:

> The market has changed, and now the tourist has much more to choose from. He's not going to come to Machu Picchu for the greatness of our ancestors. He's going to come to Machu Picchu because here we can give him security, But A-BO-VE ALL, and this is a new law of the market, because we have *GOOD VALUE!*[5] Do you know what *good value* is? *Good value* is translated as *buen valor* but do you know what it means? [It means] neither cheap nor expensive but the right price, and you know, we don't set the right price. The market decides the right price. And so, this right price, this relationship—service/cost/price—is what we need to put in our heads, not because we own Machu Picchu and we are at the *puputi*[6] (center). The world no longer has a *puputi*. The world is out there and everyone can choose, everyone can go where they want and if we give them any difficulties they will go

> somewhere else. And you know what? Our unique Machu Picchu isn't unique, there are many Machu Picchus in the world, [and] there are other places, other destinations, nature, archeology. . . . If we want to develop our country we need to be open to responsible foreign investment.

Through a process of identification, different interests are joined or pulled apart by blurring the categories that stand in the way. In this case, manipulating cultural boundaries can serve to produce a feeling of sameness or difference. As has been shown, the use of cultural identity in Latin America as elsewhere is often an effective way of organizing politically, one that can be applied against large-scale foreign investment as well (Hale 1997). By contrast, one way to change minds and facilitate foreign investment might reasonably be to assault the congruity of the cultural concepts that block capital. Juxtaposing words that might otherwise be contradictory could lead to an examination and acceptance of commonly held categories. If reinterpretations of those categories occur, one has broken the frames organizing identity. For example, the terms *Andes, Machu Picchu, Cusco,* and *the Incas* are congruous when used to give order to a local form of identity (e.g., Cuzqueño). However, note how Nieto shifted the boundary of inclusion into an identity by breaching the language normally used to describe it. According to Nieto:

> There are two kinds of Cuzqueño, the Cuzqueño by origin, the one who is born here, and the Cuzqueño by destiny, who chooses to live here regardless if they were born in Katmandu. *[The audience laughs]* Here *we* [nosotros] have a Cuzqueña by destiny. Yoselin was born in [Belgium] but she chose her destiny, and her destiny is to work with us and for us. . . . *[Margarita adds jokingly but in an amiable way that Yoselin is from Machu Picchu: "She's Machupiccheña."]*

Nieto continued:

> These people are just as much entitled to call themselves Cuzqueño as the most *[Nieto pauses for a moment, apparently trying to think up a comparison or refrain from articulating the kind of Cuzqueño he had in mind]* like the most Cuzqueño of the Cuzqueños.

Identification narratives can often be convoluted accounts that are difficult to disentangle at the moment they are performed. For instance, in the above passage, who is asked to identify with whom? According to Nieto, he and the associates of the AATC are consubstantial with those from Machu Picchu because (1) both can claim membership to the identity of Cuzqueño and (2) they share mutual experiences as small business owners in the local tourism industry. I base this largely on the way Nieto used the subject pronoun "we" (*nosotros*) to refer to who must learn the concept of "good value," and who must reject that they are either the "puputi" of the world or the owners of Machu Picchu. Ultimately, as the passage above suggests, Nieto was supporting PeruRail's investment interests in Cusco. If including PeruRail under number (1) would not already offend the sensibilities of most Cuzqueño, then number (2) would most likely be received as an untenable insult to the Machupiccheños because the financial might of PeruRail and Orient Express lies at the core of their economic despair, not to mention that the company is neither small nor local. But note that Nieto did not actually mention PeruRail by name; rather, that experiential dissonance was deflected by his much more personalized alternative of naming Yoselin, even going so far as to imply that Yoselin had a greater right to operate in Cusco because she chose it as her destiny, whereas those from Machu Picchu are merely Cuzqueño by birth. At first, Nieto fostered an impression of likeness between himself and those of Machu Picchu, only to extend this consubstantiality to Yoselin; he then converted "Yoselin" into "these people" (*esa gente*) so that ipso facto he could discreetly slip the uninvited PeruRail into the Cuzqueño identity consortium.

While it is one thing for an anthropologist to interpret the motives of an actor by scrutinizing dramaturgical performances and rhetoric, it is a more difficult task to assess the effectiveness on a group of listeners. To be sure, people were not affected in a uniform manner; there was attitudinal variation expressed by the people present at the meeting. Here I examine the question from the viewpoint of the speaker: How does a speaker know whether he/she is convincing an audience of a position? As has been shown, an audience often supplies the speaker with nonverbal vocalizations and gestures that provide "back-channel cues" to the speaker (Goffman 1981: 12). In this case, we have the amiable laughter that followed Nieto's comment. The laughter did not embarrass Nieto nor spoil his demeanor. In a curious way, the amiable spirit of the laughter perhaps told Nieto that he was being taken seriously. Margarita, no less than the vice president of Frente, accepted Nieto's framing of Yoselin, at least humorously, and even went further, granting her the honor of *Machupiccheña*.

Margarita's interjection leads us to look at the various stances people take when engaged in talk. There are many reasons why speakers make shifts, but often speakers tend to limit their choices to what is appropriate for the situation (Goffman 1981). Nevertheless, speakers often do try to manipulate the shifts in talk to control or redirect a conversational topic, and hence change the situation along with the appropriate form of talk. Speakers can and do change their stances repeatedly in a single conversational exchange, but it does not mean they change their goal, even if they sincerely express doubt and hesitation. For instance, Nieto continued his talk by talking about "corporate social responsibility" and the importance of a "code of business ethics." "We have to understand that we have to work together, live together and above all conduct ourselves in a responsible manner . . . on this topic that I and Yoselin spoke a great deal about, we agree," thereby blending his alleged concern for corporate social responsibility as the same held by Orient Express. Nieto concluded with what he referred to as "another thing I learned in Europe." Here Nieto characterizes the situation in such a way as to escape refutation of his universal claim of the value of competition.

He said:

> [O]ver there they compete with everything . . . you know what? We [Peru] know how to fight, but we don't yet know how to compete. There is a difference—he who fights destroys. He who competes moves ahead and pulls up those [people] that are behind him. (Cusco, Fieldnotes: 3-6-02)

His statement was framed as a classic if-then conditional so as to never question the destructive potential of capitalism; again globalization not as a process but an ideology, and a rhetorical strategy of persuasion. In other words, if competition is the ideal good and in Peru competition has been destructive, then it just goes to show you that what we do in Peru is not "true" competition. What Mr. Nieto does not mention is that most European countries[7] are not in the same world economic position as Peru, nor in 2002 did Europeans so harshly dissolve the structures of the welfare state as they did after the 2009 financial crisis.

The meeting continued for a couple of hours and numerous perspectives were articulated. Chela spoke in a humble fashion, claiming that the Cusco tourism agencies had a disregard for the town since Machu Picchu was generally the last stop for tourists ending their travel itineraries. Oscar retorted that the code of ethics should apply to everyone, including the tour guides. The registered tour agencies blamed the clandestine agencies operating without authorization. But finally, Nieto declared that the protestors and their platform of struggle would be responsible for decreasing tourism in Peru. Members of the tour guide association proclaimed that if the town protested they would destroy the image of Machu Picchu. "Machu Picchu is not only ours, it also belongs to the world," one said. In the end, even though the Machupiccheños had threatened to hold a stoppage if their requested changes were not made, for the time being they agreed to have it postponed.

Moreover, there was an interesting shift in language. The word *competition* was now being used as part of everyone's rhetoric. Margarita said that "competition" obliges us to stop the abuses of the tour guides that charge tourists extra. And, "competition" obliges us to stop the tour agencies from making deals with certain Pueblo restaurants, compelling the tourists to eat at their locations. And collectively as a group the agreement is that competition obliges the town to protect its image, not against Orient Express but against the *ambulantes*, the poorer folks who follow tourists to sell their trinkets. The solution was to improve the image of the town to make it more competitive. Nieto succeeded, at least in part, in having the townsfolk look for market solutions to their problems rather than protest; to create promotional packages of their own or to organize the town to make it more aesthetically appealing—to sell a better product. Unlike the state authorities who treat the Sanctuary as a homogenous entity, Mr. Nieto and the AATC had the power to more subtly redefine who was to be included in reaping the benefits of the Cusco tourism economy. They had the power to deliver the goods to an economic segment of the pueblo that was largely comprised of members of Frente and the mobilization. It showed how Frente's efforts to organize as a community of district residents fragmented because of their different economic interests and class positions compared to the varieties of groups they represented.

What transpired for the members of the artisan associations was the development of a photo-check identification system. The idea was to stop the increasing number of merchants coming to the Pueblo to take advantage of the tourism economy. Each artisan would be required to wear or have in their possession a photo ID to sell goods to tourists. If one was not already a member of an artisan association they would be excluded and prevented from doing business in the Pueblo. The upshot is that those excluded were mostly the *ambulantes*, comprised largely of poorer women and children, and whose activities were previously tolerated, but like merchants in the Cusco plaza, these people do not have a fixed market location and so resort to approaching tourists directly, along the train tracks or while tourists are dining in a local restaurant in Machu Picchu. The meeting with the AATC offered a glimpse into the dramaturgical way the neoliberal economy ordered market space in terms of exclusion or inclusion through significant encounters but often experienced as situational. The implementation of the photo ID system further exemplifies the territorial struggles carved out of the relationship between economy and governance of a tourism site. This encounter illustrates the effects of local private sector bureaucrats through personalized relationships and informal situational contexts rather, than state agents, in attaining hegemony and legitimizing state policies. This is seen more clearly when contrasted to the interactions that took place in the subsequent more formal meetings with the state authorities.[8]

STATE SECTOR PERFORMANCES

An important corollary in the expansion of the tourism economy in Cusco concerns the development of "the society of the spectacle" (Debord in Campos 2004). Following Debord, Ramiro Campos describes how social space in Cusco is organized around the production of visual commodities for tourists. He argues that under neoliberalism "landscapes and monuments become commodities for the tourist gaze" (ibid.: 2). Campos describes the development of nationalist discourses revolving around Inca identity as attempts to sanctify a landscape in resistance to market liberalization and the commoditization of life, but concludes that they are unable to stop the overwhelming power of the market economy (ibid.). While these nationalist discourses were commonly invoked in public demonstrations, as shown above in the meeting with tourism leaders, once situated in strategic interactions, we can see how regionalist sentiments summoned against neoliberalism can be appropriated. Regional identity, Incanismo, in Cusco has more recently become a form of political expression appropriated by the growing tourism industry (Flores Ochoa 1990; van den Berghe and Flores Ochoa 2000; Hill 2007). In formalized strategic interactions, the invocation of Incan identity by state authorities were too transparently understood as identification strategies. Once the players such as the Machupiccheños, state authorities and leaders of Orient Express were inserted into concrete social contexts, negotiations also took on the non-discursive quality of each group's position of power. Frente's discussions with Mr. Nieto showed that his ability to appropriate identity discourses in support of neoliberalism was in part based on his unique position in the Cusco tourism industry and his relationship with Pueblo residents as not clearly insider or outsider, and not only the content of his talk.

In the weeks that followed the first meeting with authorities, subsequent meetings were held in Cusco as well as in the Pueblo of Machu Picchu. The next two meetings were particularly important in that the limits to dialogue became apparent to the protestors. The second meeting was held in Cusco in the regional government building and was joined by the Peruvian Vice Minister of Tourism. He met with the Pueblo protestors and Orient Express (both Sanctuary Lodge Hotel and PeruRail) to resolve the conflict. The Vice Minister began by formally greeting his audience in Quechua:

> Asuan sonqo manllaiquicuna
> Muna qeipi rimaqunampa
> Lloq'anqeipi hamuni rimananchispa
> Chiamantara asuan allinta lloq'ecuni
> Rucatata q'eillata . . .[9]
> (My dear friends and countrymen, once again I come as a Cuzqueño to my beloved land of Cusco, and I am happy to see you.)

And then he shifted into Spanish:[10]

> In the first place, I don't believe this is a platform of struggle; personally, as the Cuzqueño that I am, I reject this term because I believe that the theme we must address, that we must examine, is how to improve our pueblos and improve tourism. What we need is a platform for developing tourism. . . . Here there are not two fronts, there is no border, here we have a concrete objective to develop tourism in Peru in an efficient manner in front of the world.

Here we have a similar "identification" effort, using Quechua as an address, but it was less effective. Rhetorically, the Vice Minister, like Nieto earlier, is attempting to instruct his listeners as if they were backstage, preparing a formal performance for an important audience. He explained that "Machu Picchu is the thermometer that measures the health of tourism in Peru. Whatever happens in Machu Picchu is a world event." His rhetoric, too, implied a global audience. Imagining the desires of an audience is a contest of different interests, a hegemonic field where different actors struggle to define the audience. For the Vice Minister, we see that the concern is Peru's image as being politically stable in the world economy. As he told the Machupiccheños, "I think the case of Machu Picchu is one of the most important cases . . . for Peru. I'll repeat it is a thermometer that measures the pulse of tourism in Peru and in the world. Whatever occurs there has an immense and incommensurable repercussion . . . that would tomorrow be in all the headlines of the world." Since Machu Picchu represents Peru to the world, for state officials and their external political and economic relations, those representations reflected the neoliberal Peru, either for ideological conviction, or as a matter of "keeping up appearances" for the sake of maintaining financial credibility. The Vice Minister spoke of the presidential visit by George W. Bush,[11] noting the implications for the Peruvian economy: "The tourism companies of the world say that wherever Bush goes is a good place, no one important goes to a place that has problems." He performed a similar stance as did Nieto on geopolitical knowledge, and went on to tell a story of what happened when he heard of the Machupiccheños' plans to hold a stoppage. He recounted how he was with tourism professionals when they heard of the protestors' plans to hold an indefinite stoppage at Machu Picchu. The Vice Minister role-played and assumed the voice of an imaginary tour agent conversing with a client: "Excuse me one moment, please cancel the next two weeks of trips to Peru and put them for Bali." He concluded his story with his point, "This is the way these people think."

However, for the activists experiencing corporate intrusions, the notion of a global audience is more akin to a witnessing world. As Oscar said in this respect when he threatened a stoppage, "So the world knows that this company is distorting the meaning of the Sanctuary." He responded to the comments of the Vice Minister by recounting the artisans' experience. He described the events that unfolded when the artisans protested the rules that excluded them from commerce near Sanctuary Lodge; they sold merchandise in the area around the hotel. Oscar, indignant about the abuse of power, described how police in riot gear were deployed after a few days, allegedly at the request of the hotel general manager. To the Machupiccheños, the presence of the police was what damaged the image of Machu Picchu because it revealed to the "world" the inequities they were experiencing, and made Peru appear like a police state, not to mention it jeopardized the image of Machu Picchu as a place of peace and harmony. The Machupiccheños invoked a certain meaning of the Sanctuary that emphasized how market interests took precedence over democratic ideals and social responsibility in Peru. The rhetoric that the Machupiccheños used was overwhelmingly in an idiom of abuse against them and for a call to fairness. As Oscar said to the Vice Minister, "Business under neoliberalism thinks only of profitability. . . . [T]hey don't consider social responsibility," invoking Nieto's comments a few weeks earlier. Chela and others further connected their grievances to a regionalist identity discourse, arguing that Machu Picchu is a sacred place where no commercial activity should occur, even adding that "[people] should enter barefoot." But the Vice Minister simply dismissed identity rhetoric, noting that all participants in the discussion should stay within the legal contracts that were in effect as negotiated by Orient Express and the Peruvian government. Indeed, on behalf of Orient Express he dismissed Chela's identity appeal with "market-talk" about the economy and how the decrease of tourism was due to their inadequate promotional and marketing strategies.

> We need to work very hard so that many more tourists come and to treat them very well because they are the best advertisers for our country. . . . Like some woman who goes to Machu Picchu, loves it immediately, buys something big or small and [then] says to her daughter [when she gets back home], "You know what, go to this country, it's marvelous, beautiful, take your husband, boyfriend or whoever," rather than say, "You know what, I went to Peru, they treated me bad, this and that problem."

He concluded by waving his hands emphatically, still speaking from the perspective of an imaginary Western woman, but directing criticism at the protest intentions of the mobilizers: "It's a country where you don't know if they will throw rocks at you, don't go and tell your friends not to go."

No doubt Chela and others value Machu Picchu as a sacred place, but the artisans took note of their increase in sales when they set up outside the Citadel next to Sanctuary Lodge. The original position of the protestors had been to argue the contradiction in the way privatization had been put into effect in the Sanctuary, but they changed the strategy to that of all business activities should take place in the town below, largely as a way of appealing to regionalist identity sentiment. While Chela, a person I knew well, may deeply feel the sentiment that no commercial activity should take place by the Citadel, some of the other artisans I spoke to later were hesitant to accept that line of argument, understanding that they could better compete when selling by the Citadel, and that bringing large-scale business down to the town could only undermine local commercial activity. Regardless of whether it made business sense or not, the point is that the protestors were quick to ascertain the hollow identity maneuver on the part of the Vice Minister, and perhaps he theirs as well; though the Vice Minister did agree to continue with future dialogues.

The next oration came from Orient Express, the manager of the Sanctuary Lodge Hotel (a European fluent in Spanish). He spoke the loudest by comparison to the others and in English, directly to his Peruvian lawyer seated beside him, presumably to ensure everyone heard him speak a language few understood. The lawyer then parroted his message into Spanish at a more contextually normative tone of voice to those present. I would describe his message as forceful and direct in that they had reached the limit of discussion and dialogue with the Machupiccheños, and that they could not afford the loss of revenue by closing the shops, condescendingly adding that the items they sell are "at least twenty times more expensive than any items [the artisans] sell." He rejected what he considered the harrying tactics of the Machupiccheños to obligate him to close the concession stands. At the behest of the artisans and Frente, the mayor attempted to close the shops, citing municipal regulations that the shops lacked local sellers' permits. The manager reasserted the Vice Minister's statement that Sanctuary Lodge did in fact have a legal contract with the state, and that the subcontracted shops all had the necessary authorizations to operate. He concluded:

> It will be very hard to find a solution on this point because we are not ready to give in, we are not ready to close the shops, and obviously the Frente de Defensa has done a positive protest for the last five or six days, which changed yesterday, because the police [came] and removed all of them, which has been decided by authorities, and I can assure you that in the future if again they would be disruptive *we* will take exactly the same action because *we* are not willing to give in."[12]

One cannot help noticing how the manager first claimed the decision to remove the artisans was decided by state authorities, but then goes on to insert himself as part of that decision-making process by saying that "we will take exactly the same action" in the future, and translated into Spanish as such. Unlike the private sector meeting above, the relations that were being reinforced and the identification that was being made was between the state and Orient Express.

The protestors had not, at least at this formal meeting, argued that the Sanctuary Lodge concession stands be closed, only that they be allowed to sell by the Citadel to make competition reasonable, or following Chela, that they sell in town as do the other artisans. Sanctuary Lodge made their power position far more transparent than had the state authorities. The vice minister could offer no solutions other than a promise to continue talks with residents, skirting around the aversion to dispossess multinational corporate capital to make competition fairer; he preferred instead to dispossess the artisans of what amounts to the use of public space. Sanctuary Lodge Hotel does not own the space outside the Citadel where the artisans had in "positive" protest set up their goods, but they could use the power of the state to ensure the area remained empty of any competition. While benefiting from state intervention, and the use of state resources such as the police, the Sanctuary Lodge maintained their economic stronghold. When it came to social responsibility however, the vice minister invoked the logic of market dynamics against having to act. In short, corporate capital used the language of power, the state "flowered" that power with "market talk." Great effort was made to force the people of Machu Picchu to accept market logic, and ultimately economic disadvantage, all the while dissuading them from using political means, including the right to protest and to carry out a stoppage.

The Machupiccheños often talked about how the tourism, conservation and other state authorities do not understand their lived realities. For this reason, the members of Frente invited everyone to continue talks in the town, where they could point out some of the problems firsthand and give a wider audience of district residents a chance to voice opinions; the state authorities obliged. The next meeting with authorities took place in the Pueblo cultural center about two weeks later, and was moderated by a representative of the Cusco Regional Government (CTAR). It was anticipated that the meeting would be one of finding solutions; the arbitrator in fact uttered "solutions" some twelve times in his opening lines. Present were representatives from CTAR, INC, INRENA, and the Ministry of Tourism along with other state technical advisors, the district and provincial mayor as well. The auditorium was filled with Machupiccheños from the town as well as those from the rural communities. Noticeably absent was the management of Orient Express. Somewhere in the back rows sat the Peruvian lawyers for Sanctuary Lodge and PeruRail, but not their European bosses.

As discussion began, the arbitrator stressed that if solutions were not reached on specific issues they should be bracketed and discussed later, citing the importance of maintaining the flow of discussion. After many hours of deliberation just about every issue was bracketed. However, the INC did make offers to reduce the entrance fee to the Citadel for Peruvian nationals.[13] Also, some discussion revolved around starting legal proceedings against the beer company that damaged part of the Inca sundial in the Citadel, and about retrieving artifacts from the Bingham expedition held at Yale University. These last three (reduction of entrance fees for nationals, legal proceedings and return of artifacts) were motivated largely by the nationalist tone and sentiment of the Machupiccheños. This aspect of their platform of struggle did not revolve around the theme of economic injustice as in other demands but around Peruvian identity and more so than regional identity, if one takes "regional" to mean Incanismo. I agree that identity discourses revolving around the Inca or that of "Andean mysticism" is common in the politics of the Cusco tourism industry (Hill 2007). Chela and Héctor often did express such sentiments during meetings with the townsfolk and, though tolerated by the townsfolk, I found that it had little persuasive effect as participants generally shifted discussions back into themes of unfairness, or even national and regional identity rhetoric but without the Incan romanticism. My point here is to recognize the important role of other identity discourses that are often obscured because Inca history is de facto part of the Cusco tourism industry; at the risk of making a picayune point it serves as a reminder that despite the history of Cusco Indigenismo or the current Incanismo, identity in the Cusco region understood as belonging to a national polity via the concept of citizen is also meaningful.

Archeological sites are part of a political project and the relationship between heritage and nationalism is well established (Handler 1985; Hewison 1987; Walsh 1992; Clifford 1997; Kirshenblatt-Gimblet 1998). Away from direct attention of the media, and away from the management of Orient Express, once in the town of Machu Picchu nationalist discourses not only came to life but also held a degree of influence over the state authorities. While the lawyers for Orient Express continued with their line of market and investment logic, they were put on the defensive by in effect being called traitors, "vende patrias" (national sellouts). The lawyers became flustered and felt a need to defend their patriotism. "We do identify with [Machu Picchu], we are Peruvians, the only foreigners are those who made the investment," one of the lawyers said. At one point, the lawyer for PeruRail even argued the state should retake responsibility for subsidizing train operations for the transportation services once provided to nationals, though not arguing counter to its privatization, a feeble gesture of identifying with the national control of public goods without threatening their client's business interests.

Neoliberalism like heritage is also a political project but of policies organized around an idea of an unfettered market economy to organize society (Gill 2000; Gledhill 2004). The event exposes the conflict between the two political projects, of heritage as part of national identity but used under a market economy for private profit by foreign investors. This conflict was appropriated by locals as a criticism and challenge to the state by accusing them as being the real traitors. During the event, the large number of participating district residents and their applause fed into a sense of power over both the state representatives and the lawyers for Orient Express. It also made it difficult for the authorities to control the dialogue and stifle dissent. Eber concluded the exchange with a warning to the authorities:

> If I were a director in the government I would be embarrassed to call myself Peruvian because, sirs, we are trafficking in the heritage of our

> ancestors . . . and it will be very sad for those that decide the future of Machu Picchu. We will look at your faces afterwards, sirs, when you will have to say [raises his voice], "I was the one who sold Machu Picchu!"

The language of neoliberalism, when examined in terms of the situated encounters of the speakers and performed in the institutional context of their interactions, brings into focus different modes of producing and contesting authority. The events described shows how state representatives are caught in their own double bind. The meeting with the Vice Minister showed that his authority was based on maintaining credibility with foreign investors, and the upshot was that one must adhere to the neoliberal course at the expense of social responsibility. However, authorities start to lose credibility if they appear to be on the side of foreign investors taking over Peru's cultural goods. The discussion exemplifies what Breglia notes as a "seemingly irresolvable tension between a state that needs to sell off its patrimony to be in line with global circulation of capital, and its citizenry, which heavily invests in the monuments and symbols of national patrimony as a way of defining its social identities" (2006: 17). Nationalist discourses in opposition to neoliberal programs do find their own authorial spaces, as in the town context where authorities were far more susceptible to local views, and had to appear to reject the imperialist implications of the neoliberal project, even though the net result was a lot of stalling on the part of the authorities. Mr. Nieto represented a pivotal moment when he managed to convince the mobilizers to make changes in accordance with free-market principles. By making neoliberalism an inevitable outcome of globalization he absolved the state of responsibilities that produce the dilemma faced by state agents. However, one must consider that this was not the residents' first encounter with such language about neoliberalism. In fact, their rejection of it formed the basis of their protest. By understanding the dramaturgical framing of Nieto's credibility, we can see his success in getting the town representatives to think of themselves in terms of "economic sectors" and "market dynamics," and thereby momentarily undermining the organizing principle of their protest. Their sense of district identity that they sought to cultivate among other residents and their criticisms of the state policies that had resulted in their disadvantage diminished in importance. The leaders of Frente and other mobilizers were caught in their own double bind; their sense of district identity, however broad, was nevertheless, as discussed in chapter 2, based on interests shaped by class differences.

It is difficult to point to concrete changes, except for the authorities' promise to continue dialoguing. One can point to a few important achievements made by the mobilizers. Often the gross inequalities that characterize Latin American social relations mean that people often do not envisage, much less claim, rights (Alvarez et al 1998: 12). The dialogues succeeded in getting the clear majority of the district politically engaged. Town residents sought to reclaim the use of space, as in the artisans' "commercial" protest outside Sanctuary Lodge. Also, a much wider group of residents began to understand how they were affected by neoliberal policies, and many more began participating in the discussions. The final meeting in the town drew a large supportive crowd, but it was the last time the talks with the authorities would take place in Machu Picchu, at least for these sets of issues and the remaining time that I was there. The state authorities canceled or postponed the future meetings scheduled to take place in the town. Next, I will consider the interpretations of these cancellations by the mobilizers and explore the dramaturgy of decision making among them alone in what might be considered an example of a real rather than a "staged" back-stage event, and focus on how they moved from the quotidian activities of daily life to the decision to finally hold the stoppage.

NOTES

1. See Kravel-Tovi (2012) for an excellent discussion on the usefulness of Erving Goffman's work, yet noting its relative absence in anthropology.
2. I am not applying Goffman's approach as a complete system of sociological theory but rather employing him in a piecemeal fashion for specific situations that are likely to require strategic interactions between social actors. See Geertz's critique of Goffman in *Local Knowledge: Further Essays in Interpretive Anthropology*, Basic Books, 1983: 24–27.
3. At the time of this fieldwork in 2001/02, PeruRail had a monopoly on transportation. In around 2010 the new company "Inca Rail" (a joint Peruvian-Colombian venture with U.S. and British shareholders) began transportation operations as well.
4. I have not been able to find a town in Chile named "Condorito," or for that matter that the Euro currency is made there. His reference is most probably to the famous Chilean comic book character by that name that he used metaphorically as a place name to make his point.
5. Italics mean he used the actual words in English and no translation was required.
6. Puputi is a Quechua term for navel. Nieto is making a reference to the way the Incas referred to Cusco as the navel, or center, of the world; hence in this context I translate it as "center."
7. Note to reader: Mr. Nieto's reference is on Western European countries. Eastern European countries joined the European Union in 2004 after this fieldwork was completed. The Euro currency appeared in 2002 during my fieldwork.
8. As these meetings lasted between 6 and 8 hours, space does not permit me to cover every possible item discussed, nor do I wish to burden the reader with all the details. Rather, by necessity I discuss the outcome abstractly, restricting examples to what furthers the argument.
9. I wish to thank Nayruth Yanez for the translation from Quechua to Spanish.
10. In an effort to make it easier on the reader, large quotes in Spanish are translated and appear in English only. In this event I included some Quechua to better show the reader how the diglossia was performed as an appeal to identity, but noting that the Spanish, Quechua and English language shifts were important to my analysis in this meeting.
11. U.S. presidential visit to Peru, March 2002.

12. Italics mine.

13. The INC did eventually reduce entrance fees for all Peruvian nationals, in part as a result of this meeting, which was a noteworthy accomplishment on the part of the mobilizers.

SIX

Protest and Memories of Violence

Maybe they'll make us disappear.
—Héctor, Machupicchu Pueblo

I stood in Plaza Manco Capac not knowing exactly what to do. It was mid-May and we were a couple of hours short of noon, but the sun was already intense. I had prepared to spend the day in a meeting between the Machupiccheños and the authorities. I arrived only to find the plaza empty of the participants. The artisans of the Joyitas Association were busy setting up stands for a *chiriuchada,* or a *chiriuchu* benefit, to raise funds to legally establish themselves as an artisan association in the public registry.[1] The newly implemented photo-check system required independent artisans and vendors to formalize an association and to list their members to gain the proper identity cards to do business in the town.

The position that many had, as residents in the Sanctuary of Machu Picchu, is reminiscent of how Deborah Poole describes the use of national identification cards during the civil war against the Shining Path as both a source of "vulnerability" and "guarantee" that one's identity would not be construed by authorities as an enemy of the state (2004: 36). Living under the shadow of a national icon, that logic may be more intense, and pervades to the level of local activity and life. For the artisans and vendors, the photo-check system provided the hope that making a living is secured, and exclusion avoided. Machu Picchu is a symbol of peace and harmony, and yet it also reflects a national history of violence. Decisions made by residents of this protected area carry the weight of that history, from the way it is popularly described as undiscovered, untouched by the Spanish conquest and shielded from the dirty hands of colonialism, to the history of land struggles and to the hopes and meanings of an identity card. In Poole's terms, what lies "between threat and guarantee" is also for the Machupiccheños reverberated through the unique geography of their town (ibid.: 37). The town is the bottleneck of tourism that the industry cannot bypass. The townsfolk could bring tourism to a halt, and so they had the clout to elicit a degree of cooperation on the part of the authorities. However, the use of that power made for a very fragile circumstance; the Machupiccheños believed that not far behind the appearance of cooperation was the willingness of authorities to use violence to rid themselves of a problematic population.

HOW THE TOWN BOILED OVER

After a few minutes of waiting, Héctor and "Adolfo" approached me from Pachacútec Avenue. Héctor seemed agitated; things had changed. As we stood in the plaza with the sun pounding us, Héctor said that CTAR had called the leaders of Frente the previous day to inform them that a delegation would arrive in Cusco too late to make it on time to catch the train to Machu Picchu. However, they had offered to change the location of the meeting, and offered to make a PeruRail train wagon available to take the leaders to and from Cusco. But Héctor expressed concern about going to Cusco. He feared that it was a police ploy to arrest them and silence their protest. "This is dangerous" (*ésto está peligroso*), he said, waving his hands to emphasize his concerns. Adolfo proposed a different reason for the sudden change on the part of the authorities: "[They] did this with the intention of changing the stage."[2] He felt that it was a strategy by the authorities to take the activists out of the context of their own pueblo, and away from the "home team" advantage. The result would be that in Cusco large numbers of town residents would not be able to attend the meeting on such short notice, reducing their participation. But, Héctor feared something worse from the authorities. "Maybe they'll make us disappear" (*derepente nos desaparecen*). Héctor was visibly upset at this change of plans. "How could they change the location at the last moment?" he asked. He felt it was intended as an insult. "How is it that they don't have time for the town that brings [Peru] the most money?" From Héctor's point of view the only way the authorities would take them seriously would be to hold a Pueblo-wide stoppage, but his question was also a search for the true motives; behind the rhetorical *how could they* was a *why would they*.

Héctor was particularly angry over a journalistic slur discrediting their protest. "They are portraying Oscar as if he were a lunatic," he said, referring to an article published in the magazine *Caretas*, a well-reputed Peruvian political magazine, and written by a well-respected columnist.[3] Two editions later the Ambassador of Finland wrote a letter to the editor applauding the comments of the author. And in that subsequent issue there was a lengthier article on the politics of Machu Picchu entitled "Aguas Hirvientes," or boiling waters, a play on the often-cited name

"Aguas Calientes" (hot springs) for the town of Machu Picchu, but more a reference to the troubling resistance and dissent by the Machupiccheños.[4] The writer ingratiated himself with the ambassador, thanking him for his extraordinary patience, and of course for the Finnish funds as well.

Héctor was troubled. Again, he searched for concealed motives. "How is it possible that they ridicule our people, such a serious and important magazine, how could they print these kinds of commentaries?" He mentioned a photo he had seen in the same magazine of Ms. Luther, the director of PeruRail, with the Vice Minister of Tourism they had met with previously.[5] "The Vice Minister was supposed to be helping the Machupiccheños." To Héctor, the fact that they were posed together, with their postures and smiles, suggested that the Vice Minister was giving preferential treatment to PeruRail. The conversations and interactions in the meeting they had with him certainly bolstered that impression. After all the negotiations with the authorities, it seemed to Héctor that all they had received were deceptions, and that their efforts were reduced by the media to a handful of malicious words caricaturing them as "crazy." Héctor said that those who have power just buy off the press to bring the Pueblo into disrepute and discredit their cause.[6]

Charo walked hurriedly down Pachacutec Avenue, agenda book in hand. She joined us in the plaza and listened to Héctor finish his grievance. He soon quieted down and turned to Charo to get the latest scoop. Charo said that the pueblo would assemble in the plaza to decide to continue to talk with the authorities or to break with them and begin the stoppage. Charo asserted her personal verdict. "Already [the authorities] have suspended many meetings and we have tolerated enough, so no more!"

But just then, the local train pulled into the station so Héctor went off to see if by chance the authorities had arrived on that train rather than the earlier tourist train. He returned with a negative report. Adolfo and Charo began analyzing the situation, describing it like a game of chess. "You have to move the pieces strategically and deceptively, [first] they say yes then they say no, it's all a game." Adolfo wrinkled his forehead. "It seems to me that their strategy is to divide the pueblo, discredit the leader of Frente [Oscar Valencia]," he said, still talking about the magazine article. Adolfo continued, "It's regrettable that they have resorted to such low blows as calling [Oscar] a lunatic." Adolfo even spoke of the possibility of Frente having a "mysterious" car accident. His remark seemed to trigger a fear in Charo. She appeared worried that they may have gotten into more trouble than she had anticipated. Charo rarely sounded so hesitant. She feared the power of PeruRail and the Sanctuary Lodge and like most of them felt that as foreign companies they would surely be given preferential treatment by her own government. From her perspective, Peru would never place limits on foreign investors because they would fear losing economic credibility in the "eyes of the world." "With whom did we get mixed up with?" she asked. Héctor rejoined, "They're bringing us to the point of exhaustion. We should have gone to Cusco but in our own train." He spoke about the frustration of being dependent on PeruRail, the same entity they are fighting, to take them to Cusco. Adolfo heightened Héctor's concern, saying in a semi-serious way, "Getting us to use their train could be a strategy for [getting rid of us] with a bomb." They all entertained the idea that the Peruvian government would not hesitate to blow up the train with all the activists. Charo could not resist a stab at morbid humor by pretending to be reading a newspaper headline; she played on the contents of the recent magazine article by pronouncing: "The lunatics of the Pueblo are dead." Their comments, among other things, also exemplify how the privatization of the transportation system in the sanctuary created a sense of vulnerability that in turn fueled suspicion among Machupiccheños.

The heat of the sun deepened and we moved to the shade. A man dressed in a black suit passed us, briefcase in hand. He looked like the lawyer for Sanctuary Lodge they met at the town meeting discussed above. "Is that him?" they said repeatedly. Charo suspected that they must have their own informants in the Pueblo, feeding them information on the activities of the mobilizers. At that moment Chela, seeing us from the opposite side of the plaza, sauntered across to us; she greeted us in her amiable shy fashion. Curious about our assembly, she asked, "What are you guys up to?" The group momentarily lost cohesion as people chatted separately. Chela spoke privately with Charo. Adolfo reflected aloud to himself, but also to whoever was in earshot. "It's that they're changing the stage on us, and we have to be careful because at the end of the tunnel everything stops." Héctor spoke as obliquely as Adolfo, but a bit more concretely. "It's that they're making fun of us."

Then, Oscar appeared. "Buenas días." Suddenly the group pulled together, but so excited at Oscar's arrival that everyone spoke at once. As it quieted down, Oscar went straight to the topic of the day. He said, "We can no longer believe in the usefulness of talking to any of them. First, we come to an agreement but later when you hold them up to it, they say they 'don't know' anything about it." Oscar was referring to the INC agreement to lower the entrance fee into the Citadel to half price for Peruvian nationals. Despite their agreement, the INC continued to charge the regular twenty-dollar entrance fee. He cursed the bureaucracy! "Sofía," who had been listening all along from her store entrance, approached to give some advice. "It's not our fault," she quipped, "it's an institutional problem; we should organize ourselves like they did in Arequipa," referring to the way protestors in Arequipa effectively organized themselves against President Toledo's privatization efforts, as discussed in chapter 1.

Oscar pulled the group tighter around him to explain the situation with the authorities. He said that the authorities called him from Cusco, asking Frente to meet them there because they were going to arrive too late to catch the train to the Pueblo. "They wanted us to go to Cusco by train." Héctor interjected, "But Don Oscar, this is a strategy; they're trying to tire us out." Adolfo again alleged that authorities had more brutal motives: "Maybe it's an assassination attempt?" They laughed. Oscar played along. He announced, "Yes, and later they'll say, 'the thirty-five members of Frente are dead,'" and like Charo, he also pretended to be reading an imaginary journalistic caption. They continued laughing, but Héctor wore a somber face, reminding them of the recent history of the civil war violence. "Yes, like what happened to those people in Uchuraccay." He was talking about the 8 journalists killed in the village of Uchuraccay in Ayacucho in 1983, allegedly by campesinos who thought the arriving journalists were Shining Path terrorists. Héctor, like many in Peru, suspected that the campesinos had been deceived by the Peruvian military, or that the military were the ones to carry out the assassinations. Oscar agreed. "You see how they killed those eight journalists. It's that they were a strong opposition to the government, they were making the government dance (*zapatear*), that's why they made them 'disappear.'"

The conversation progressed into a discussion over the history of politics and presidents in Peru. Oscar claimed that the best president Peru ever had was Juan Velasco, because of his agrarian reform. "With the politics of the agrarian reform, 'sir, you see your land, it's going to be for the campesinos,'" he said as if talking to a hacendado. Héctor reflected over the agrarian reform and the bitter resentment that followed from the hacendados. For Héctor the agrarian reform was not as successful as in Oscar's depiction. Héctor explained that hate and resentment over the agrarian reform was still pervasive in Peru, and that racism persisted. He spelled out the history of Peru through the proverb "Necessity has the face of a heretic and is mother to all vice" (La necesidad tiene cara de hereje, es madre de todos los vicios), which captured the way the need for money breeds corruption. Oscar added that now there are new challenges. "Before there was imperialism and that was fatal; then capitalism came and destroyed our economy; and now the world is globalized," to which Chela added, "Neoliberalism is the new political economy in fashion." For Oscar, the solution to the problems created by neoliberalism was to create a political mix of socialism and capitalism. He reasoned that the two by themselves would at best only address a limited set of needs, and at worst create extremes in power or wealth. Oscar maintained that a balance of some kind would form a better system, if only one is willing to combine the most constructive aspects of each.

The group was hungry and the chiriuchu was ready to be served. We shuffled to the other end of the plaza where they purchased their meal consisting of hen, *cuy* (guinea pig), corn omelet, fish eggs, cheese, toasted kernels of white corn, q'ochayuyo (a lake version of seaweed), and sausage. Since the meal did not appeal to me I opted not to eat. The gang passed me pieces from their plates, as they criticized me for being such a gringo; I ate. The group picked at their plates savoring each piece, pulling apart the fish eggs with their hands. As the group occupied themselves with their plates, Adolfo declared, as he ate his cuy, "We need nourishment, Napoleon lost at Waterloo for lack of food. Not to mention that one can't philosophize without food." Oscar added, "Naturally," and just continued eating.

With the meal finished, the group reconvened on a nearby bench. It was now noon and the plaza was scorching from the heat of the sun. Officer Martin from the local police precinct arrived. As the town's regularly posted police official, Officer Martin was treated like a friend. Oscar turned to him. As president of Frente he wanted the officer to witness their statement. "We are present," he declared, "but the authorities have not fulfilled [their part of] the bargain. The pueblo waited until the arrival of the local train, fulfilling to the end the democracy[7] of the dialogue. Therefore, Officer, the pueblo has the free reign to conduct a strike." "Yes, yes, I'm recording everything," said the officer.

Charo felt that the magazine article that portrayed Oscar and the members of Frente as lunatics now prevented them from conducting a reasonable dialogue with the authorities. "How dare they say that we are a town of lunatics?" By calling the mobilizers "crazy" the magazine helped discredit their stand in the talks. Charo was furious over this depiction. She spoke with determination, saying, "For that alone we are going to do our talking [to the authorities] with a stoppage." However, Chela wanted a wider level of participation before making the decision and insisted they should call for a town meeting. Margot responded with a more practical attitude, "Let's do it once and for all, what are we waiting for?" "No more!" a woman cried referring to the maltreatment from the authorities. "How dare they kick us around, after one institution failed us, to hell with everyone else," shouted Eber. Adolfo tried to calm people from the intensifying emotional stances. "We cannot be passionate," he declared, "we have to think clearly." They paid little mind as Oscar stirred the group. "Remember, neighbors, that it's acceptable to break from the talks because the authorities did not fulfill their part."

Still, even at this point the group retained some hope that the authorities would arrive late. "Let's wait another half hour," Oscar said. He was worried that he would be seen as the person dictating the decisions rather than trying to communicate the "will" of the pueblo; that leadership role might make him legally culpable should something go badly during the stoppage. He wanted the people there to voice their position. He asked, "What do we do, do we hold a stoppage?" The heat was sweltering. Stifled by the sun, the group moved again, this time to a shady area. There, Alfredo, the president of the workers' association, and later Raúl and Emilio, joined the group. They gathered in a circle speaking all at once. Most seemed resolved to conduct a strike.

Oscar posed: "What do we do if the president of CTAR sends a fax asking to reschedule a meeting for Monday or Tuesday?" A cluster of people spoke at once, "No, it's already too late." Oscar echoed the response as a question, "So we're not accepting any more meetings?" Héctor raised his voice above the others. "No, we no longer want a meeting!" Chela, in a well-composed voice gave her advice. "Oscar, I suggest that we hold a meeting with at least a majority of the pueblo. We alone can't make that decision." Oscar nodded but continued, "What happens if now or later the president or vice minister calls and says, 'ladies and gentlemen we can't come, and we ask you for a new date for next week,' what do I tell them?" Héctor was willing to reschedule a meeting. Oscar seemed to look for more resolve and asked, "So we accept a meeting?" Again, there was an avalanche of voices saying, "No, No!" José turned to Héctor. Somewhat agitated Jorge said, "Come on Héctor, it's the fourth time they cancelled." Chela tried to find a middle ground. "If they call you, tell them you don't know because in the evening we are going to hold a [town] meeting.'" Once more a stampede of voices trampled one on top of the other: "No, that's it," "No, they've ridiculed us," "What good is it if they've already deceived us two or three times?" Charo agreed with Chela's viewpoint. "Señor Oscar, if they call you, you tell them that we will hold a meeting tonight and the majority of the town will decide whether to accept or not." The group went into a loud chatter.

Oscar yelled out, asking the group yet again, "How should we respond, because all things considered they are surely going to call saying 'we want a new meeting on Monday or Tuesday or whenever,' should we accept or not, should we say 'enough, we have withdrawn from the talks,' what should we say? Speak out, what should we tell them?" Everyone spoke at once trying to get his or her voice heard. Irma, like Charo, raised her voice to say she agreed with Chela, "That's why I say the same as Chelita that in a meeting this evening we let the majority decide." Others agreed as well that "naturally, a meeting, we can't just decide ourselves." Jorge blocked out the presence of the others and spoke directly to Oscar as if he were conversing privately. "Señor Oscar you tell them you know what, the pueblo has broken away from dialogue and in a meeting this evening the pueblo will decide what they want to do." Upon hearing Jorge, Chela modified his statement. "You have to tell them that *they* are the ones who broke the dialogue, and they are to blame." Oscar agreed, "Of course, they're the ones at fault. 'You don't come to my house [town] to disrespect me, now you can leave; I don't want to talk to you.' To say that we're gonna ask [the whole pueblo for consensus?] if it's either 'yes' or 'no' and if we want to go on strike, then let's do it."

The leadership role comes with risks of accountability that Oscar was well aware of and he needed to emphasize that the decision was not his alone. "I want you to know that Oscar Valencia has never acted alone." We [Frente] always consulted you, the leaders of the associations, and it's recorded in the minutes that everything we've done is according to you. . . . Now I don't want to sound or appear as if I'm taking control but if we're going to break with the dialogue, then we break it and goodbye, you see, no dialogue."

Yet many still did not agree that a stoppage should be organized without a broader town consensus. As Héctor noted, without broader consensus a stoppage would only fail. "So many times when we go on strike the masses don't show up and there is no widespread support." Oscar responded to Héctor's skepticism about the level of support among the pueblo that illustrates the ecology of decision making between the Machupiccheños and the state authorities. For Oscar, the situation had to be "carefully managed." For him, community participation in all town meetings previously had not been low, generally attracting about a hundred or so residents to discuss local problems. On this issue, however, he felt that decisions had to be made with fewer participants. "When we deal with too many people," Oscar said, "we also have to deal with passionate and emotional points of view." He felt the leaders of various associations were sufficient for initiating a stoppage.

The predicament of these actors is strikingly different from the way governing authorities can diffuse accountability. This calls attention to the different risks incurred by the different stakeholders. State representatives are not saddled with the same consensus-building techniques, as are the Machupiccheños living there. What is for Oscar a situation that needed to be carefully managed, a problem of building town support, is in terms of policy making on the part of state representatives something far less democratic. To be sure, decision making on the part of state representatives involves building consensus to some degree, but it is concealed from public view. Bureaucrats are assigned their offices and desks to which they routinely report regardless of the plans they execute. They have the advantage of giving off few warning signals before they move to action. To this, protestors can only gather clues obtained in public locales such as in noticing an increased police presence in the streets after bureaucratic decisions are made. On the other hand, the members of Frente and their supporters were known publicly and therefore Oscar's attempt at building a town-wide consensus further exposed him to scrutiny from authorities and makes him, and associates, vulnerable to being held legally culpable should serious problems arise during the stoppage. In short, authorities can preserve the element of surprise in ways that resident organizers could not. For Oscar, the public nature of building consensus meant potentially being identified as "the leader" and labeled "the agitator" in advance to any action (he was already labeled derogatorily in some of the newspapers and magazines). He was aware of his position and predicament when he said; "I want to make it clear that Oscar Valencia is not giving orders to anyone." He communicated his concern—"I feel like I'm between two swords, one in front from the pueblo and the other behind me from the authorities and the law, so I can't just say outright 'let's hold the stoppage.'"

Emilio, standing quietly listening to everything that was going on, spoke for the first time, in a low voice. "Let's go on strike once and for all, why do we have to tolerate so much? A resounding 'yes,' came in near unity from the crowd. Again, many people in the group spoke at the same time, and a myriad of voices burst out:

" . . . We did the same two years ago when we held a stoppage . . . "
" . . . Like on the fifth of February . . . "
" . . . All day,"
" . . . Transportation and everything,"
" . . . The people, damn it, the people have stopped believing in us."

However, not all were convinced of the decision and some were outspoken against it. Sofía spoke in a gentle but concerned voice that expressed an opposing position on the decision to strike and hold a stoppage. She reminded them of the laws that make it possible to take legal action leading to prosecution and jail terms against protestors who block the roads. "I believe that maybe we should take a different approach, a little more intelligent." Before she could finish, numerous voices quickly jumped out against her and accused her of not identifying with the pueblo or only being interested in making money:

"In our final hour, after all we've been through, we're gonna get scared?"
" . . . How many laws have [the authorities] themselves broken?"

Sofía got defensive saying, "I'm not defending this government. I'm just letting you know." One woman replied in pungent and sarcastic voice, "We already know." Sofía attempted to reply, but she appeared flabbergasted—"Because one talks, and says 'yes,' they should, but you know, and later, later they back down." Sofia's opposing voice was nevertheless a reminder that power lies in the state. The public nature of organizing dissent leads not only to the problem of building consensus but clearly in building the collective courage needed to take a decisive stand; this required feeding the momentum in the direction people wanted to take but first had to overcome fear of reprisal. Planning the stoppage also required a lot of preparation in forming committees and arranging signs and pickets for getting the message across, since a stoppage in Machu Picchu would attract a great deal of media attention.

Oscar reviewed the reasons for conducting the strike with the others. "Look, the INC has agreed to a resolution and we can't believe that the director has not sent the orders from Cusco to Machu Picchu, and after fifteen days they continue to charge twenty dollars when they should be charging only ten. We can't believe that Yoselin does not have the power to order the [sales people] on the train not to sell tourist memorabilia. So then what agreements and resolutions are we talking about? Well, if it's a fight they want, let's give them a fight. They'll attack Oscar. They'll take it all out on Oscar, I also want you all to think about that, I'm sure that maybe on Wednesday they could take legal action against me, but I'm not going to be afraid of that. I'm not afraid!" Oscar finally wanted to know if the decision to hold a stoppage was fine with all of them. Almost everyone agreed, but Sofía, who was reluctant to decide without including wider participation. Raúl addressed her in a frustrated voice: "If we've given them one truce, then another truce, the plane didn't arrive, the rain, enough already, the cry of stoppage has already been made." And somebody concluded, "It's about time." With Raúl's statement, the decision to hold a stoppage was finalized to be held on May 29, 2002.

One of the most attention-grabbing aspects of the above incident is the way fear and uncertainty is expressed through recollections of the civil war against the Shining Path and other historical events. Conservation problems are not just a question of conflicting heritage meanings nor of the global relationships in which people are embroiled. The participants express a distrust of the state, and conservation efforts are an extension of the motivation for that distrust in the way they relate their current struggles against the effects of neoliberalism with past state violence. While the Shining Path terrorized many civilians, the government also incorporated similarly brutal tactics, and was responsible for many of the civilian deaths, thus magnifying the atmosphere of fear throughout Peru (Poole and Renique 1992, 2003). With state activities couched in secrecy and the population under the constant surveillance of police forces, people endured general roundups of demonstrators and arbitrary detentions. Popular leaders, and particularly members of left-wing organizations, were arrested, tortured and/or killed (ibid.). As Poole and Renique describe it, "[T]housands of people suffered systematic police harassment and arbitrary detention; journalists, lawyers, and relatives of alleged subversives were executed, arrested, or disappeared" (2003: 3).

Social interaction is not a more empirical body of evidence or void of interpretation. The interaction order is as abstract and conceptual as are the concepts of "power" or "class" (Lemert and Brananman 1997). History and culture shape interaction at all levels. What we see in the interactions between residents is that decision making on the part of the above protestors is marked by the presence of their history. What these Machupiccheños tried to come to grips with was the fact that Machu Picchu is of vital importance to the state, and that they in this relationship are disposable. The suspicion that the move to Cusco was a plot, the remarks about being eliminated or arrested along with the morbid humor about the assassination of the "crazy" members of Frente all reflect fear and awareness that the government would see their intentions as too transgressive.

There was a sense among the participants that a "critical distance" between permissible activity and justification for violence from the state had been breached. By initiating a stoppage, they would bring an important moneymaking engine of the government and private interests to a halt, not to mention attract negative media attention. For that reason it was necessary through their conversations and interactions to advance the rationale that it was the authorities that broke the spirit of the talks, not they.

The state, business interests, intellectuals and labor banked their hopes on a kind of "El Dorado." Strong was the sense that a single resource could do so much for the economy and the nation. In addition, the negative press coverage helped to discredit the protestors' cause by framing them as irrational, and as holding back national progress. Many Machupiccheños were not so different in terms of the hopes that tourism revenues could provide, but they do live there and that prompted a fair amount of hesitation and criticism from many other Peruvians: "What are they doing there?" or even "What right do they have to be there?" were common questions. In fact, outside of Cusco and the regional area, many Peruvians I encountered were surprised to learn that people live and make a life in the Sanctuary, that it constitutes a political district.

THE STOPPAGE

On the morning of the stoppage about thirty protestors, mostly Frente and their close supporters, gathered at the juncture between the train tracks and the bus road that leads to the Citadel. The rows of artisan stalls along the road, normally filled with ceramics, t-shirts and other cloth goods were bare, appearing as wooden skeletons. The artisans/vendors arrived, carrying plastic bottles, partially filled with pebbles, to use as rattles. Eber beat his drum and sounded the *pututu* (seashell horn); they chanted: *The people united will never be defeated! (¡El pueblo unido jamás será vencido!).* The crowd grew quickly to about seventy people as they made their way along the train tracks, inspecting whether the restaurants had closed in support of the stoppage. The train platform, usually crammed with chairs and tables and bustling with tourists looking for a meal, was vacant. The group settled across from the PeruRail ticket office just outside the plaza by the train tracks, and as the crowd continued to grow so did the police presence.

The protestors stayed within the legal requirements by notifying the regional authorities of their stoppage. At the same time PeruRail had pressured the Cusco Prefect to terminate the stoppage, but the prefect refused their request, invoking the residents' constitutional right to protest. PeruRail appeared to comply with the stoppage, suspending arrival and departure services. Nevertheless, on the day of the protest they had scheduled a 5 PM departure train. Was this an act of provocation? How could the protestors stop the train without blocking the tracks and hence breaking the law? Police in riot gear took up positions behind the train yard fence.

Oscar spoke over the megaphone to inform the crowd of the national media interest in their protest. He noted the hypocrisy of PeruRail changing the schedule even as they informed media sources of their support and willingness to cooperate with the Machupiccheños. Oscar declared that if the state authorities did not contact them with resolutions they would continue the stoppage indefinitely. People shook their rattles, beat their drums, sounded the pututu, and held up banners against privatization, such as "Fight Against Privatization" (La Lucha contra Privatización) and "Enough of Privatization" (Basta de privatización). The participants commenced a march through the Pueblo, with police tagging behind. Raúl took over the megaphone: *¡Esta es, aquí está, la respuesta popular! (This is it, here it is, the people's response).* They circled the town (see figure 6.1), pausing momentarily in various locations to speak of abuses. One such pause was above the Pueblo near the entrance to the hot springs. On the way down and through Plaza Manco Capac, about 200 people descended like a long snake. Again they passed the PeruRail office; many defiantly rang the train signal cord as they went by.

On the road to the Citadel the group suddenly encountered a line of police in helmets and riot gear. The protestors marched forward. The police stayed firm, batons in hand. The protestors continued. The police buttressed their formation. The protestors got closer. The police stared ahead with hard faces. The two groups were now face-to-face. The tension was released, either by command or established orders of the day, when the police parted and let the group pass. Although the protestors were at least a good kilometer away from the Citadel, and in the valley below it, the police were poised to prevent them from even going in that direction. Apparently, the police surrendered the path only when it was clear the protestors were not attempting to bring their demonstration to the Citadel of Machu Picchu.

The protestors then set up their demonstration at the train yard and were determined not to let the 5 PM train depart. Oscar warned them not to block the train or the tracks so they moved to the sides of the track. Not long after the protestors settled at the train yard Officer Martin arrived with word that a tourist had fallen from a path on Mt. Huayna Picchu and needed to be medically evacuated as soon as possible to the hospital either in Cusco or Urubamba. Oscar and the officer rushed over to the medical station; I followed closely behind. There, a young Irish tourist lay strapped to a stretcher to immobilize her back from further injury. Oscar assured her in competent English that everything possible would be done to get her to a hospital; he assured her that there would be no resistance against a departing train. Oscar also personally assured the police as well

Figure 6.1. Photo of protest march during the pueblo stoppage. The front banner denounces privatization and plans to build a cable car (May 2002). (Photo taken by Pellegrino Luciano)

as PeruRail that an emergency train wagon would be met with no resistance on the part of the protestors. Back at the train yard gate Oscar instructed the crowd of the situation, and they complied, further clearing the area of banners that might be taken as a blockage. Yet PeruRail delayed evacuation for over an hour. A Canadian woman, the tour coordinator for the injured party's tour group, approached the protestors accompanied by police. Looking rather pale in the face, she appealed to the protestors to please not block the train as her client needed urgent medical assistance. The demonstrators looked at her somewhat dumbfounded as they had never intended to block the train, and close to an hour had gone by from the time they assured authorities that the train would have free passage because of the emergency. Suspicions grew among the protestors, especially when it was discovered that some tourists were beginning to congregate a quarter of a mile down the tracks. The crowd grew skeptical, believing that PeruRail was trying to take advantage of the situation. As they became more impatient, Oscar tried to calm them down by saying, "Don't be provoked by PeruRail." It appeared to the crowd that PeruRail was intentionally misinforming the tour coordinator in stating that the protestors were not permitting the train to pass.[8]

By chance, I encountered the coordinator some two weeks after the incident, and approached her for her account. Although I had somewhat expected she would express hostilities at the protestors, this was not the case. She and her tour group felt that the problem with the delay was caused by PeruRail's unwillingness to send out an otherwise empty train because of the cost. According to her, she was furious that company representatives tried to get the injured tourist and members of her group to sign an affidavit stating that the delay was the fault of the protestors, even before her medical situation was stabilized; nobody signed. Even though few if anyone was privy to all the details as the event occurred, the commander of the riot police[9] had already made up his mind about who was to blame. As the injured tourist was placed onto the train, the commander faced Oscar with arms folded, head turning and eyes rolling. Oscar assured him that the passage had been clear and that PeruRail was at fault for the delay. The commander moved closer to Oscar, a finger pointed at him, and said as he parted company, "You are responsible (Ustedes son responsables)."[10] It was a rare sight to see Oscar appear sheepish and worried, but Regina and other women were less intimidated as they yelled back to the commander that he had no right to speak to them in that tone and manner.

Certainly, the state is not a monolithic entity, but rather its agents often act in contradictory ways and is an example of how under neoliberalism one hand of the state is radically divorced from the other (Bourdieu 1998: 2); one element of the government can uphold the right to protest as another element is involved in repressing it. In placing much more weight on economic laws of the market, neoliberal principles offer a way out for governing officials handling political dissent. When resources are privatized the state removes itself as arbitrator of those resources, turning political dissent into an attack against the private property of others rather than a dispute with the state's role in creating inequality. The confrontation between state forces and the residents makes apparent how privatization can politically dispossess. The people-power the residents have, to create change, is based on their unique situation to stop the flow of tourism, and bring the tourism economy to a standstill. State authorities will tend to negotiate, since any brutal display of force on their part would run the risk of damaging the commercial image of Machu Picchu as a symbol of man in harmony with nature. Indeed, just a few hours into the stoppage the authorities called Oscar on his cell phone, pleading to Frente to reenter negotiations; they rescheduled a meeting for just two days later.

Frente met with the authorities in Cusco just a couple of days after the stoppage. They mustered the support of most of the townsfolk, leaving the Pueblo virtually empty as hundreds joined in a march through the streets of Cusco and on to the regional office. The problems in Machu Picchu had by then received world media attention. As can be expected, one could hear a diversity of commentaries among the spectators: "The people of Machu Picchu are too tranquil, they don't know how to protest"; "The people of Machu Picchu are always causing problems with tourism"; and other off-the-cuff variations of "the people are right or wrong."

Despite the march, the upshot of the meetings was that the authorities again had few decisions and provided the protestors with no resolutions to their problems. However, it succeeded in arranging for Frente to move discussions higher up in the central government and arranged meetings with officials at the national offices in the capital Lima along with representatives of Orient Express.

NOTES

1. Chiriuchu, a Quechua term referring to eight cold dishes of food. As a Cusco specialty, it is specifically eaten for the festival of Corpus Christi, but of late it has also become a dish for any sort of special occasion.

2. As a point of interest to the reader, this sentence by Adolfo about "changing the stage" (cambio de escenario) motivated me to consider Goffman's notions of back/front stage as a form of analysis.

3. "Lugar Común," by Augusto Elmore, *Caretas,* May 2, 2002, Edición 1719.

4. "Aguas Hirvientes," by Alberto Sanchez Aizcorbe, *Caretas,* May 16, 2002, Edición 1721.

5. "Niky Express: Nueva y Espectacular Manera de Llegar a Machu Picchu," *Caretas,* May 9, 2002, Edición 1720.

6. While I cannot be certain, Héctor was apparently alluding to the way the Peruvian media were implicated in a bribery plot orchestrated by ex-president Fujimori's spy chief Vladimiro Montesinos.

7. I am not sure why Oscar uses the word "democracy." I do not know exactly what he means by it, but my interpretation is that he means to use it similarly to the metaphor of "spirit," as in "the spirit of the dialogue."

8. Video recordings provide evidential documentation of the protestors' lawful response from the moment Oscar was informed of the accident and his prompt reaction as well as the residents clearing the train track area so as not to appear to be blocking the passage of the train.

9. Not to be confused with the *comisario.*

10. The statement was largely made in the context of a warning should there be any medical ramifications for the injured tourist on account of the delay. The issue was eventually dismissed as it became clear that the tourist's medical condition was stabilized.

SEVEN

Sweet Dreams and Accommodations

> Do you think other pueblos like Arequipa survive only by tourism, I don't think so! We have to fight, maybe do a hunger strike.
>
> —Chela, Machupicchu Pueblo

> What are we going to do, fight against them forever? I don't want to fight for all my life.
>
> —Margarita, Machupicchu Pueblo

Under neoliberalism, national heritage monuments are primarily appraised in monetary values as economic assets in a world economy. Conservation agencies in protected areas are often steered to protect capital investments, even as the state depends on such places for the continued cultivation of national sentiment (Harvey 2005: 85; Breglia 2006: 17). The Sanctuary of Machu Picchu simultaneously represents Peruvian identity as it does competitiveness and individual gain. The aggressive push for market solutions as the only viable course for success shapes desires, even for those who fight against it. As I hope I've shown throughout this ethnography, the organizers of the protest are too shaped by these desires and their class interests. But for them this produces a contradictory social image compared to the public personas they had committed themselves to as opponents of privatization. The political and economic potential of Machu Picchu are a source of dreaming for a better future across class divides, but those dreams also intermingle with insecurity and fear brought about by the state's determination to serve direct foreign capital. The lives and actions of people who live in Machu Picchu show the class-contradictory ways neoliberalism shapes subjectivity, and social relationships.

After the stoppage and throughout the month of June 2002, news about anti-privatization riots in the city of Arequipa filtered into Machu Picchu. Many watched images of protestors hurling rocks at the police on

TVs in restaurants and other public areas, making for lively discussions. Two people were killed in the clashes and a state of emergency was declared in the region. In addition, there was a two-day national-level stoppage in support of Arequipa and the fight against privatization. In the city of Cusco, as in Arequipa, protestors started a hunger strike in the Plaza de Armas. Here was certainly an opportunity to articulate local protest in Machu Picchu to wider national dissent against the drive towards neoliberal policies. In town, I found that the reaction to the images and development of protests at the national level, though mixed, were generally supportive of the protestors in Arequipa. Chela and Héctor expressed their left politics, assumed the risks and were far more prone than others to join the larger movement against privatization.

Yet, in Machu Picchu neither demonstration nor participation was planned. Oscar, as leader of Frente, did nothing to sway the Machupiccheños to participate in the national stoppage. For him, the current struggles against PeruRail and Sanctuary Lodge were local problems, problems that should stay within the confines of the district and Sanctuary. In effect, it was the first time since the Machu Picchu protests began that he argued to separate their struggle from the wider anti-privatization engagements across Peru. When I asked Oscar for his reasons he maintained that his rationale was based on his knowledge of the political figures behind the national stoppage and their alleged motives. Oscar was a supporter of the Toledo regime, and his position was that the Toledo government was floundering under the pressure of all the anti-privatization protests taking place in Peru. He felt the government might be on the verge of collapse. His view was that it would benefit ex-president Alan Garcia and his APRA political party, and argued that APRA was behind the protests in Arequipa. Alan Garcia did again ultimately become president in Peru's 2006 elections. However, Toledo would have four years in office still ahead of him. Oscar had rescaled the protest in Machu Picchu around his own political party affiliations, and his aspirations to become the next district mayor of Machu Picchu. And indeed, he ran for and won subsequent mayoral elections after my fieldwork stay in 2002.[1] Despite Toledo's privatization push, Oscar apparently chose to support his party rather than one he opposes, despite his anti-privatization stance. Oscar's position illustrates how, as David Harvey contends, local mobilizations "constantly intermingle" with broader political movements, but despite the need for organizing on a larger level, often break from them for their own local material and political interests (Harvey 2001: 191). These shifts reveal the common human contradictions of lived experience. The very wealthy of the world have the privilege of defending their class interests, all the while appearing as helping the poor through "charity," "donations" and other purported "good-hearted" offers. The middle class and the poor have less privilege in this respect and face a more complicated set of not only struggles but also seductions for improving themselves economically. Neoliberal ideology cultivated ecotourism and nature conservation projects, as it has in everyday life, around a sentiment of limitless gain or as a "metaphor" of an "ever-growing pie" with a sufficient slice for everyone (Igoe and Brockington 2007: 434). As I grew to know many of the mobilizers in Machu Picchu I was interested to see if or how people juggling the temptations of neoliberals' ideological promises of wealth clashed with their public commitments. Discrepancies in the "performance of self" constrain actors from easily moving away from protesting privatization, as desires for wealth become incongruous with their past performances and public identities. Even if "life makes hypocrites of us all," it does not make it as we please; there are restrictions and factors that shape how one's public image aligns with class interest.

While Machupiccheños struggled to make sense of the power relations they confronted, they were also forced to confront their own contradictions. Though the mobilization opposed large big-money corporations, most townsfolk owned commercial enterprises ranging from market posts to mid-level family-owned businesses; it was no surprise that they wanted market opportunities. They criticized big business based on its size and power, using terms like "monster" to distinguish the large from their own level and participation in the economy; even so, many had their own growth aspirations. The protestors may have been against neoliberal privatization policies, "*los neoliberalistas*" as Margarita would say, but most were not against market prospects, or for that matter capitalism. The Machupiccheños, like people everywhere, differed in just exactly what role profit should have in their lives, and they too took different positions on the idea of a free-market economy. Recall that for Oscar, investments were fine if capitalism was "socially responsible."

I bring this account to a finish, as abrupt as ethnographic endings often are, by focusing on the dreams and imagined futures of two prominent women in the struggles of Machu Picchu. The ethnographer's value, if there be any, is at least to note the humanity of it all—to show the intricacies of people, unforeseeably fragmented, spirited yet prosaic as they struggle to produce their lives as coherent and dignified, and as this case would have it, what neoliberalism meant to them living in this highly charged political landscape. In separate events, Margarita and Chela provide different perspectives on questions about the nature of their protest and to what degree one's individual economic interests are subordinated to such a protracted struggle. What is the ultimate goal of the protest and where are its limits?

In a small gathering at Margarita's hotel, Frente members and some of the leaders of the different associations discussed their plans for Lima. Margarita began by proudly reading her email communications with "Mr. Abraham Garcia," a high-ranking official for Orient Express in Lima. Mr. Garcia had asked Margarita for Frente's travel itinerary to the capital where they were to next meet with the state authorities. He invited her to have dinner with him upon her arrival. Margarita told the group that she declined the invitation because of a conflict of interest, but she informed him of the date and time of the group's arrival, and stated that Frente could meet with him rather than just her alone. She noted that she replied asking him if he could arrange a meeting with the prominent members of Lima's tourism industry as a way of helping to promote the restaurants and hotels of Machu Picchu. The group reacted strongly against her for asking favors from a man with whom they were fighting and against whose company they were protesting. Margarita defended her actions: "But why is everything demonized, everything exaggerated?" she asked. After listening to what was being said, Oscar jumped into the conversation. "Look you can't trust these people . . . for them everything is about money, they don't understand that what we want is that they don't do business at the entrance of the Sanctuary, and that they come down [from the Citadel] and compete with the pueblo." In effect for Oscar it was about making competition fair. Oscar recounted a story of Sanctuary Lodge offering him an office in their hotel for his work as leader of Frente. Oscar said he rejected their offer. "I already know the talk, eventually you'll learn also that, excuse me for the vulgar comment, 'the mouth eats and the ass pays.'" There was raucous laughter. The idiomatic expression conveyed the notion that Orient Express was only using Margarita and the present offer would have later reprisals. As Margarita's example shows, credibility as a mobilizer can easily be questioned. Oscar emphasized that he did not take the offer, perhaps addressing accusations against him that were buzzing from the small talk of the town of him "taking offers" or "selling out." These interactions illustrate how the mobilizers too had an image and public persona to maintain and defend. They also had dreams of financial growth.

Margarita retorted defensively but was being honest about her position, "No, no, you don't understand, the only thing I want is to take advantage of his offer and his willingness to speak to us." The group, however, was concerned about the class realities between the townsfolk and Orient Express. "You can never confide in them," Oscar said, "because in the first place they are at another economic level . . . that's only their strategy and they know from where to penetrate . . . We're never going to be at their level, you have to understand that!" "It's true Marga," Marina said, "'the mouth eats and the *behind* pays,'" softening up Oscar's more vulgar phrasing. "It's that we are fighting against them and if they do us any favors we are going to be obligated to them." Regina quieted down and then agreed. "It's better not to owe anyone anything." Feeling defensive, Margarita still resisted. "But I'm only responding [to Garcia's email] because he is expressing the will to be on good terms with the pueblo." Surprised at Margarita's excuse, Regina blankly pointed out that she was just being manipulated. Margarita continued defending her position, "But what I want is that he [Sanctuary Lodge] integrates himself into our [hotel and restaurant] Association." The others, jolted by her statement as naïve, responded with "are you crazy" and comments to that effect. Margarita was genuine about her economic interests and stubbornly stood fast to her position. She exclaimed, "You see everything as evil." "Look Marga," said Oscar, "what you'll realize is that after he's integrated into your association, little by little he'll get you removed as president and then he'll be in charge, leaving you with neither space nor vote." To which the discouraged Margarita uttered, "What are we going to do, fight against them forever? I don't want to fight for all my life."

The different socioeconomic realities between small-scale entrepreneurs in Machu Picchu and Belmond/Orient Express are often summarized by the expression "the big are big and the small are small." Many in the tourism professions of Cusco note the history of the city tourist agencies. When the large agencies of Lima and elsewhere entered the tourism associations of Cusco, they ended up taking over the industry. Marina reiterated that expression, "The big are never going to be part of us little ones, and they are never going to be part of the pueblo." Yet Margarita still argued against them, "Why such resentment? If we don't unite [with them] we're never going to achieve anything, for the rest of our lives we're going to be in one fight after another."

The group pondered over the postures of the big companies. I found it interesting to hear what actions would show district support from the Orient Express. For Oscar, if Orient Express were friendly toward the economic interests of the townsfolk they would "be respectful" and at least add another train wagon for the porters carrying tourist equipment on the Inca Trail. "But no, they say 'I'll put in another wagon if I'm exempt from taxes.' . . . If Garcia were friendly he would have stopped his commercial activity around Sanctuary Lodge [or allowed the artisans to do business there]." The townsfolk had been struggling for over a year without any cooperation from the company. As Oscar noted about Garcia who now wished to join the pueblo associations only after a long struggle and after they had gained the attention of authorities in Lima, "What kind of cooperation is that?" The main point from their perspective was for Orient Express and the conservation authorities to stop "rigging" their economy, and to make competition fair, an acceptance of the ideals of neoliberalism but a challenge to its hypocrisies that often goes unquestioned or normalized as business as usual. Regina warned Margarita by addressing her as leader of her association rather than as a member of Frente. "You, [Ms.] Hotel and Restaurant Association, don't ask them for anything!" Margarita was unwavering though. "I'm only taking advantage of his offer," she said. Regina chastised her for supporting PeruRail and Sanctuary Lodge, coming close to accusing her of being a traitor. She declared, "You're putting down the pueblo and making them out to be good." The conversation quieted down, and the group turned to their travel plans to Lima, but they remained strongly at odds with Margarita's attitude.

In contrast to Margarita, Chela, the president of the artisans and small-sellers' association, provides a different take on the pueblo struggle, what it meant and what their goals were. If Margarita wished to free herself from her commitment to the protests, and bring her public persona in line with her desires for greater profit for her own business, Chela wished to move in a more radical social direction. That same day, Chela chastised the members of her artisan association for not getting more involved in the struggles against Orient Express. For Chela, the protests involved a much greater willingness to engage in a long-term struggle of resistance against capitalism. In a loud and angry voice, which was highly unusual for the soft-spoken Chela, she said:

> Everything is tourism, for me it's an embarrassment to say that we only live from tourism. . . . It's embarrassing to hear the gringos say that 'this pueblo lives on my money.' Do you think other pueblos like Arequipa survive only by tourism, I don't think so! We too [like Arequipa] must fight; maybe do a hunger strike. . . . When will we stop begging Sanctuary Lodge? Now, this meeting was to hand out the photo IDs and only for that reason you all have come. . . . We have not done anything against its privatization. . . . For how long are we going to be hanging on to the tourists just waiting for the high season? My companions, let's search for alternatives!

Chela's more progressive social stand largely fell on deaf ears. Many of the artisans and vendors were poor and in financial hardship; they struggled to secure their own livelihoods. What, if not promote the sale of their products, was the president of the artisan association supposed to do? Chela's stance for a more radical position did not resonate with their needs. Their own dreams of economic improvement had become invested in obtaining an ID card that permitted them to sell their products legally in the town.

The comparison of these two prominent women of the pueblo is not meant to praise or criticize one over the other; both participated tirelessly in demonstrations, and in courageously challenging the authorities and even police. Margarita and Chela both looked at the same social horizon but invoked different futures and directions. For Margarita, the question was how long were they to continue to engage in protests. For Chela, it was how long could they hold back. For Margarita, the goal of the protest was more akin to opening opportunities to do big business, and metaphorically speaking, to "run with the wolves." Chela's, on the other hand, conveyed much more of a social vision of change, of searching for alternatives to neoliberalism. As president of her association she worked with the architect of the new artisan market (as described earlier in the encounter with the Finnish Ambassador), to help redesign the project to include many more artisans and small merchants otherwise excluded from the original project; she met with the Ambassador as well to emphasize the unfairness of excluding so many people, rather than just defending her own interests in the market. The point is that different people saw their protest as having different ends, and different ends leading to different directions; mobilizations end as do relationships. The maintenance of credibility by the protest leaders was more complex than simply winning the approval of residents in the way of "us," the Machupiccheños, versus "them," the corporate and governmental elite. Perhaps, had Frente imposed a more radical position against neoliberal ideology from the start of their protests, rather than Oscar's "socially responsible capitalism" approach, then they might have connected their struggles to the broader struggles that were taking place around the country, but it is unlikely that they would have built broad-based support from the restaurant and hotel sectors, or from the small-scale entrepreneurs such as the artisans and artisan sellers. The seductive power of neoliberal ideology cultivates desires for wealth and exaggerates opportunities across class difference, but also as we have seen throughout this extended essay, the neoliberal state which combines corporate interest with governing authority cultivates greater fear, leaving people feeling easily threatened and distrustful. Despite the willingness of Frente to negotiate, traveling to Lima to meet government authorities left the members of Frente nervous, divided in their interests and goals, and very uncertain about how authorities would react to their protests and demands. As Marina said, "God knows what they will do to us in Lima."

Accounting for the complexity and differentiation of the actors involved forces anthropology to resist the grand narrative explanations that fail to fully appreciate the subjectivity and contradictions people experience under neoliberalism. The protests began with the issue of defending political autonomy, property rights and the protection of the local economy from large capital investments and state control. Throughout the course of the dispute, the Machupiccheños questioned the authority of other nations such as Finland to make decisions in their district because of foreign debt agreements with Peru. They dealt with the entrenched practices of their government that provoke memories of violence and fear, and reproduce a climate of distrust where no one can be sure of a person's allegiance.

What I hope to have shown throughout this book is how neoliberal policies were brought to life, enacted and performed at a critical juncture in Peru's economic shift. Residents of Machu Picchu live in a protected area that despite the popular representations of the landscape is a competitive capitalist environment that usurps their energy and confidence, manipulates existing insecurities, and arouses their suspicion of state authorities, and yet simultaneously cultivates desires and dreams for wealth in a place where they make not just a living but a life; the Machupicchenos struggle to define their district of Machu Picchu as a place to live, a way of making a livelihood as well as something to conserve. For many, the right to make a living in the Sanctuary is based on the fact that it is their political district, giving them the jurisdictional right to live there; only second are they inhabitants of a protected area. But to accomplish their objectives, the Machupicchenos must, in their various ways, adjust to the strict regulations of the Sanctuary by means of tactical maneuvers, while maintaining an image of compliance. As a population, the inhabitants of the Sanctuary constantly risk being discredited by conservation authorities. The Machupicchenos are continuously blamed and stigmatized for not having the appropriate identity meant for the Sanctuary, or for destroying the ecology. The state authorities use heritage to erode the civil status of residents and control land for the benefit of whoever brings in the most money. Corporate investments in the Sanctuary to a large degree define what is good for the Sanctuary, an ethnographic illustration of David Harvey's observation that neoliberalism involves capital accumulation by dispossession. Dispossession entails the state ensuring that direct foreign investments are protected above the interests of their own citizenry, though that process is neither neat nor complete. I have suggested in this study that for the state, favoring corporate interests over their citizenry comes with a price. For those citizens who experience the contradiction it is not uncommon to find the accompanying attitude that the potential for democracy in Peru wanes with the expansion of privatization as it further commercializes every aspect of life. For the Machupicchenos we see from the attempt to form a pueblo train company to compete against PeruRail to the acceptance of a commoditized identity and the implementation of a photo ID system, life in the district is increasingly disciplined, and political participation increasingly governed, by a perspective initiated by small-scale entrepreneurs as a response to corporate intrusions. For some the outcome is better than for others, as the ambulantes who are excluded from making a legitimate living and face much harder conditions show. Just as dispossession of the local entrepreneurs involves discrediting and blame, economically better-positioned residents can pass blame along. Each rung in the class hierarchy is a group of people that live by a different shade of dispossession.

On an early July evening, as people began departing from a town meeting, women from the artisans and small-sellers' association gathered outside in the main plaza. They had their new photo IDs in hand, laughing at the way their faces came out looking like mug shots.

I returned to Machu Picchu in the summer of 2007 and noticed changes taking place. Occasionally, I would chance upon some of the Machupicchenos in Cusco over the years when I had the fortune of returning to Peru, and they would speak of great changes taking place. However, the challenges of life in completing my studies, job searches, marriage and a child meant that it wasn't until August of 2016 when I had the opportunity to return and speak to some of the residents who were active in the rebuilding of Machupicchu Pueblo. It was emotional, as I imagine is the case for many ethnographers, to return to where one spent time getting to know people through the fieldwork experience. I was astounded at the changes and found it to be a very different place from when I lived there. Machupicchu Pueblo was no longer that "frontier town" it appeared to be fourteen years earlier. The town was no longer just a transit depot for travelers but a destination incorporated into the touristic experience of visiting the Citadel of Machu Picchu. The population of the town had grown considerably, estimated at approximately 7,000, now over double the 2002 number.[2] I could see a large influx of capital investments from a variety of sources. There were banks and ATM machines. Belmond/Orient Express continued its hotel and train operations; the transportation economy was now shared with another train company that some such as Margarita claim to allegedly be a sister company disguising the continued monopoly of transportation. There were also new national- and regional-level hotel chains such as Casa Andina. The Finnish projects were complete and the town had potable water and a well-built artisan market that was redesigned to be more spacious and inclusive than the original plan. Much of the infrastructural change was founded on municipal and residential capital; even some of the national chains operated their hotels on rented residential space.

When I met Margarita, she looked untouched by the years, still fashionable in dress and demeanor, as she greeted me with a big smile and saying, "our CNNNNN man," recalling the nickname. We sat in her hotel where years ago the conversation above about the limits of the protests took place. She confessed to me that she looked back at the period with some nostalgia. "The pueblo had never been as unified," she said. She spoke of how Oscar had turned authoritarian as mayor, imposing his policies without feedback and stifling any dissent. "He used the *serenazgo* like spies to inform him of people criticizing his administration," she said.[3] After the Lima trip Margarita gradually distanced herself from the Frente group and was not interested in assuming a municipal post after Oscar won the election. True to her position described in the above debate, Margarita focused on her hotel business which was doing quite well; it had expanded and now had a professional staff. She nevertheless felt that the mobilization and the protests had achieved what no mayor was able to achieve in the history of the town and district. "We were always left abandoned [by the central government]," she said. What they had succeeded in doing, from her perspective, was getting the central government to stop pretending they didn't exist as a jurisdiction or hoping that they would disappear. "You remember how the town was a chaos," she said to me. According to Margarita, one of the major outcomes resulting from their trip to Lima in 2002 was their municipality receiving a 1.2-million-dollar grant from the government.

The town had been "beautified," as residents remarked, with stone works and statues representing Inca style and history, noticeably absent in the town during my fieldwork. The municipal building itself had been reconstructed using a stone facade. A large statue of Pachacútec now stood in a remodeled Plaza Manco Capac. The stadium that was under construction was completed, and in addition connected to an entire sports and exercise complex. Formerly, the town barrios were unpaved, especially in living areas as opposed to the plaza and principal avenue where hotels and restaurants were concentrated and that led to the hot springs, but now the whole town was largely enclosed in concrete and stonework. The town had commodified its image to a much greater extent, an issue that as we recall above was what conservation authorities preferred as the proper identity, but that the residents often eschewed as being artificial and not reflective of who they were as a community. Also, Frente failed in changing the law that prompted their collective response against the collusion of state and foreign investments. Their effort was to have the town recognized as an "urban zone," exempting them from property restrictions; however, they did not change the conservation mandates. Margarita recalled how in Lima, government officials reassured them that despite possession status of land, their infrastructural investments were secure. She and other hotel proprietors such as Emilio were less perturbed about not having property titles and far more confident that their homes or establishments would never be expropriated or at least that they could never lose their investment capital. Once the image of the community articulated with the market, dispossession appeared to be less of a threat.

Noticeably absent were ambulantes, but as anticipated, there were many new faces in town and children back then are now adults. There was clear upward social mobility of some of the people I knew. For instance, Quintina, who previously sold chicken and fries from a small cart in the Plaza Manco Capac, now ran two food posts in the renovated central market. I hung out with her in the market, reminiscing about the old days and chatting about the changes. Her daughter Sharon, twelve at the time of my fieldwork but now with a family of her own, still worked alongside her mother in the plaza in one of the posts, busily attending to customers.

I recognized Guido, though he not me initially. By chance, we again met along the banks of a river, although a different one from our first conversation years ago along the Vilcanota; this time we met by the Aguas Calientes. He had left Machupicchu Pueblo only some three years earlier in pursuit of work and had recently returned with his fiancée to start his own business venture, a campground for hikers. As we chatted he expressed the same amazement at the social and infrastructural changes, noting how he got lost walking through now unfamiliar streets. He described the transformation as an "explosion." All the town barrios were now full of locally owned hotels and restaurants, the majority geared to foreign tourists rather than the once common local "house" restaurants serving residents or locals; many converted their homes into business establishments for tourism. The developments were in fact incremental, but as Guido's own surprise suggests, there had been exponential growth in the last few years. According to government estimates and park officials, Machu Picchu began averaging over a million visitors annually, 2,500–5,000 per day since 2012 depending on the season. Even on the low end it surpasses World Heritage UNESCO limits. There was a much larger migrant labor force presence in the town. The old establishments of hotels and restaurants, no longer simply run by family along with one or two workers, were now staffed and even managed by hired employees. The labor needs in town were so great that they lacked sufficient living quarters to house people. The residents preferred using their available living space for tourists rather than for housing workers. I found some workers living in substandard conditions in makeshift unsanitary constructions with no running water, out of public view at one far end of the town.

Emilio, who was not an original Frente member but certainly a principal supporter of the mobilization, had done quite well economically. We sat inside his now finished multistory hotel talking about the meaning of the protests and the stoppage of 2002. He scoffed at the past, "It was a different time, a different reality." For Emilio, the bus consortium that generated funds for the municipality, but was still somewhat of a fledgling company for resident investors during my fieldwork, was now a major engine of wealth for those investors; Emilio was one of them. He told me of their success but was coy about details. "Go see for yourself," he said, referring to the number of tourists standing in line to take a bus to the Citadel. The tourist line snaked some 200 meters along the newly stone-paved promenade along the Aguas Calientes River. The past was different for Emilio. Back then they were battling Orient Express, the project to build a cable car, the privatization of the train and other incursions into their economy. They battled conservation agencies and even plans to move the town population to a different location entirely. They fought and they won, from his perspective. Emilio was now against protest or conducting a stoppage to address problems with conservation agencies or corporate favoritism. He made clear his position against Oscar's continued political endeavors as participant in a different Frente now organized at a larger provincial level.[4] Oscar was in Urubamba, according to Emilio, behind a stoppage that now protested in a certain irony the monopoly of the bus consortium in Machu Picchu, among other things, attempting to move it out of the district and to Urubamba in order to reallocate control and funds of the buses to the provincial level.[5] Emilio made disparaging comments, making clear he had no trust or support in Oscar politically, but certainly it was not in his economic interests either. Emilio was always an intelligent businessman but also as before, a community leader. He was aware of the need to address the living conditions of the migrant labor force. He supported and even backed educational projects for the district. In fact the town had made considerable investments in the schools, supplementing teacher salaries out of municipal funds. For Emilio, it was more about a question of trust and credibility. What he expressed in his opposition to protests and stoppages and Oscar is reflective of a current common sentiment in Peru about anti-privatization politics from presidents Toledo to Humala—against empty, politically left discourse that prove to be mainly self-serving.[6] It's reflective of a popular sentiment that helped usher in the current president of Peru on his largely neoliberal agenda in 2016. Oscar's politics had remained remarkably consistent, at least in image, as a center-left fighter against neoliberal greed. Nevertheless, the original Frente members that helped give rise to Oscar's political vocation had long disbanded. Oscar's tenure as mayor was fraught with tensions and accusations of abuse by the former group and others that ultimately led to mistrust and opposition from the "old guard" of the town. In 2007 Oscar lost as the incumbent candidate but was nevertheless reelected in 2010; his second term resulted in a recall election after 22 months in office.[7] Yet, he was undeniably a key player in the mobilization strategies that first got the attention of the Sanctuary authorities and the Peruvian government described throughout this book. In addition, it was also his mayoral administration that carried out some of the projects to turn the town into a more commercially attractive place.

Regardless, Chela and Héctor, for instance, expressed disdain and were no longer on speaking terms with him. We sat in a courtyard one evening outside their same modest home full of tools and artisan materials. I spoke with the still charming couple who years earlier had danced as Inca royalty; they greeted me with a hug but chastised me for being gone so long. Chela looked back at the protests with strong feelings. Once Oscar was in office it became clear to her that he had used them for his own political ambitions. The disagreements between them and Oscar over his authoritarian style of making decisions about the town had gotten personal even after his first election. Chela conveyed resentment over how Oscar received unwarranted credit for the accomplishments really made by the artisans and sellers, mainly women. They formed the support base for the mobilization, stoppage and his election. "It was the Sindicato de Artesanos y Pequenos Comerciantes de Machu Picchu," she declared, adding how "Oscar would have never been able to do it without them. They struggled, took time off from their work and demonstrated." Chela was animated but still in a gentle soft-spoken voice advised me, "That's what you should let people know."

NOTES

1. According to Peru's National Office of Electoral Processes (ONPE) 2002 Mayoral District elections, out of 8 candidates Oscar won 35.652% of the vote; the incumbent mayor held 11.304%. For full results see https://www.web.onpe.gob.pe/modElecciones/downloads/RyM2002/Resultados.pdf.

2. There were 8,332 residents in the District of Machu Picchu based on the 2015 National Census. The last census to provide the distribution between urban and rural populations for districts was in 2007, which showed a distribution in the District at 85% urban. See Insituto Nacional de Estadisticas e Informatica (www.inei.gob.pe). Assuming the percentage distribution remained the same for 2015, the town would currently have 7,083 registered permanent residents, which is more than double the 2002 figures. These figures should be understood as relative in that it indicates the number of registered residents not the actual number of people living in the town. In addition, these figures do not account for long-term migrant workers.

3. The serenazgo are a security and vigilance patrol in Peru operated at the municipal level.

4. Though I spoke to Oscar by phone and we attempted to meet for an interview, he cancelled, and under my time restrictions, we never met.

5. The event was billed in the national press as the first conflict for Peru's newly elected President Kuczynski and his neoliberal agenda. See *La Republica*, "Paro en Urubamba, el primer conflicto de PPK," August 3, 2016. This topic is part of ongoing research and I am not able to adequately discuss these developments here.

6. It is not my intention to imply that an anti-privatization platform is limited to the politics of these presidencies but to call attention to neoliberal politics in the post-Fujimori era as discussed in the introduction and in subsequent chapters. It should be noted that even President Alberto Fujimori won the 1990 elections that ushered him into a decade-long administration, partially on an anti-privatization platform that distinguished him from his contender Mario Vargas Llosa who ran on a pro-privatization agenda.

7. Note to reader: A mayoral term in Peru is 4 years. According to Peru's National Office of Electoral Processes (ONPE), the recall elections took place on October 23, 2012. The results were 1,657 votes in favor of recall; 1,229 against it. See https://www.web.onpe.gob.pe/modElecciones/elecciones/elecciones2012/Resultados-Ubigeo-Distrital.html.

References

Alvarez, Sonia E., Evelina Dagnino, and Arturo Escobar. 1998. "Introduction: The Cultural and the Political in Latin American Social Movements." In *Cultures of Politics, Politics of Cultures: Re-Visioning Latin American Social Movements*, edited by Sonia E. Alvarez, Evelina Dagnino, and Arturo Escobar, 1–29. Boulder, CO: Westview Press.

Barlett, Peggy. 1999. "Introduction." In *Globalization and the Rural Poor in Latin America*, edited by William M. Loker. Boulder, CO: Lynne Rienner.

Bartra, Roger. 1974. *Estructura Agraria y Clases Sociales en Mexico*. Mexico D.F.: Ediciones Era.

Basilico, Mathew, Jonathan Weigal, Anjali Motgi, Jacob Bor, and Salman Keshavjee. 2013. "Health for All? Competing Theories and Geopolitics." In *Reimagining Global Health: An Introduction*, edited by Paul Farmer, Arthur Kleinman, Jim Yong Kim, and Mathew Basilico. Los Angeles: University of California Press.

Beatty, John. 1997. "Language and Communication." In *Cross-Cultural Topics in Psychology*, edited by Leonore Loeb Adler and Uwe P. Gielen. Westport, CT: Praeger.

Beatty, John, and Junichi Takahashi. 2001. *Intercultural Communication*. Cincinnati, OH: Atomic Dog.

Bender, Barbara. 1998. *Stonehenge: Making Space*. Oxford: Berg.

Bingham, Alfred. 1989. *Portrait of an Explorer: Hiram Bingham, Discoverer of Machu Picchu*. Ames: Iowa State University Press.

Bingham, Hiram. 1909. *The Journal of an Expedition across Venezuela and Colombia, 1906–1907*. New Haven, CT: Yale Publishing Association.

———. 1911. *Across South America: An Account of a Journey from Buenos Aires by Way of Potosi*. Boston: Houghton Mifflin.

———. 1913. "In the Wonderland of Peru." *National Geographic* April: 387–583.

———. 1913. "The Discovery of Machu Picchu." *Harper's Monthly* 127: 709–719.

———. 1922. *Inca Land: Explorations in the Highlands of Peru*. Boston: Houghton Mifflin.

———. 1930. *Machu Picchu, a Citadel of the Incas*. National Geographic Society. New Haven, CT: Yale University Press.

———. (1948) 1981. *Lost City of the Incas: The Story of Machu Picchu and Its Builders*. Westport, CT: Greenwood Press.

Blim, Michael. 2000. "Capitalism in Late Modernity." *Annual Review of Anthropology* 29: 25–38.

Bonhomme, Julien. 2012. "The Dangers of Anonymity: Witchcraft, Rumor and Modernity in Africa." *HAU: Journal of Ethnographic Theory* 2 (2): 205–233.

Bose, Christine E., and Edna Acosta-Belen, eds. 1995. *Women in the Latin American Development Process*. Philadelphia: Temple University Press.

Bourdieu, Pierre. 1998. *Acts of Resistance: Against the Tyranny of the Market*. New York: The New Press.

———. 2003. *Firing Back: Against the Tyranny of the Market* 2. New York: The New Press.

Bowen, Sally. 2000. *The Fujimori File: Peru and Its President, 1990–2000*. Lima: The Peru Monitor.

Braun, Bruce, and Noel Castree, eds. 1998. *Remaking Reality: Nature at the Millennium*. London: Routledge.

Breglia, Lisa C. 2006. *Monumental Ambivalence: The Politics of Heritage.* Austin: University of Texas Press.

Brunner, Edward. 2001. "The Maasai and the Lion King: Authenticity, Nationalism, and Globalization in African Tourism." *American Ethnologist* 28 (4): 881–908.

Bulmer-Thomas, Victor. 1994. *The Economic History of Latin America since Independence.* Cambridge: Cambridge University Press.

Burke, Kenneth. 1945. *A Grammar of Motives.* New York: Prentice-Hall.

———. 1950. *A Rhetoric of Motives.* Berkeley: University of California Press.

———. 1966. *Language as Symbolic Action: Essays on Life, Literature, and Method.* Berkeley: University of California Press.

Calhoun, Craig. 1998. "The Public Good as a Social and Cultural Project." In *Private Action for the Public Good,* edited by W. Powell and L. Clemens. New Haven, CT: Yale University Press.

Campos, Ramiro. 2004. "Pilgrims, Spectacle, and the Sacred Space of the Inkas: The Geography of Neoliberalism, Monuments and World Tourism in Cusco, Peru." Master's thesis, Hunter College, City University of New York.

Carlotto, Victor. 2001. *Plan para la Mitigacion de Desastres del Poblado de Machu Picchu—Aguas Calientes.* Cusco: Instituto Nacional de Recursos Naturales, Ministerio de Agricultura.

Centro de Estudios Regionales Agrarios Bartolome de Las Casas y Pacifica. 2001. *Diagnostico Participativo del Sector Rural del Santuario Historico Machu Picchu.* Lima: Centro Bartolome de las Casas/Pacifica.

Cernea, Michael M. 2005. "Restriction of Access Is Displacement: A Broader Concept and Policy." *Forced Migration Review* 23: 48–49.

Certeau, Michel de. 1984. *The Practice of Everyday Life.* Berkeley: University of California Press.

Chase, Jacquelyn. 2002. "Introduction: The Spaces of Neoliberalism in Latin America." In *The Spaces of Neoliberalism: Land, Place and Family in Latin America,* edited by Jacquelyn Chase. Bloomfield, CT: Kumarian Press.

Clifford, James. 1997. *Routes: Travel and Translation in the Late Twentieth Century.* Cambridge, MA: Harvard University Press.

Cody, Francis. 2009. "Inscribing Subjects to Citizenship: Petition, Literacy Activism, and the Performativity of Signature in Rural Tamil India." *Cultural Anthropology* 24 (3): 347–380.

Cohen, Daniel. 1984. *Hiram Bingham and the Dream of Gold.* New York: M. Evans.

Colloredo-Mansfeld, Rudi. 2002a. "Don't Be Lazy, Don't Lie, Don't Steal: Community Justice in the Neoliberal Andes." *American Ethnologist* 29 (3): 637–662.

_____. 2002b. "An Ethnography of Neoliberalism: Understanding Competition in Artisan Economies." *Current Anthropology* 43 (1): 113–137.

———. 2009. *Fighting like a Community: Andean Civil Society in an Era of Indian Uprisings.* Chicago: University of Chicago Press.

Comaroff, John L. 1998. "Reflections on the Colonial State, in South Africa and Elsewhere: Factions, Fragments, Facts and Fictions." *Social Identities* 4 (3): 321–361.

Coombe, Rosemary J., and Lindsay M. Weiss. 2015. "Neoliberalism, Heritage Regimes, and Cultural Rights." In *Global Heritage: A Reader,* edited by Lynn Meskell. Malden, MA: Wiley Blackwell.

Coronil, Fernando. 1997. *The Magical State: Nature, Money and Modernity in Venezuela.* Chicago: University of Chicago Press.

Corrigan, Philip, and Derek Sayer. 1985. *The Great Arch: English State Formation as Cultural Revolution.* London: Basil Blackwell.

Cox Hall, Amy. 2012. "Collecting a 'Lost City' for Science: Huaquero Vision and the Yale Peruvian Expeditions to Machu Picchu, 1911, 1912, and 1914–15." *Ethnohistory* 59 (Spring): 293–321.

Crabtree, John. 2002. "The Impact of Neo-liberal Economics on Peruvian Peasant Agriculture." *Journal of Peasant Studies* 29 (3 & 4): 131–161.

Cronon, William, ed. 1996. *Uncommon Ground: Rethinking the Human Place in Nature.* New York: W. W. Norton.

Das, Veena, and Deborah Poole, eds. 2004. *Anthropology in the Margins of the State.* Santa Fe, NM: School of American Research Press.

Degregori, Carlos Ivan. 1990. *Que Deficil Es Ser Dios: Ideologia y Violencia Politica en Sendero Luminoso.* Lima, Peru: El Zorro de Abajo Ediciones.

———. 1997. "After the Fall of Abimael Guzman: The Limits of Sendero Luminoso." In *The Peruvian Labyrinth: Polity, Society, Economy,* edited by Maxwell A. Cameron and Phillip Mauceri. University Park: Pennsylvania State University Press.

de la Cadena, Marisol. 2000. *Indigenous Mestizos: The Politics of Race and Culture in Cusco, Peru, 1919–1991.* Durham, NC: Duke University Press.

de Soto, Hernando. 1989. *The Other Path: The Invisible Revolution in the Third World.* New York: Harper and Row.

Denzin, Norman K. 2003. "Much Ado about Goffman." In *Goffman's Legacy,* edited by A. Javier Trevino. Lanham, MD: Rowman & Littlefield.

Desforges, Luke. 1998. "State Tourism Institutions and Neo-liberal Development: A Case Study of Peru." *Tourism Geographies* 2, no. 2: 177–192.

Durand, Francisco. 1997. "The Growth and Limitations of the Peruvian Right." In *The Peruvian Labyrinth: Polity, Society, Economy,* edited by Maxwell A. Cameron and Phillip Mauceri. University Park: Pennsylvania State University Press.

———. 1998. "Collective Action and the Empowerment of Peruvian Business." In *Organized Business, Economic Change, Democracy in Latin America,* edited by Francisco Durand and Eduardo Silva. Miami, FL: North South Center Press.

Edelman, Marc. 1995. "Rethinking the Hamburger Thesis: Deforestation and the Crisis of Central America's Beef." In *The Social Causes of Environmental Destruction in Latin America,* edited by Michael Painter and William Durham. Ann Arbor: University of Michigan Press.

———. 1999. *Peasants against Globalization: Rural Social Movements in Costa Rica.* Stanford, CA: Stanford University Press.

———. 2001. "Social Movements: Changing Paradigms and Forms of Politics." *Annual Review of Anthropology* 30: 285–317.

Edensor, Tim. 1998. *Tourists at the Taj: Performance and Meaning at a Symbolic Site.* London: Routledge.

Escobar, Arturo. 1995. *Encountering Development: The Making and Unmaking of the Third World.* Princeton, NJ: Princeton University Press.

Featherstone, Mike. 1991. *Consumer Culture and Postmodernism.* London: Sage.

Femenias, Blenda. 1999. "Mapping Race onto Region: Indigenistas and the Creation of Peruvian National Museums." Paper presented at the 98th annual meeting of the American Anthropological Association, Chicago, Illinois, November 17–21.

Ferguson, James, and Akhil Gupta. "Spatializing States: Toward an Ethnography of Neoliberal Governmentality." *American Ethnologist* 29, no. 4: 981–1002.

Flores Ochoa, Jorge A. 1990. *El Cusco: Resistencia y Continuidad.* Cusco: Centro de Estudios Andinos.

———. 1995. "El Turismo Crece, Hay que Estar Preparados: Medio Ambiente y Turismo." *Opciones* 4: 31–33.

———. 1996. "Buscando los Espiritus del Ande: Turismo Mistico en el Qosqo." In *La Tradicion Andina en Tiempo Modernos,* Senri Ethnological Report 5, edited by H. Tomoeda and L. Millones. Osaka: National Museum of Ethnology.

———. 2004. "Contemporary Significance of Machu Picchu." In *Machu Picchu: Unveiling the Mystery of the Incas,* edited by Richard L. Burger and Lucy C. Salazar. New Haven, CT: Yale University Press.

Foucault, Michel. 1977. *Discipline and Punish: The Birth of the Prison.* New York: Vintage Books.

———. 1988. "The Political Technology of Individuals." In *Technologies of the Self,* edited by L. H. Marin, H. Gutman, and P. H. Hutton. Amherst: University of Massachusetts Press.

———. 1991. "Governmentality." In *The Foucault Effect: Studies in Governmentality*, edited by Graham Burchell, Colin Gordon, and Peter Miller. Chicago: University of Chicago Press.

Ganti, Tejaswini. 2014. "Neoliberalism." *Annual Review of Anthropology*. 43: 89–104.

Geertz, Clifford. 1983. *Local Knowledge: Further Essays in Interpretive Anthropology*. New York: Basic Books.

Gill, Lesley. 1994. *Precarious Dependencies: Gender, Class and Domestic Service in Bolivia.* New York: Columbia University Press.

———. 2000. *Teetering on the Rim.* New York: Columbia University Press.

Gledhill, John. 2004. "Neoliberalism." In *A Companion to the Anthropology of Politics*, edited by David Nugent and Joan Vincent. Malden, MA: Blackwell Publishing.

Goettlich, Andreas. 2011. "Power and Powerlessness: Alfred Schutz's Theory of Relevance and Its Possible Impact on a Sociological Analysis of Power." *Civitas* 11, no 3: 491–508.

Goffman, Erving. 1959. *The Presentation of Self in Everyday Life*. New York: Anchor Books.

———. 1961. *Asylums: Essays on the Social Situation of Mental Patients and Other Inmates*. Garden City, NY: Anchor Books.

———. 1963. *Stigma: Notes on the Management of Spoiled Identity.* New York: Simon and Schuster.

———. 1969. *Strategic Interaction.* Philadelphia: University of Pennsylvania Press.

———. 1972. *Relations in Public: Microstudies of the Public Order*. New York: Basic Books.

———. 1981. *Forms of Talk*. Philadelphia: University of Pennsylvania Press.

Goldfarb, Jeffrey C. 2007. *The Politics of Small Things: The Power of the Powerless in Dark Times*. Chicago: University of Chicago Press.

Goldstein, Daniel M. 2004. *The Spectacular City: Violence and Performance in Urban Bolivia*. Durham, NC: Duke University Press.

Green, Duncan. 2003. *Silent Revolution in Latin America: The Rise and Crisis of Market Economics in Latin America*. 4th ed. New York: Monthly Review Press.

Guillet, David. 1979. *Agrarian Reform and Peasant Economy in Southern Peru*. Columbia: University of Missouri Press.

Hacking, Ian. 2004. "Between Michel Foucault and Erving Goffman: Between Discourses in the Abstract and Face-to-Face Interaction." *Economy and Society* 33, no. 3: 277–302.

Hale, Charles R. 1997. "Cultural Politics of Identity in Latin America." *Annual Review of Anthropology* 26: 567–590.

Hall, Edward T. 1989. *Beyond Culture*. New York: Anchor Books.

Handler, Richard. 1985. "On Having Culture: Nationalism and the Preservation of Quebec's Patrimoine." In *Objects and Others: Essays on Museums and Material Culture*, edited by George W. Stocking, Jr. Madison: University of Wisconsin Press.

———. 2012. "What I'm Reading: What's Up, Dr. Goffman? Tell Us Where the Action Is!" *Journal of the Royal Anthropological Institute* 18: 179–190.

Handler, Richard, and Eric Gable. 1997. *The New History in an Old Museum: Creating the Past at Colonial Williamsburg*. Durham, NC: Duke University Press.

Harvey, David. 1990. *The Condition of Postmodernity*. Oxford: Blackwell Publishers.

———. 1996. *Justice, Nature, and the Geography of Difference*. Oxford: Blackwell Publishers.

———. 2003. *The New Imperialism*. Oxford: Oxford University Press.

———. 2005. *A Brief History of Neoliberalism*. Oxford: Oxford University Press.

Hertzfeld, Michael. 1992. *The Social Production of Indifference: Exploring the Symbolic Roots of Western Bureaucracy*. Chicago: University of Chicago Press.

Hewison, Robert. 1987. *The Heritage Industry*. London: Methuen.

Hill, Michael D. 2007. "Contesting Patrimony: Cusco's Mystical Tourist Industry and the Politics of Incanismo." *Ethnos* 72 (December 4).

Hojman, David E. 1994. "The Political Economy of Recent Conversions to Market Economics in Latin America." *Journal of Latin American Studies* 26, no. 1: 191–220.

Hunefeldt, Christine. 1997. "The Rural Landscape and Changing Political Awareness: Enterprises, Agrarian Producers, and Peasant Communities, 1969–1994." In *The Peruvian Labyrinth: Politics, Society, Economy*, edited by Maxwell A. Cameron and Phillip Mauceri. University Park: Pennsylvania State University Press.

Igoe, James. 2004. *Conservation and Globalization: A Study of National Parks and Indigenous Communities from East Africa to South Dakota.* Belmont, CA: Wadsworth.

Igoe, James, and D. Brockington. 2007. "Neoliberal Conservation: A Brief Introduction." *Conservation and Society* 5, no. 4: 432–449.

Instituto Nacional de Recursos Naturales. 1998. *Plan Maestro del Santuario Historico de Machu Picchu.* Lima: Ministerio de Agricultura Publisher.

Jelin, Elizabeth, ed. 1990. *Women and Social Change in Latin America.* London: Zed Books.

Jones, James C. 1995. "Environmental Destruction, Ethnic Discrimination, and International Aid in Bolivia." In *The Social Causes of Environmental Destruction in Latin America,* edited by Michael Painter and William Durham. Ann Arbor: University of Michigan Press.

Joseph, Gilbert M., and Daniel Nugent, eds. 1994. *Everyday Forms of State Formation: Revolution and Negotiation of Rule in Modern Mexico.* Durham, NC: Duke University Press.

Kay, Cristobal. 2002. "Agrarian Reform and the Neoliberal Counter-Reform in Latin America." In *The Spaces of Neoliberalism: Land, Place and Family in Latin America,* edited by Jacquelyn Chase. Bloomfield, CT: Kumarian Press.

Kirshenblatt-Gimblett, Barbara. 1998. *Destination Culture: Tourism, Museums and Heritage.* Berkeley: University of California Press.

Kravel-Tovi, Michal. 2012. "Rites of Passing: Bureaucratic Encounters, Dramaturgy, and Jewish Conversion in Israel." *American Ethnologist* 39, no. 2: 371–388.

Lagos, Maria. 1994. *Autonomy and Power: The Dynamics of Class and Culture in Rural Bolivia.* Philadelphia: University of Pennsylvania Press.

———. 2002. "Livelihood, Citizenship, and the Gender of Politics." In *Locating Capitalism in Time and Space: Global Restructuring, Politics and Identity,* edited by David Nugent. Stanford, CA: Stanford University Press.

Larson, Brooke. 2004. *Trials of Nation Making: Liberalism, Race and Ethnicity in the Andes, 1810–1910.* Cambridge, UK: Cambridge University Press.

Lash, Scott, and John Urry. 1987. *The End of Organized Capitalism.* Madison: University of Wisconsin Press.

———. 1994. *Economies of Signs and Space.* Thousand Oaks, CA: Sage.

Lefebvre, Henri. (1974) 1998. *The Production of Space.* Oxford, UK: Blackwell Publishers.

Lemert, Charles, and Ana Branaman, eds. 1997. *The Goffman Reader.* Cambridge, MA: Blackwell.

Loker, William M., ed. 1999. *Globalization and the Rural Poor in Latin America.* Boulder, CO: Lynne Rienner Publishers.

Low, Setha. 2000. *On the Plaza: The Politics of Public Space and Culture.* Austin: University of Texas Press.

Lowenthal, David. 1997. *The Heritage Crusade and the Spoils of History.* New York: Cambridge University Press.

Luciano, Pellegrino A. 2006. "Neoliberalism, Heritage Conservation, and the Resulting Dispossession at Machu Picchu, A Protected Area in the Peruvian Andes." *Applied Anthropology* 26, no. 1: 26–36.

———. 2011. "Where Are the Edges of a Protected Area? Political Dispossession in Machu Picchu, Peru." *Conservation and Society* 9, no. 1: 35–41.

Lutz, Catherine A., and Jane L. Collins. 1993. *Reading National Geographic.* Chicago: University of Chicago Press.

MacCannell, Dean. 1973. "Staged Authenticity: Arrangements of Social Space in Tourist Settings." *American Journal of Sociology* 79, no. 3: 589–603.

———. 1976. *The Tourist: A New Theory of the Leisure Class*. New York: Schocken Books.

MacCormack, Carol, and Marilyn Strathern, eds. 1980. *Nature, Culture and Gender*. Cambridge: Cambridge University Press.

Mackenthun, Gesa. 1997. *Metaphors of Dispossession: American Beginnings and the Translation of Empire, 1492–1637*. Norman: University of Oklahoma Press.

Malkki, Liisa H. 1997. "National Geographic: The Rooting of Peoples and the Territorialization of National Identity among Scholars and Refugees." In *Culture, Power, Place: Explorations in Critical Anthropology*, edited by Akhil Gupta and James Ferguson. Durham, NC: Duke University Press.

Mallon, Florencia E. 1983. *The Defense of Community in Peru's Central Highlands: Peasant Struggle and Capitalist Transition, 1860–1940*. Princeton, NJ: Princeton University Press.

———. 1995. *Peasant and Nation: The Making of Postcolonial Mexico and Peru*. Berkeley: University of California Press.

Manning, Philip. 1991. "Drama as Life: The Significance of Goffman's Changing Use of the Theatrical Metaphor." *Sociological Theory* 9, no. 1: 70–86.

———. 1992. *Erving Goffman and Modern Sociology*. Stanford, CA: Stanford University Press.

———. 2000. "Credibility, Agency, and the Interaction Order." *Symbolic Interaction* 23, no. 3: 283–297.

Marx, Karl. 1990. *Capital*. Vol. 1. London: Penguin Books, in association with New Left Review.

Maxwell, Keely. 2004. "Lost Cities and Exotic Cows: Constructing the Space of Nature and Culture in the Machu Picchu Historic Sanctuary, Peru." PhD diss., Yale University.

Mayer, Enrique. 1991. "Peru in Deep Trouble: Mario Vargas Llosa's 'Inquest in the Andes' Reexamined." *Cultural Anthropology* 6, no. 4: 466–504.

———. 2002. *The Articulated Peasant: Household Economies in the Andes*. Boulder, CO: Westview Press.

———. 2009. *Ugly Stories from the Peruvian Agrarian Reform*. Duke University Press.

McTigue, Kevin, and PromPeru Summer Internship Program. 1997. *Peru: Beyond the Reforms*. 1996 PromPeru Summer Internship Program Field Reports. Lima, Peru: Commission for the Promotion of Peru.

Mendoza, Zoila S. 2000. *Shaping Society through Dance: Mestizo Ritual Performance in the Peruvian Andes*. University of Chicago Press.

Meskell, Lynn. 2002. "The Intersection of Identity and Politics in Archeology." *Annual Review of Anthropology* 31: 279–301.

Nas, Peter J. M. 2002. "Masterpieces of Oral and Intangible Culture: Reflections on the UNESCO World Heritage List." *Current Anthropology* 43, no. 1: 139–143.

Nash, June. 1979. *We Eat the Mines and the Mines Eat Us: Dependency and Exploitation in Bolivian Tin Mines*. New York: Columbia University Press.

———. 1994. "Global Integration and Subsistence Insecurity." *American Anthropologist* 96, no. 1: 7–30.

———. 2001. *Mayan Visions: The Quest for Autonomy in an Age of Globalization*. New York: Routledge.

———. 2005. "Introduction: Social Movements and Global Processes." In *Social Movements: An Anthropological Reader*, edited by June Nash. Malden, MA: Blackwell Publishing.

Neruda, Pablo. 1961. *Selected Poems of Pablo Neruda*. New York: Grove Press.

Norman, James. 1968. *The Riddle of the Incas: The Story of Hiram Bingham and Machu Picchu*. New York: Hawthorn Books.

Nugent, Daniel, and Gilbert M. Joseph. 1994. "Popular Culture and State Formation in Revolutionary Mexico." In *Everyday Forms of State Formations: Revolution and the Negotiation of Rule in Modern Mexico*, edited by Daniel Nugent and Gilbert M. Joseph. Durham, NC: Duke University Press.

Nugent, David. 1997. *Modernity at the Edge of Empire: State, Individual and Nation in the Northern Peruvian Andes, 1885–1935*. Stanford, CA: Stanford University Press.

———. 2002. "Erasing Race to Make the Nation: The Rise of 'the People' in the Northern Peruvian Andes." In *Locating Capitalism in Time and Space: Global Restructuring, Politics and Identity*, edited by David Nugent. Stanford, CA: Stanford University Press.

Oliver-Smith, Anthony. 1969. "The Pishtaco: Institutionalized Fears in Highland Peru." *Journal of American Folklore* 82, no. 326 (Oct–Dec): 363–368.

Ortiz de Aevallos, Augusto. 2000. *Plan de Ordenamiento Urbano del Poblado de Machu Picchu*. Cusco: Programa Machu Picchu.

Ortner, Sherry B. 2011. "On neoliberalism." *Anthropology of This Century* May (1): http://aotcpress.com/articles/neoliberalism/.

Pastor, Manuel, and Carol Wise. 1992. "Peruvian Economic Policy in the 1980s: From Orthodoxy to Heterodoxy and Back." *Latin American Research Review* 27, no. 2: 83–118.

Patterson, Alan. 1990. "Debt for Nature Swaps and the Need for Alternatives." *Environment* 32, no. 10: 4–13, 31–2.

Peet, Richard, and Michael Watts, eds. 2004. *Liberation Ecologies: Environment, Development, Social Movements*. 2nd ed. London: Routledge.

Peña Berna, Jose. 1997. "Cambios Sociales, Turismo y Desarrollo: Machu Picchu—Pueblo." Master's thesis, Universidad Nacional de San Antonio Abad del Cusco.

Phillips, Lynne. 1998. *The Third Wave of Modernization in Latin America: Cultural Perspectives on Neoliberalism.* Wilmington, DE: Scholarly Resources.

Poole, Deborah. 1997. *Vision, Race and Modernity: The Visual Economy of the Andean Image World*. Princeton, NJ: Princeton University Press.

———. 1998. "Landscape and Imperial Subject: U.S. Images of the Andes, 1859–1930." In *Close Encounters of Empire: Writing the Cultural History of U.S.-Latin American Relations,* edited by Gilbert M. Joseph, Catherine C. Legrand, and Ricardo D. Salvatore. Durham, NC: Duke University Press.

———. 2004. "Between Threat and Guarantee: Justice and Community in the Margins of the Peruvian State." In *Anthropology in the Margins of the State*, edited by Veena Das and Deborah Poole. Santa Fe, NM: School of American Research Press.

Poole, Deborah, and Gerardo Renique. 1992. *Peru: Time of Fear*. UK: Latin American Bureau.

———. 2003. "Terror and the Privatized State: A Peruvian Parable." *Radical History Review* 85: 150–163.

"Prof. Hiram Bingham of Yale Makes the Greatest Archeological Discovery of the Age by Locating and Excavating Ruins of Machu Picchu on a Peak in the Andes in Peru; Lost City in the Clouds Found after Centuries." 1913. *New York Times*, June 15.

Rivero, Oswaldo. 2001. *The Myth of Development: Non-Viable Economies of the 21st Century*. London: Zed Books.

Robertson, George, Melinda Mash, Lisa Tickner, Barry Curtis, and Tim Putnam, eds. 1996. *FutureNatural: Nature, Science and Culture.* London: Routledge.

Roseberry, William. 1989. *Anthropologies and Histories: Essays in Culture, History, and Political Economy*. New Brunswick, NJ: Rutgers University Press.

———. 1991. "Potatoes, Sacks, and Enclosures in Early Modern England." In *Golden Ages, Dark Ages: Imagining the Past in Anthropology and History*, edited by Jay O'Brien and William Roseberry. Berkeley: University of California Press.

———. 1994. "Hegemony and the Language of Contention." In *Everyday Forms of State Formation: Revolution and Negotiation of Rule in Modern Mexico,* edited by Gilbert M. Joseph and Daniel Nugent. Durham, NC: Duke University Press.

Rothenberg, Tamar Y. 1994. "Voyeurs of Imperialism: The National Geographic Magazine before WWII." In *Geography and Empire*, edited by Anne Godlewska and Neil Smith. Oxford, UK: Blackwell.

Rubin, Jeffrey W. 1997. *Decentering the Regime: Ethnicity, Radicalism, and Democracy in Juchitan, Mexico.* Durham, NC: Duke University Press.

Said, Edward. 1997. "Invention, Memory, and Place." *Critical Inquiry* 26 (Winter): 175–192.

Sanabria, Harry, 1999. "Consolidating Status, Restructuring Economies, and Confronting Workers and Peasants: The Antinomies of Bolivian Neoliberalism." *Comparative Studies in Society and History* 41, no. 3: 535–562.

Scarritt, Arthur, 2015. *Racial Spoils from Native Soils: How Neoliberalism Steals Indigenous Lands in Highland Peru.* London: Lexington Books.

Schutz, Alfred. 1970. *On Phenomenology and Social Relations.* Chicago: University of Chicago Press.

Scott, James C. 1985. *Weapons of the Weak: Everyday Forms of Peasant Resistance.* New Haven, CT: Yale University Press.

———. 1990. *Domination and the Arts of Resistance: Hidden Transcripts.* New Haven, CT: Yale University Press.

———. 1998. *Seeing Like a State: How Certain Schemes to Improve the Human Condition Have Failed.* New Haven, CT: Yale University Press.

Seligmann, Linda J. 1993. "The Burden of Vision amidst Reform: Peasant Relations to Law in the Peruvian Andes." *American Ethnologist* 20, no. 1: 25–51.

———. 1995. *Between Reform and Revolution: Political Struggles in the Peruvian Andes, 1969–1991.* Stanford, CA: Stanford University Press.

———. 2000. "Market Places, Social Spaces in Cusco, Peru." *Urban Anthropology* 29: 1–68.

———. 2004. *Peruvian Street Lives: Culture, Power, and Economy among Market Women of Cusco.* Urbana: University of Illinois Press.

Shadlen, Kenneth C. 2000. "Neoliberalism, Corporatism, and Small Business Political Activism in Contemporary Mexico." *Latin American Research Review* 35, no. 2: 73–106.

Silverberg, Robert. 1968. *The Mound Builders.* Athens, Ohio: Ohio University Press.

Silverman, Helaine. 2002. "Touring Ancient Times: The Present and Presented Past in Contemporary Peru." *American Anthropologist* 104, no. 3: 881–902.

Smith, Gavin. 1989. *Livelihood and Resistance: Peasants and the Politics of Land in Peru.* Berkeley: University of California Press.

Smith, Neil. 1984. *Uneven Development: Nature, Capital, and the Production of Space*. New York: Blackwell.

———. 1996. "The Production of Nature." In *FutureNatural: Nature, Science and Culture,* edited by George Robertson, Melinda Mash, Lisa Tickner, Barry Curtis, and Tim Putnam. London: Routledge.

Smith, Neil, and Anne Godlewska. 1994. "Introduction: Critical Histories of Geography." In *Geography and Empire,* edited by Anne Godlewska and Neil Smith. Oxford: Blackwell.

Starn, Orin. 1991. "Missing the Revolution: Anthropologists and the War in Peru." *Cultural Anthropology* 6, no 1: 63–91.

Stephen, Lynn. 1997. *Women and Social Movements in Latin America: Power from Below.* Austin: University of Texas Press.

Stern, Steve J., ed. 1987. *Resistance, Rebellion, and Consciousness in the Andean Peasant World: Eighteenth to Twentieth Century.* Madison: University of Wisconsin Press.

Stobart, Henry. 2006. "Devils, Daydreams, and Desire: Siren Traditions and Musical Creation in the Central-Southern Andes." In *Music of the Sirens,* edited by Linda Phyllis Austern and Inna Naroditskaya. Bloomington: Indiana University Press.

Tamayo Herrera, Jose. 1981. *Historia Social del Cusco Republicano.* Lima, Peru: Editorial Universo.

Taussig, Michael T. 1997. *The Magic of the State.* New York: Routledge.

Taylor, Charles, 1995. *Philosophical Arguments.* Cambridge, MA: Harvard University Press.

Tsing, Anna. 2000. "The Global Situation." *Cultural Anthropology* 15, no. 3: 327–360.

Urry, John. 1990. *The Tourist Gaze: Leisure and Travel in Contemporary Societies.* London: Sage.

Valcarcel, Luis Jose. (1927) 1972. *Tempestad en Los Andes*. Lima, Peru: Editorial Universo.
———. 1964. *Machu Picchu: El mas famoso monumento arqueologico del Peru*. Buenos Aires: EUDEBA.
Valderrama Fernández, Ricardo, and Carmen Escalante Gutiérrez. 1996. *Andean Lives: Gregorio Condori Mamani and Asunta Quispe Huamán*. Austin: University of Texas Press.
van den Berghe, Pierre L., and Jorge Flores Ochoa. 2000. "Tourism and Nativistic Ideology in Cusco, Peru." *Annals of Tourism Research* 27, no. 1: 7–26.
Vilas, Carlos M. 2004. "Water Privatization in Buenos Aires." *NACLA Report on the Americas*, 38, no. 1: 34–40.
Walsh, Kevin. 1992. *The Representation of the Past: Museums and Heritage in the Post-Modern World*. New York: Routledge.
Weber, Max. 1978. *Economy and Society*. Berkeley: University of California Press.
Weismantal, Mary. 2001. *Cholas and Pishtacos: Stories of Race and Sex in the Andes*. Chicago: University of Chicago Press.
West, Paige, James Igoe, and Dan Brockington. 2006. "Parks and People: The Social Impact of Protected Areas." *Annual Review of Anthropology* 35: 251–277.
Williams, Raymond. 1973. *The Country and the City*. New York: Oxford University Press.
———. 1980. *Problems in Materialism and Culture*. London: Verso.
———. 1989. *Marxism and Literature*. London: Oxford University Press.
Wolf, Eric. 1957. "Closed Corporate Communities in Mesoamerica and Central Java." *Southwestern Journal of Anthropology* 13: 1–18.
———. 1982. *Europe and the People without History*. Berkeley: University of California Press.
———. 1986. "The Vicissitudes of the Closed Corporate Peasant Community." *American Ethnologist* 13, no. 2: 325–329.
Zapata Velasco, Antonio. 1999. *Guía de Machu Picchu*. Lima, Peru: Instituto de Estudios Peruanos.
Zevallos Medina, Oscar. 1998. *The Enigma of Machu Picchu: Five Hundred Years After*. Cusco: Millennium Editors.

Index

AATC. *See* Association for the Tourism Agencies of Cusco
adaptation: competition and, in protests, 104; inner resources and personal narratives used for, 52; to power, 47; tactics as mode of, 51
agrarian reform, 25, 52; 1969 law of, 24; opinions on, 125
agriculture, 27
Aguas Calientes. *See* Machupicchu Pueblo
ambulantes (street sellers), 33, 36, 47–48
Andes: identity in, 3; perceptions of, 24; reform in, 6
Aobamba River, 78
artisan market, 12, 70–77; photo ID system for, 111, 121, 144; unveiling of new, 88–93
Association for the Tourism Agencies of Cusco (AATC), 97, 103–111
Asylums (Goffman), 3

Bacahuaman, Francisco, 28
baggage carriers (*cargadores*), 34, 68, 80n8
Batra, Roger, 6
Belaúnde, Fernando, 24–25
Bingham, Hiram, 10, 19, 37n8–37n10; *Machu Picchu: A Citadel of the Incas* by, 21; portrayal of, 22–23; Vilcabamba discovered by, 20
Breglia, Lisa C., 91
brequeros (train workers), 28
Brunner, Edward, 42
bureaucracy, 105; Frente cursing, 124; in Machu Picchu, 83–84; navigating through, 98; role in economy, 95–96
Burke, Kenneth, 102

campesinos, 25–26, 98; blaming of, 43, 86; civil-parade march and protests of, 97; community right of, 46; conservation authorities opinion on, 41–42; development projects promised for, 77; dress of, 52–53; possession status of, 64–65; traditionality of, 44–46
Campos, Ramiro, 111–112
capital: conservation agencies protecting investments of, 137; corporate intertwined with local, 75; mobilization of, 73; public goods facilitating, 6, 42; reorganization of public goods for, 46; train system needing, 73
capitalism, 5, 46, 103; coercive practices of, 86; emergence of, 59; resistance against, 142; as socially responsible, 139, 143
cargadores (baggage carriers), 34, 68, 80n8
Carnival, 17, 37n2
Chambi, Martin, 37n12
chasqui boys, 32–33
chicha, 27, 38n22, 51, 61n16
Church, Frederic Edwin, 21
Citadel of Machu Picchu. *See* Machu Picchu
class, 64, 75, 130; concern surrounding realities of, 140; divisions of, 12, 65; interests of, 137; wealth and, 73
commercialization, 9, 41, 47, 54
Commission for the Promotion of Peru, 16n4
commoditization, 57, 111–112
community: campesinos' right to, 46; leadership in, 148; traditional festivals of, 43–44. *See also* rural communities

competition: adaptation and, in protests, 104; as legal, 72; for PeruRail, 144; privatization creating, 8; value of, 107, 110–111
conservation agencies, 13, 41, 91, 147; capital investments protected by, 137; goals of, 51; regulations of, 20, 57
conservation authorities, 54, 60, 117–118, 122; accountability lacking in, 123–128; campesinos opinion from, 41–42; criticism by, 92; Frente meeting with, 15, 96–98, 119, 123, 134–135; as rigging economy, 141
Consorcio de Empresas de Transporte Turístico (CONSETTUR), 32
Corihuayrachina, 27–28, 38n20, 84–85
Corporación de Turismo del Perú (COTURPERU), 30
CTAR. *See* Cusco Regional Government
culture of fear, 96
currency, devaluing of, 36
Cusco, 23, 30, 34, 47
Cusco Indigenismo, 23
Cusco Regional Government (CTAR), 116, 127

dance, 16n13, 39–40, 40, 60n2
debt-for-nature agreements, 8, 65–66, 77, 80n2–80n3
de Certeau, Michel, 46, 47, 51, 52
de Soto, Hernando, 7, 25, 49, 67, 95–96
displacement, 6, 10, 65
dispossession, 5, 22, 43, 54, 66; encouragement from, 52; justification for, 59; in Latin America, 6–7; in protected areas, 91; threat of, 57, 146
domestic labor, 12
dramaturgy, 101, 107, 118, 119, 130

economic policies: of Fujimori, 69; Machupiccheños lives influenced by, 86; proponents of, 101, 103
economic realism, 64
economy: bureaucracy role in, 95–96; conservation authorities rigging, 141; corporate threat to, 79; loss of control over, 71; Peru shift in, 143; property ownership and survival of, 25; restructuring of, 16n3; Sanctuary law changes influencing, 50; secondary adjustments and understanding, 58. *See also* neoliberal economy; tourism economy
Empresa Nacional de Ferrocarriles (ENEFER), 69, 80n10, 80n12
exclusion politics, 19
exportation, of natural resources, 14

festival of the cross, 45
Finland, Ambassador of, 88–91, 99n4, 122–123
floods (*huaycos)*, 44, 55–57, 61n23, 61n26, 77–78
Fondo Nacional para Áreas Naturales Protegidas por el Estado (PROFONANPE), 67, 91
Foucault, Michele, 59
free market, 52, 72, 86
free thinkers (*pensadores liberales*), 5
Frente de Defensa de los Intereses de Machu Picchu (The Front in Defense of the Interests of Machu Picchu), 10–13, 128–130, 140–142, 143; achievements made by, 118–119; bureaucracy cursed by, 124; conservation authorities meeting with, 15, 96–98, 119, 123, 134–135; depiction of members of, 126; fear of, 130; institutions confronted by, 80; justice demanded by, 126–128; long term results of, 145
Fujimori, Alberto, 7–9, 18, 25, 35, 69, 149n6

Ganti, Tejaswini, 3–5
garbage collection, on Inca Trail, 54
Garcia, Abraham, 139–140, 141
Garcia, Alan, 138
GDAT. *See* Group for Debates in Anthropological Theory
Gill, Lesley, 63–64
globalization, 35, 83, 106

Goffman, Erving, 3, 15, 46, 52, 102, 107–108, 119n2
greed, 56–57
Green, Duncan, 103
Group for Debates in Anthropological Theory (GDAT), 3

hacendados, 53
haciendas, 24, 25, 27
Hall, Amy Cox, 21
Harvey, David, 5, 46, 59, 138
hotels, 30, 32, 36, 69
huaycos. *See* floods
Huayllabamba, 27–28, 38n20, 52
Huayno music, 14

identification: concept of, 102; language utilized in, 112–113; narratives of, 108–109; power of, 107; process of, 108
identity, 15, 22–23; in Andes, 3; as commercialized, 9, 41, 47; commoditization of, 57; dance as representation of, 39–40; Machupicchu Pueblo lacking, 39, 44; Machupiccheños as symbol of, 18–19; organizing of, 108; as racialized, 6
Igoe, Jim, 42
Imperio de los Incas, 31
INC. *See* Instituto Nacional de Cultura
Inca Civilization, 18, 21–22, 54
Incanismo, 13, 111–112, 116–117
Inca Trail, 17, 54; hiking of, 30–31, 70; regulations for, 38n23, 50, 99n2; rural communities on, 27
indigenous populations, 22
industrialization, 28
INRENA. *See* Instituto Nacional de Recursos Naturales
Instituto Nacional de Cultura (INC), 16n7, 26, 40–41, 98, 116, 120n13
Instituto Nacional de Recursos Naturales (INRENA), 26, 27–28, 52–53, 83; master plan implemented by, 66; as not cooperative, 98; plants and wildlife distinguished by, 61n21
insubordination, 47–53
intangibility, 42–43, 72
Intihuatana (sundial), 9–10

J. Walter Thompson firm, 16n7

Lagos, Maria, 73
land, 27; allocating of, 75; as national resource, 17; redistribution of, 24, 25; restrictions on usage of, 26
land invasions, 24, 37n15, 80n1
landscape, 20, 21, 41, 111–112
landslides, 77; fear of, 55–56; in Machupicchu Pueblo, 54–57; Machupiccheños observing, 57; positive outcomes from, 60
leadership, 12–13; accountability of, 127–128; in community, 148; legal implications of, 126
liberalism, 5, 6
looping, 51
Luther, Yoselin, 104, 123, 130

Machu Picchu, 75–79, 103, 114, 130; bureaucracy in, 83–84; climate in, 17; as commodity, 24, 54, 111–112; discovery of, 18–19; global institutional alignments of, 87; infrastructure advance in, 145, 146–147; institutional vision for, 85; intangibility in, 42–43; labor needs of, 147; as marketing strategy, 7–10; market value of, 107–108; media attention of, 60; municipal funds of, 77; as national trust, 17; neoliberal economy introduced in, 59; political and economic potential of, 137; population statistics of, 149n2; proliferation of organizations at, 93–94; property regulations of, 1; as public good, 17; taking over tourism of, 141; Valencia as mayor of, 138, 149n1; as World Heritage Site, 25, 26
Machu Picchu: A Citadel of the Incas (Bingham), 21
Machupicchu Pueblo, 18, 28, 58; beautification of, 146; composition of, 31–32; family histories in, 64–65; identity lacking in, 39, 44; landslides in, 54–57; map of, 3, 29; mayor not

supporting, 76; rebuilding of, 145; 60th anniversary festival of, 39–41; struggle opinions of, 141–142; tourism economy in, 34; tourism establishments in, 32
Machupiccheños, 1, 79–80; adjustments needed of, 144; authority confronted by, 87, 89–93; clearing out of, 77–78; commercial activity restricted for, 72; criticism of lifestyle of, 131; economic policies influencing lives of, 86; everyday life of, 1; as identity symbol, 18–19; landslides observed by, 57; lived realities expressed by, 116; loss of control of, 98–99; nationalist tone of, 116–117; power of, 122; as progressive, 142; protests planned by, 67; social life of, 44; support desired by, 104; tourists interactions with, 50–51
Mandorpampa, 25
Maryland and Delaware Railroad Company, 81n17
Master Plan, 43, 66
Maxwell, Keely, 26
media attention: of Machu Picchu, 60; of stoppage, 134–135
Metropolitan Museum of Art, 21
El Mirador, 31
mobilization, 1, 13–14, 54; of capital, 73; credibility and, 140; in election year, 78–79; against privatization, 65; strategies of, 148
motor vehicles, 67–68, 80n9
municipal politics, funds for, 75–80
Museo Peruano de Arqueología, 23

National Geographic Society, 21
National Institute of Culture, 60n3
national trust, Machu Picchu as, 17
Native American Indian mounds, 22
neoliberal economy, 95–96; changes in, 54; Machu Picchu introduced to, 59; social interaction in, 46–52
neoliberalism, 15, 57, 117; alternatives to, 142–143; as fashionable, 63, 125; foundation of, 42; free market and, 52; language of, 101, 103–104, 118–119; as polysemic, 3–5; profitability priority of, 114; radical separation under, 134; sentiments against, 112; social interaction framed by, 1–3; subjectivity experience under, 143; in terms of power, 46; violence and, 130
neoliberal reforms, 49, 72–73
Neruda, Pablo, 20
NGOs, 8, 18, 63–64, 67, 84; communication of, 99; influence of, 95–96
Nieto, Jorge, 104–113, 119n6–119n7

OAS. *See* Organization of American States
Ollantaytambo, 27, 38n21
Organization of American States (OAS), 9
Orient Express/Belmound corporation, 8, 30, 40, 66–67, 112; distrust in, 140; high-end market of, 48; hotels owned by, 32; investments made by, 36; legal contracts of, 114; monopoly of, 71; purchases by, 69; support for, 141
Las Orquideas, 31
The Other Path (de Soto), 67

Pampaccauha, 96
patriotism, 117
pensadores liberales (free thinkers), 5
persuasion, process of, 102
Peru: economic shift in, 143; image of, 7–8; national law of, 60n5; tourists preconceptions of, 49; Vice Minister of Tourism of, 102, 106, 112–113, 123; Yale University partnership with, 16n8
PeruRail, 8, 10, 69–72, 81n16, 98; accusations against, 76–77; blocking of, 54–55; competition for, 144; control of, 103; monopoly of, 119n3; power of, 123; stoppage response of, 131; suspicions of, 132
platform of struggle (*plataforma de lucha*), 60, 96, 105
Plaza de Armas (central plaza, Cusco), 47–49, 138
PMP. *See* Programa Machu Picchu

police: arrest ploy of, 122; brutality by, 50; efficiency of, 96; presence of, 87–88, 113–117, 128; stoppage activity of, 131–132
politics of blame, 43
Poole, Deborah, 20–21, 22, 121
porters (*porteadores*), 27, 38n27, 70
possessors (*posesionarios*), 18
power: as abstract, 130; abuse of, 113; adaptation to, 47; Fujimori dictatorial, 35; of governing authority, 94; of identification, 107; of Machupiccheños, 122; money, sovereignty and, 18; neoliberalism in terms of, 46; of PeruRail, 123; of Sanctuary Lodge, 123; specific relationships of, 52; struggle of relations of, 139
privatization, 1, 13, 63; coercion made effective by, 99; competition created by, 8; concerns about, 1; contradictions to, 86; of credit agencies, 24–25; distrust from, 67; implementation of policies of, 47; mobilization against, 65; opposition to, 9; platform against, 149n6; riots against, 137–138; of train system, 46; of transportation services, 67; trust undermined by, 95
PROFONANPE. *See* Fondo Nacional para Áreas Naturales Protegidas por el Estado
Programa Machu Picchu (PMP), 8–9, 43–44, 65–66; blame from, 93–95; head of, 91; lack of improvement from, 85
PromPeru, 8, 16n5
property ownership, 1, 25, 42
property regulations: of Machu Picchu, 1; protests against, 67
protests, 54–55; in civil-parade march, 97; commitment to, 142; competition and adaptation in, 104; discrediting of, 122–123, 131; goals of, 139, 142; Machupiccheños planning, 67; organization of, 75; outcome of, 15; pleas in, 89–91; as regular occurrence, 39
public goods, 5, 37n4; capital facilitation through, 6; Machu Picchu as, 17; reorganization of, for capital, 46

Q'ente, 25–26

race: discrimination of, 49; Peru definitions of, 16n6
Radio Machu Picchu, 11
regionalism, 23
ruins, restoration of, 30
rural communities: haciendas forming, 25; on Inca Trail, 27; life in, 27–28; tourism as variable in, 27; wealth of, 77

Sacred Valley, map of, 19
San Antonio de Torontoy, 25–26, 28–29
Sanctuary laws, 1; confusion surrounding, 84; economic consequences of change in, 50; enforcement of, 64
Sanctuary Lodge, 32, 69–72, 81n15–81n16, 115–116, 123, 140
Sanctuary of Machu Picchu: authority of, 83; boundaries of, 28, 37n18, 50; map of, 4; original inhabitants of, 85; total institution similarities with, 46–47
Santa Rita de Q'ente, 25–26
Schutz, Alfred, 83–84, 88
Scott, James C., 46, 47
secondary adjustments, 47, 51, 58
Seligmann, Linda, 49
Shining Path, 1, 7–9, 121; fear through recollection of, 130; influence of, 35–36; terrorists of, 125
Silverberg, Robert, 22
Silverman, Helaine, 48
Smith, Gavin, 72
social change, 16n12, 142, 146
social interaction, 46–52, 130
solidarity bonds, 49
Spanish Conquest, 20
speech acts, 105, 109
stage notion, 102, 107–108
Starn, Orin, 1

stoppage: decision making around, 125–130; escalation of, 131; injury during, 132, 135n10; as lawful, 135n8; legal requirements for, 131; march during, 133; media attention of, 134–135; PeruRail response to, 131; police activity during, 131–132; reflection on, 147; Valencia giving instructions for, 132
street sellers (*ambulantes*), 33, 36, 47–48
sundial (Intihuatana), 9–10

tactics: as adaptation modes, 51; de Certeau view of, 47; spatial stories based on, 87. *See also* secondary adjustments
Taylor, Charles, 37n4
technological equipment, perception of, 14
Tempestad en los Andes (Valcárcel), 23–24
Toledo, Alejandro, 9
total institution, 46–47, 58
Touring and Automóvil Club del Perú, 30
tourism: developers of, 25; as ecological/cultural, 22; ethics of, 110; growth of, 22, 54; heritage and, 3; icons of, 47; income generated by, 30; Machupicchu Pueblo establishments of, 32; as mystical, 61n11; Peruvian Vice Minister of, 102, 106, 112–113, 123; as rural community variable, 27; seasons of, 38n33; stopping of, 10; taking over Machu Picchu, 141; threatening of, 54–55
tourism economy, 13; alliances within, 72–73; benefit recipients of, 111; of Cusco, 30, 34; elites favored in, 57; exploitation in, 70; in Machupicchu Pueblo, 34; marketing to, 54; necessities of, 104–105; opportunities in, 34; profits from, 91; spacial control of, 48–49; at standstill, 134; struggle turned to security in, 105–106; worker salaries and conditions in, 33–34
tourists: cultural engagement of, 50; expectations of, 9; expected behavior of, 14; food sold to, 68; heritage experience of, 50; language barriers of, 49; Machupiccheños interactions with, 50–51; Peru preconceptions of, 49; products purchased by, 72; time pressures of, 71
train system: bombing of, 35–36; building of, 14; capital necessary for, 73; criticism of development of, 74–75; for export, 29–30; extending of, 29–30; importance of, 67–68; investors for, 73–74; privatization of, 46. *See also* PeruRail
train workers (*brequeros*), 28
TRAMUSA bus company, 66
transportation services: helicopter use for, 80n7, 80n13; privatization of, 67; quality of, 70; responsibility for, 117

Uchuraccay, 125
UGM. *See* Unidad Gestión Machu Picchu
UNESCO, 18, 26, 54
Unidad Gestión Machu Picchu (UGM), 53, 66
unification, 141, 145
UN World Heritage Committee, 24
Urban Plan, 43–46
Urban Renewal, 16n3
Urubamba River, 28, 69

Valcárcel, Jose Luis, 23–24, 37n13–37n14
Valencia, Oscar, 11, 60, 67, 74, 83; discrediting of, 123; distrust in, 147; as hopeful, 87; as Machu Picchu Mayor, 138, 149n1; options presented by, 127; political opinions expressed by, 124–125; priorities of, 138; proper behavior instructed by, 102–103; resentment for, 148; speech acts of, 104–105; stoppage instructions given by, 132; understanding of, 135n7
Vargas Llosa, Mario, 7, 149n6
Velasco, Juan, 24, 125

Vilcabamba, 20
Vilcanota River. *See* Urubamba River
violence: commodity undermined by, 60; justification for, 131; of land invasions, 24; memories of fear and, 143; of military, 7–8; national history of, 121; neoliberalism and, 130

water project, 92, 99
wealth, 12; class and, 73; desire for, 143; privilege of, 138–139; relationships structured from, 42; of rural communities, 77
weapons of the weak, 47
women: domestic labor demands of, 12; as politically engaged, 12–13; as social change protagonists, 16n12
World Heritage Sites: humanity heritage represented in, 41; Machu Picchu as, 25, 26; monetary appraisal of monuments in, 137; requirements of, 60n4

Yale University, 10, 16n8

About the Author

Pellegrino A. Luciano is assistant professor of anthropology at the American University of Kuwait, Department of Social and Behavioral Sciences/Anthropology. He completed his doctoral work in anthropology at the Graduate Center of the City University of New York.

CPSIA information can be obtained
at www.ICGtesting.com
Printed in the USA
BVHW041811290120
570880BV00015B/176

9 781498 545969